WAKE UP FOR
ASCENSION

To a New Earth or Leave

Robert E. Pettit, PhD

Emeritus Associate Professor

Wake Up For Ascension

To a New Earth or Leave

First Impressions Printer & Publisher
1901 S. Stewart
Springfield, Missouri

Printed in the United States of America
Publication March 2010

Contents

Section V. Light Body Awakening Sequence 109

Section VI. Dimensional Consciousness Features ..139

Acknowledgments

To each Research Associate who has participated in the Subtle Energy Research (SER) program for the past twenty years, I thank you for your dedication and the contributions that have made possible the assembly of the information presented within this book. Your suggestions of references, Internet Web sites, and workshops, in addition to your spiritual talents, have opened up many new avenues of knowing. These many insights have provided a foundation for working with subtle energy. With these insights we have been able to conduct a large number of remote spiritual healing sessions. Over these twenty years, more than 850 individuals throughout the United States have helped open up new understandings of a multitude of procedures and techniques that have helped guide the design of many research experiments. Another 255 have benefited from the results of these experiments. Many of you reading these two books can now benefit from those efforts.

Writing and summarizing the material for this second book has also been an exercise in responsibility, dedication, discipline, awareness, and a willingness to be open to receive guidance from many Spiritual sources. This book has been designed to help those who are in the process of activating their fifth dimensional state of consciousness Light Body and are on a spiritual path to graduation, ascension, and arrival on the "New Earth."

Special thanks to the editors, Betty Pettit, Patricia Pike, Irene Jennings, Harriett Gray, Isa Ra and Kim Notz. Also a special thanks to the staff and assistants who respond to the many calls for help from throughout the United States: Larry Sorensen, Suzy London, MD, Linda Case, Francosis Pellissier, Betty Pettit, Sharon Berry, Don Yows, Jackie Cohen, Janet Rainey, Kim Notz, George Ward, Maurice Portilla, MD, Nayda Portilla, Steve Fox, Nira Granott Fox, Cheryl Bright, and Carol Handing.

Some of the many Research Associates who assisted are:

Annette Gore	Tom Lynch	Loretta Lines
Rosie Kuhn	John Luttrell	Geoffrey Luttrell
Kenneth Shaw	Stephanie Flanders	Alicya Simmons
Vicki Buffington	Donald Miles	Cynthia Luttrell

Rebecca Thomas

David Pettit
Bridget Sorensen
Lisa Christian
Kelly Lousey
Christopher Pettit

Dorothy Combs
Patty Kumm
Maria Smith
Betty Wood
Kathleen St John

David Hudspeth
Christy Campassi
Christine Lurski
Marlene Coats
Neal Anderson

Randy Scherer
Shannen Twaddle
Judy Modglin
Vicki Bolton
Donna Reiber

Bonnie Hansen
Elaine Checkly
Barbara Blevins
Simone Little
Marvin Kubik

Elynn Light
Lei Hill
Patty Kumm
Mauricio Portilla
Lawrence Hansen

Susan Neander
Frances Townsend
Gary Batten

Valerie Lynch

Martha James
Delwin Houser
William Luttrell
Bradley Smith
Michael George

Leonard Ripley
Sandra Letson
Leroy Wood
Jennifer Hudspeth
Shellie Hudspeth

Vicki Miles
Barbara Baine
Cher Barlevi
Gregory Coats
Paula Bordelon

Sandra Schaff
Rick Pinckert
Pat Janus
Donna Taylor
Frances Hebert

Judith McClung
David Massey
Marina Pierce
Rosemary Lanza
Nina Miller

Jan Pryor
Bruce Thomas
Cathleen Howard
Barbara Johnson
Russell Barrett

Allese Hauroutunian
Inbal Farber
Paul Gresham

Dorothy Gilkes

Debbie May
Sharon Pettit
Joanna Himes
Rebecca Winks
Sharie Cochran

Faina Engel
Kathy Middleton
Lea Carleton
Amy Wagner
Mindy Hudspeth

Steve Thompson
Bonnie Thompson
Lorie Spiegel
Jason Ellis
Harrison Spiegel

Michael Middleton
Venetia Poirot
Shelly Hume
Jody Janati
Geddy Hamblen

Chris McCombs
Deborah Massey
Toni Tindel
Patricia Kubik
Paul Gryglas

Kelly Norri
Chareen Thomas
Carolyn Jones
Charles Kuchulis
Lisa Glover

Jennifer Kenning
Tyson Goodman
Nancy Evans

Deborah Oakes	Peter Jurouskis	Janice Eicher
Annette Murphy	Rosemary Lanza	Nancy Coats
Mariett Laneer	Jessica Schuman	Carla Stine
Linda Stowe	Jesse Nochella	Robert Parma
Anne Hartikka	Carol James	Tom Stine
Pamela Boyke	Katharina Kaffl	Sharon Louise
Letitia Jackson	Jason Wagner	Adele French
Lyle Christensen	Roxy Baxter	Nancy Kriesky
Juli Ann Benett	Betty Axthelm	Stephen Bredesen
Lucy Lutkowski	Dan Morris	Sundi Bright
Arlie Paulson	Jack Frazier	Suzanne Frazier
Jaimie Ware	Daly Smith	Kathy Slentz
Cyreal Burgett	Greg Slentz	Lea Carleton
Jacque Tindel	Terry James	Brad Eberhart
Michele Francesconi	Martha Moore	

Thanks also to the hundreds of additional individuals throughout the United States and world who have assisted the research.

Thanks to the faculty and staff of the Department of Plant Pathology and Microbiology at Texas A&M University, College Station, Texas, for their encouragement and support during my twenty-seven years with them. Thanks for the grant support for research activities form many different sources. These grant funds provided an opportunity to travel, conduct research, and attend conferences in forty-four states of the United States and twenty-seven different countries of the world.

Credit for book cover art "The Blue Marble West Photo" of the Earth is given to the National Aeronautic and Space Administration, Goddard Space Flight Center. The composite photograph was taken 700 km above Earth on board the Terra Satellite in 2001.

Finally, I would like to thank my wife, children, grandchildren, and great-grandchildren for their support throughout the eighty years of my incarnation on planet Earth. I have been grateful for the patience, support, and encouragement of my mother and father, brother, and family, as I have journeyed down a road still unfamiliar to many others and me.

* * * * * *

Section I. Introduction

The Purpose for Being on Earth

The author of this book has worked with his High Self to design each sentence and paragraph to insert information beyond the words you are reading.   Therefore, to receive maximum benefit during reading, connect with your Higher Self and receive pictures, feelings, and an inner knowing that rings true to the deepest part of your being. Set aside those messages that do not ring true currently and move on to that inner knowing that will brighten your path "Now."

A majority of humans on Earth sense that some dramatic changes are taking place. Some sense there is less time to complete a task. Also, they observe political and economic changes. Many believe these changes are long overdue. However, there are many other associated changes taking place. There are significant Earth changes and climatic changes. Good evidence indicates the glacial ice on Earth is melting. Earthquakes and volcanic activity have increased in recent years. Very few ask why the changes are occurring and seem to take little interest in figuring out the cause for all of these changes. Many humans go about their normal activities very unaware that they also must change or vacate planet Earth. Yes, you read correctly. The old Earth will cease supporting human life in the near future. There are several reasons for this upcoming change. Several of these reasons will be discussed within this book. In addition, we will discuss what your responsibilities are for yourself, family, friends, and the Earth.

There are many preparing for the upcoming changes and have been preparing for many lifetimes. You may be one who is preparing. Others may need your help if you have some understanding about how to prepare. Preparation will need to take place within a multitude of your daily activities.   The primary change will be internal, a change in consciousness. A change in the way you live. This change means there is no need to go and hide or go inside the Earth to obtain safety.

For some the challenge is -- they do not know what to do. Their thoughts are on survival. Well there is no way to survive unless you know what survival means currently. One important question you can ask is --

have I become entranced with the physical third dimensional world of physical things. Am I mainly going though life using my five senses to determine how to face each new day?

These individuals are essentially asleep consciously. In addition, many have given their power away by allowing others to control their thinking and decision-making. One good example is the skyrocketing business of health care of the sick and dying. One of the largest businesses in the United States is the medical business. Individuals by the thousands are flocking to doctors and hospitals for help to stay healthy. They have forgotten that it is their responsibility to take care of their own health. Many have given their power over to the doctors, drug companies, and hospitals.

There is much more than the physical world you detect with your five senses. There is an invisible world all around you that is just waiting for your awareness. To understand the reality of the physical world you are required to tap into that invisible unseen world of thoughts, and of spirit. Within the unseen world of spirit, you can discover who you are, where you came from, and where your going. Obviously, you are aware of that unseen world just waiting for you to visit. A majority of scientists, historians, theologians, philosophers, channelers, and many other groups realize there is an unseen world that is just as real as the physical world.

All Spirits and Souls inhabiting human vehicles are believed to have originated from All THAT IS, SOURCE, Creators, and God/Goddess, and other creations within the spiritual realm. Each individual spirit with a Soul appears to have an evolutionary purpose. Most humans came to Earth to discover that purpose and find their way back home to SOURCE.

The lower frequencies of Earth, previously third and fourth (DMC) are typical of several planets where linear time, duality, and separation offers each Soul unique opportunities for evolutionary development. When we each came into third dimensional world, we lost our conscious memory of other experiences and spiritual desires. Different groups of controllers who believe they know what is best for you and me have manipulated many humans on Earth. As a result, our free will has been greatly restricted, even taken away in some cases. The purpose for this loss of free will has adversely influenced many humans. They are unsure what they should do while here on Earth. All of the guidance from their parents, schools, churches, government, etc. has largely failed to create happiness and a sense of well being. Consequently, very few individual realize the most important task they have is to evolve spiritually.

Thus, we should ask the question, what is the most appropriate way to evolve spiritually? This question suggests the need for another question. Where can I find out what my responsibilities are to family, friends, society and myself? Assuming that one of your goals was to shift to a higher state of dimensional consciousness, then the question: What is required to make that shift?

Before coming to Earth, you were at a higher state of consciousness. In order to incarnate within the third Dimensional State of Consciousness (DMC) on (physical) Earth you moved out of the fourth DMC (astral) where you had some capability to know. As you evolve back to the fourth DMC, your sensing system will be altered, where words will be replaced with a heightened intuition. As a result, you will know all thoughts, feelings, troubles and challenges of others. There is no deception and no desire for deception.

Under these conditions within the fourth DMC, the Soul lacked polarity. Thus, there were very few challenges to keep you occupied. Therefore, you and I actually volunteered to come to Earth. We were informed somehow that Earth was a place with challenges where we could fine-tune our internal desire to evolve spiritually. We believed that by working through the challenges on Earth we could keep busy and in the process grow spiritually.

You have volunteered as a part of an experiment. You dropped down to the lower densities of Earth for the value of experiencing new challenges. When you shifted down to the lower third DMC frequency, you had to give up your memory. You started this life with somewhat of a clean slate consciously. Within the third DMC, a lack of knowing along with pain and suffering have created many challenges that have forced individuals and groups of Souls, to seek out solutions to these challenges. Meeting the challenges and coming up with solutions is what you came to experience. That process has rapidly accelerated the evolutionary status of Earth's inhabitants. That is, compared to the amount of spiritual progress you were making within the fourth DMCs and above.

3

To gain approval to come to Earth you also had to leave your higher states of consciousness and accept your lower states of mind. These lower states of mind contain a strong element of dysfunction, a collective mental illness. Christians call this dysfunction "sin", more accurately translated means, "to miss the mark". Some of these dysfunctions (limitations) have been purposely implanted in the human energy system to slow spiritual development. For example, our Soul has been unevenly distributed within our bodies. Generally, a larger percentage lies on the left side. As a result, humans live out of balance; unskillfully and/or blindly thus, they suffer and cause suffering. These dysfunctional behaviors include inflicting harm on other life forms -- people, animals, plants, the Earth, and the solar system. Fear, greed, and desire for power appear to be some of the motivating (driving) factors that bring about a misinterpretation of human relationships. These dysfunctions appear to have been carried over from our many parallel past and future realities, into the current "Now" time frame. As these dysfunctions surface, they manifest in many ways such as sickness, crime, planning sexual strategies, being critical, defending your space, conducting war, pollution of the soil, air, and water, and self inflicted punishments of all sorts.

Part of our challenge is our lack of understanding of the indivisible world many scientists call the "Quantum World." To comprehend that world will require a new way of viewing everything that has become so familiar. Before you were born physically and incarnated within a physical body, you existed in some other form. Many call that form -- a spirit form. That spirit form is the "Real You." The physical body is merely a vehicle for the spirit to ride in. Your spirit had quantum features before your arrival on Earth. What does it mean to have quantum features? In addition, even if you do have quantum features, what difference does that make?

By understanding some basic features of the quantum world, you can gain a better understanding of why you are here and what is currently taking place all over the Milky Way Galaxy, the solar system and on Earth. To understand the quantum world will take some effort. However, that effort will pay significant dividends.

Your willingness to choose to understand or just forget the whole idea of trying to figure out what is happening, could determine your future survival and potential to transition to a New Earth. Everyone on Earth has been and is constantly faced with making decisions and choices. The process of making choices is one of humanities major activities. The current choices available will possibly be one of the most important choices you will make during this lifetime.

You have come to a point in history when you will be required to make a choice whether you want to or not. You could avoid making the most important choice of your life. You could choose the easy way and refuse to choose. That will be a choice. You can even stop reading now and not even know what that important choice was. Then you can carry on as usual and be unprepared for the greatest change that has taken place, within the past 24,000 years.

The coming change goes by many names. Some have called it "The End of The Age," others have called it "The Shift," some religious groups call it "The Rapture." Regardless of what name you use to describe the coming events, surrounding the year 2012, some potentially dramatic changes are taking place and will continue to take place. A very descriptive term is "The Shift of the Ages." After 2012, all existing evidence indicates the world you have become so familiar with will gradually disappear.

Make a concerted effort to understand that you are composed of many complex energy patterns. The human energy system is composed of a multitude of energy frequencies within various dimensional designs. Thus, the human energy bodies as a group have been called multidimensional. You are much more than a physical, mental, and emotional body. To come to that realization should spur you on to realize that you have more to take care of than just your physical body.

At the top of the list is the choice to take care of your Soul Body and Emotional Body. These two bodies should have some priority in your life. Obviously, your energy system is composed of a large number of other bodies that need your attention. If you are not familiar with all of your energy bodies, may I suggest you make an effort to study about each one and how they function to create your realty. The physical body you spend so much time thinking about is less than one percent of your total reality.

One of your first steps in preparing for the future is to realize that your consciousness determines your future. One of your major purposes for coming to Earth was to evolve consciously. To change consciously means to change the way you think and act. For the majority of people to make that shift in consciousness, may require a change in their belief systems. Many of your old beliefs of what is real and false will have to be studied carefully to determine if they meet the requirements to make a meaningful shift in consciousness. In a majority of the cases, you will have to give up many of your false beliefs. That means "waking up" to fine tune your discernment capabilities and take on new beliefs that are more accurate. Your new beliefs will of necessity help you understand what a dimensional shift. Those new beliefs will help you anticipate and prepare for "The Shift" or as many are calling the date of December 2012, "The End of The Age."

When you made your recent decision to incarnate on Earth, (during the end of several Universal Cycles) your spiritual self realized that Earth would go through some dramatic changes during your lifetime. You also realized there would be an opportunity to graduate and ascend together with many others. This mass ascension event is scheduled to allow an undetermined percentage of Earth's population to simultaneously graduate and ascend. That is, energetic conditions are in progress so that "mass" (millions simultaneously) physical body ascension is a probability during this lifetime on planet Earth. Ascension will allow you to pass through a dimensional doorway (portal) to a "New Earth." To transition from one density or dimensional state of consciousness to the next higher one requires a generalized degree of internal accomplishments and/or internal preparations.

An analysis of human activities upon planet Earth indicates that a majority of the population is either spiritually asleep or have forgotten about their spiritual contract they agreed to and signed off on. Each human on Earth came with a contract worked out before birth for this incarnation. Because many do not remember their contract, they are unaware of their purpose for being on Earth. Every human, animal, and plant came here to Earth for a purpose. Since all of these creations came from "One Source of Light," every creation is connected. In addition, each creation now senses the current duality experiment on Earth is over. This experiment has been relatively successful. In other words, many have evolved spiritually and they are ready to move on.

The coming "End of The Age" is not the end of the world. The coming events are the ending of one age and the awakening or beginning of a completely new and different age. The old third dimension Earth is rapidly shifting from third density to fourth density and then on to fifth density. As a result, you have an opportunity to evolve with the planet and transition to the "New Earth." "The End of The Age" has been correlated with planet Earth's movement within the Milky Way Galaxy. The solar system is moving out of a dark period into a light period. A massive band of light called the "Photon Belt" will support the light period for the coming 2,160 years.

To be a part of this "New Earth" and evolve consciously will require that you shift from third density to fourth density and on to fifth density. Those shifts in density are an inside job involving a shift in consciousness from third dimensional consciousness to fourth dimensional consciousness and on to a fifth state of dimensional consciousness. Frequency, density, and levels of dimensional consciousness are different concepts but correlated.

To make that shift will require that each individual interested in graduating and ascending will need to awaken or activate his or her Light Bodies. That procedure involves going through a series of steps influenced by new energies coming from the Great Central Sun around which our solar system rotates. These new high frequencies have been and are currently changing every planet within the solar system. Thus for you to ascend with the solar system and planet Earth you will need to adjust your energies to those higher frequencies. If your energies fail to match those of the Earth, the only alternative you have is to physically die and leave your body on Earth. Once your spirit passes over into the spirit realm, you will then have other choices and decisions to make concerning your future spiritual evolution.

Again, realize that one of your major purposes for coming to Earth was to evolve spiritually by learning how to raise the frequency of your various energy systems up to the higher densities. This process involves shifting your internal energies to higher states of dimensional consciousness. All component parts of creation are also involved in these evolutionary steps from the low frequencies to the higher frequencies. It is helpful to understand that everything within the universe is energy and that all energies vibrate at specific frequencies. For example, the emotion of

Love is a higher frequency "thought form" compared to the "thought form" of fear. Individual creations that exhibit the frequencies of Love vibrate at a higher frequency compared to those who vibrate at the lower frequencies of fear. Thus, one technique for assisting your spiritual evolution is to take on and radiate the consciousness of love.

To make the transition from the old third dimension Earth to the new fifth dimension Earth will require that you fine-tune your discernment capabilities. The ability to discern means to judge well. That is, having the capability to know right from wrong.

Why is discernment so important? Oftentimes humans go through life making decisions and choices based upon what their parents, friends, school, church, politicians, bankers, doctors, psychotherapist, counselors, gurus, spiritual advisors, and others have instilled within their consciousness. Notice how these programmed individuals have lost their ability to discern, and decide for themselves. Many have allowed various outside "thought forms" ideals about reality to be programmed into their minds at different levels of mind called the conscious, subconscious and superconscious minds. They have inadvertently allowed others to control their lives and take their power away. They are living a reality and system of beliefs that are quite distant from the reality as designed by the Creators.

The time has come to "take your power back" and use discernment by listening to and receiving guidance from the still small voice of God/Goddess within and/or your "High Self." Strive to sharpen your intuition and live your life in harmony within unity (Christ) consciousness, without losing your individuality.

Surprises await those who depend on the advice of others and have difficulty in discerning the most appropriate paths or choices for their life. I repeat, a future ordained (programmed) for you by the whims (thoughts) of someone else's agenda means giving your power away. As a result, you can anticipate that you will be having a multitude of future surprises. Some of which could be painful.

Discernment may not provide you with a quick fix but it will empower you to make informed decisions and wise choices before you go digging into the unknown. The choices you make "Now" will determine your future for thousands of years.

One effective discernment procedure, a means of receiving internal guidance, is to still the mind and enter the void between thoughts.

8

The still small voice of God/Goddess and your High Self speaks within the void or quiet time of meditation and contemplation -- between your thoughts. Discernment is a process that re-collects and awakens your own intuitive skills of determining your future life. With an efficient intuition, your future becomes self-assured.

The days of living blindly on automatic pilot will have ceased in the later part of 2012. Everyone on Earth can now make a decision to live within a state of heightened awareness for the next three years. Those who so choose to shift their consciousness to the higher dimensions will reside within an awareness that embodies all those desirable features you have prayed for and dreamed of. Some would call this preparation process, "Preparing for The Coming of Heaven on Earth." Throughout history a multitude of preparation procedures have been available, many of which could have taken you down a blind road. That is, "the blind leading the blind." Other more spiritually designed paths or roads would normally take many lifetimes to complete.

In addition, every person living on Earth within a state of victim consciousness, poverty consciousness, and conditional love consciousness is depriving themselves of the desirable features of God/Goddess Love. Anyone living with a multitude of illusion about the chosen path has limited his or her future achievements. Your consciousness determines your future, not your false beliefs. Remember God/Goddess does not withhold anything from you ever. Humans create the withholding as one of their lessons.

For those humans who succumb to the emotion of fear during these changing times, they (together) will collectively make the decision to pass up graduation until some future "Now" time. Those who fail to shift their consciousness to a higher vibratory rate (frequency) they are faced with an opportunity to incarnate on another third dimension planet. That planet will allow them to continue their duality lessons and many challenges related to good and poor choices.

Most all third dimension life on Earth will gradually disappear within the next few years. When this occurs, those who have failed to prepare for ascension and graduation will simply leave their physical body ("die"). They will return to the spiritual realm according to the level of their development and spiritual attainment. Those who have prepared to ascend may transition to the "New Earth" from the spirit realm. Many other options are also available as they always have been.

The illusion of space and time were created for your use within the third–fourth dimensions. In reality, "All Is One." There is no space and time. These illusions of space and time will become obvious when you shift your consciousness into the fifth dimension. There will be no space and no time upon the New fifth dimensional Earth.

Earth as a Duality School - Learning to Create

As you realize that Earth is a "Creator School," a school for perfecting your skills of creation, then the available challenges help you understand the reasons for coming here. To create means to learn how to manipulate energies. Everything on Earth and within the Universe is composed of energy. All energies originated from the energy of Light. Thus, everything detected by your sensing system is a component part of Light. The Light energy has been separated out into an untold number of different frequencies. Each frequency represents a specific vibratory pattern that gives recognizable features to each creation.

Love energy, a major component of Light is the essence energy of God/Goddess. The basic human energy systems, commonly called Spirits, were created in the image and likeness of God/Goddess. Likewise, evidence is surfacing that not only did Source Light Energy create humans, that Light Energy was also the basic creative energy for all the creation of everything. Since all of creations came from "One Source Light," then every creation is interconnected. We all are one in Spirit. Therefore, since we are all connected, each component part of creation has an influence on all other parts of that creation.

To carry this analogy one-step further, since all originated from the Creator then each component part of the creation has creative abilities. Every part of creation has a purpose. Our challenge is to determine what those purposes are and make effective connection to proceed in our spiritual evolution. We came to take advantage of the duality school called Earth. Here on Earth we have an opportunity to create from various energies supplied by Mother Earth and the Spirit realm.

All of the physical features of what you term the world around you are creations brought into existence by the efforts of spirits in one form or another. Humans as creators have learned how to make cars, houses, airplanes, and how to work with nature to grow food.

The lower third dimension Earth school is a place where the concepts of duality are available for gaining an understanding, learning differences between right and wrong, and determining the most appropriate procedures for creating. Through working within the many activities associated within "Creator School, and with repeated incarnations into a physical body each individual has the assignment of creating a structured Soul. That individual Soul is to be created in the likeness of the forces that created your Spirit. To create that Soul involves understanding what true spirituality is. True spirituality comes from Source" and has very little correlation with fear based manipulating belief systems.

While residing upon the Earth one major evolutionary technique involves creating challenges and then learning how to solve those challenges. These challenges were created in line with the contracts each soul agreed to before coming to Earth. Before coming to Earth our Spiritual body met with a review board (committee) in which decisions were made on how each person could make progress spiritually during their upcoming incarnation. That is, what activities could most appropriately assist the Soul in its spiritual evolution during the upcoming incarnation? A majority of humans on Earth have repeatedly incarnated within a third dimension (third density) physical body to complete these agreed upon lessons.

As mentioned, humans come to Earth with a contract that outlines those activities they agreed to carry out while incarnated here. Following each physical death, a review is carried out on the other side of the veil to determine the degree of progress. This review is primarily carried out between incarnations (lives) as each spiritual entity is preparing for a new contract. In many cases, the review also considers other parallel lives (so called past, future, and parallel lives) in relation to the one you just completed. When you examine your series of contracts over many lifetimes, you detect a specific pattern that relates to your time tract, time path, and time line. In all cases, you will discover your individuality and purpose for incarnating time after time.

During the latter process of the review, each spirit, with their accompanying Soul, is provided an opportunity to make suggestions and eventually agree upon a new contract as approved by a spiritual committee. The overall purpose of such repeated contracts and repeated incarnations is to become more God/Goddess like as recorded in the makeup of the individual Soul.

Each Soul is a part of the "Explorer Race" that came to Earth for the value of struggle and discomfort. This "Explorer Race," composed of several different races chose to carry out a series of experiments. One of the major objectives of these experiments was to develop an ability to learn how to accept each race and individual present unconditionally. In addition, many came to explore and develop their curiosity about one of the most beautiful planets in the Milky Way Galaxy. Through these experiences, including a multitude of related experiments, you have been in the process of creating an infrastructure that seeks to perfect your Soul self from within.

One objective for these experiences is to learn how to accept struggle and develop an interest in going elsewhere in the Universe. Again, the overall purpose for coming to Earth was for spiritual growth. When you graduate and have learned how to travel throughout the Universe you will be able to blend your consciousness with many other creations on different planets.

No one is saying or stating that struggle by itself is good and that you should continually look for more struggles. However, that struggle has helped create within your consciousness a need to survive and cherish life. It has also created a lust for life that has come from experiencing the discomforts of living upon a third dimension -- duality planet. Thus, one major purpose for your presence on Earth is to instill within your consciousness a desire to live.

Keep in mind that on many other planets there is no desire to live and ride around in a third-dimensional body. On these other planets, a majority of Souls have lost their desire to live in a physical body. Many have given up hope. One of their main desires is to incarnate on a planet where they can regain their desire to live physically.

There is value in experiencing a physical body with the associated mental and emotional features, even though in reality you are a spiritual body without physical form. You are also here on Earth to strengthen your mental and emotional bodies. The strength of these two bodies correlates with your changes in dimensional consciousness. Remember, the spiritual body survives death, needs your daily attention and lives eternally. As your eternal spirit evolves consciously, that change causes God/Goddess within to becomes more, since all of creation is interconnected.

Your Soul, the seventh density component part of your Oversoul reality, is essentially a large part of your personality. Your Soul was created to evolve and designed so that you would want to survive. You then could appreciate the many opportunities to enjoy all the variables associated with experiencing duality. That is, enjoy experiencing many challenges and sufferings upon a third dimension planet. Here on Earth you have an opportunity to imagine, go places, see new things, and have different experiences. All of these activities are designed to help you appreciate life in a physical body.

Through my experiences of working with many people, I have noted that some people have become disillusioned, (discouraged) about remaining on Earth to complete their lessons. Some wonder, why they can't just go back into the spiritual world where there are not so many challenges. They continue on to state, "Now that I have discovered how difficult these lessons are let me know when the next bus is leaving. I want to go back home as soon as possible!"

You volunteered to come to Earth at this specific time in history. You came here to learn how to experience a physical life, learn to create, and strengthen your Soul so you could assist other evolving civilizations throughout the Universe. The physical life you are living may not be easy. In addition, the procedures for qualifying for graduation and ascension may require considerable dedicated effort. However, in the long haul it will be worth it as you reflect on those efforts. You will come to realize that the effort was will worth every minute you spent.

You knew that it would not be easy when you volunteered to come. By your request, you were seeded (placed) here on Earth in spirit form for a purpose. You then chose to inhabit a physical body for the experiences available. That vehicle has been genetically engineered may times in an attempt to perfect it. There are jumps within the evolutionary pattern of the human form where advanced Extraterrestrials assisted in shifting the genetic base. Those shifts in genetic features have helped create the physical vehicle for your Spirit to maneuver here on Earth. From a scientific perspective, there are no missing physical links in the evolutionary path of human development.

Graduation and ascension are in part about appreciating the physical experience, appreciating the opportunities of each life lived on many different planets. Then you can clear away all those discomforts (negative thought forms, discordant programs, and other imprints) collected over many lifetimes and move on into a completely new world, a "New Earth." When you arrive upon that fifth dimension "New Earth, additional opportunities will become available. To qualify to take your physical body with you to the "New Earth" will require several preparations. Since fifth dimensional consciousness means you awaken your "Light Body;" then we suggest you determine how to awaken and activate your "Light Body" as soon as possible.

On most planets within the Universe, the conditions are not as harsh as they are here. One some planets the conditions are more harsh. The extreme conditions on Earth have helped strengthen the human energy systems. All humans on Earth are interconnected. Thus if someone can live at sixty below zero, and another can live at over 120 degrees Fahrenheit, then everyone on the planet is influenced by those abilities and they are recorded within your genetic codes. Thus, spirit indicates that the survival process of each individual on Earth influences the genetic makeup of every human on Earth. Everyone on Earth is inter-connected because of the original patterns of creation.

That strengthened genetic code brought about by the collective consciousness, also strengthens your Soul. Soul development involves a transition from lower density forms and/or lower states of Dimensional Consciousness to Higher Frequency Vibrational States. One key component of that process of Soul evolution is the implanting of LOVE energy into all of your energy bodies. LOVE energy heals everything.

These Earth related experiences will influence your capabilities, in helpful ways for eons to come. Within "Creator School' you have learned how to alter the energies to create and to alter the energies of planet Earth. As you travel and work on other planets as a fifth dimension entity, you will realize that time and space are illusions. Once within fifth dimension you can easily travel to other planets. There you will discover that many of these civilizations are declining, on the wane. They are dying out just as the Zeta Rectulians were when they were given permission to create hybrids with Earthlings. Our United States government officials signed contracts to allow the Zeta (Grays) to develop agreements with select

14

females and then implant them with some of their genetic features. The objective was to gain back their emotions and ability to reproduce sexually. That experiment has been successful and the hybrids that have formed, from those experiments, have helped create a new race, on a different planet. In the future, you could, in a similar way help many other distant civilizations needing help.

Through all of your experiences and that of all other humans on Earth, the collective consciousness has signaled that a large percentage of the population is now ready for a change. Many would like to graduate from the low-density third dimension Earth. From a third dimension perspective the clock is ringing, just a few minutes remain. Between the time you read this message and December 2012 will indicate how much preparation time you have remaining. Events are moving fast ever since the Harmonic Convergence in 1987. Obviously, you have a limited amount of time to finalize your preparations for graduation and ascension. However, you still can prepare to graduate and ascend.

Planet Earth, a school for Spiritual evolution, is in the process of making dramatic changes during a very brief period of history. Humans have a choice to either adapt to these changes or leave third dimension Earth. Thus, the question that needs considerable clarification is what methods are available for making the necessary preparations and adaptations. In order to understand the processes of making changes, it will be important to know why you are here on Earth and understand the creative process that brought you into existence. You are here now because you believed you had the desire and willingness to learn how to adapt without extensive training. You also came to learn how to control all of the negative emotions associated with fear. That ability to control fear will be one of your strongest features in the next few years as many unfamiliar events take place. As you avoid fear and practice acceptance of everything taking place, you will know that all is in Divine order and you will accomplish your goals.

Up to this point in history, Universal design has given humans a level of protection. That protection was designed to help ensure your opportunity to face the coming events with mental and emotional strength. To take advantage of that protection you must ask for it. There are many Spiritual entities just waiting for your request for help. They cannot interfere with your free will or your contract, nor will they live your life for you.

Thoughts originating from the heart and mind create everyone's reality – what you think you can create. As a part of Earth school, we create our challenges of sickness, pain, and suffering in order to come up with workable solutions. Giving your power away to others for solving your created challenges, could limit your creative accomplishments.

You created the challenges to give you the opportunity to come up with solutions. Thus when you fail to take care of your body and it becomes diseased, you need to act positively. Then you have an opportunity to determine why you are having to deal with these disease symptoms. Keep in mind the symptoms of an imbalance are not what created the disease or challenge. Every imbalance has an emotional and mental basis. Thus, the appearance of symptoms is the expression of a much more complicated cause. Your goal then should be to determine the causes and use the tools available to eliminate those causes.

Obviously, you would be more comfortable by eliminating the symptoms. In general, that is what many "health care practitioners" attempt to do, eliminate the symptoms so that you think the challenge has been solved. The use of drugs to eliminate or reduce the severity of a disease symptom can be very dangerous. In a majority of situations, drugs create many more problems than they solve.

The only person that can heal you is you. No one ever healed someone else. Another person or spirit can help supply healing energy, but in the final analysis, your body will heal itself when given the opportunity. Others helpers are available, including spiritual help. Spirit can help by altering up to 77% of the imbalance. The other 23% is your personal responsibility.

One challenge that a large percentage of the Earth's population is faced with is relatively new. Many humans have damaged immune systems. Because of this breakdown, there is an increased susceptibility to a host of disease inciting agents. This immune system breakdown has created a health crisis. In addition, the controllers know this and have developed a host of new disease inciting agents designed to limit your life span on Earth. There are many health related scientific experiments, the results of which have been withheld from public view. The establishment keeps many alternative helpful health care practices, those that could greatly reduce the immune system stress, away from public awareness. The philosophy is that the release of those procedures would be harmful to the current multi-million dollar health care system. In order to maintain this massive health care system it is highly undesirable to help patients regain their health. The objective is to keep them coming back for more treatments. Regardless of the complicated nature of the archaic health care system, those humans who have the capability to meet these many challenges will survive and evolve along their chosen time line.

One very important consideration is to make sure your originally designed energy patterns are intact and functional. All creations have a spiritual component and holographic template (blueprint) that helps create the many human energy bodies and physical vehicle. These blueprints help create the etheric body, which is a replica of the physical, mental, and emotional bodies. To download these ideal etheric templates (blueprints) into the other bodies requires the removal of all blocking energies. This subject is quite involved and will need your future study and careful attention.

As the planet shifts to a higher state of dimensional consciousness, so will your holographic template need to be upgraded. Thus, you need to request that your holographic template be upgraded to accept the new high frequency energies that can assist in your Light Body Awakening. You will need a healthy body to pass through the portals to the higher states of dimensional consciousness.

In order to maintain a healthy body, one of your first challenges is to use your creative skills and wisdom to not only repair your immune system, but to repair all the damage created following its breakdown. The choice is now available for you to decide where you want to live in the near future. It will be very difficult and even undesirable to make the required adaptations to various new energies without a healthy body. Thus to choose to transcend to the higher dimensional states of consciousness will of necessity require that you take advantage of all of your creative skills. Those creative skills can help you create a new healthy body.

We begin our review of the many aspects of meeting the challenges of creating a healthy body by pointing out the importance of understanding many different terms. How can you create a healthy body if you are unfamiliar how a healthy body functions?

For example understanding these terms are good concepts for starters: Oversoul, consciousness, transcendence, space-time, DNA encodements, High Self, emotional stability, illusions, biophotonics, Photon Belt, Light Body, stem cells, metabolism, chakras, Mer-Ka-Ba, adenosine-tri-phosphate, ribonucleic acid (RNA), quantum consciousness, scalar waves, axiatonal lines, and spin points. The point is that in order to gain an understanding of your creative potential you need to become familiar with many of the descriptive terms that help you understand that process. By gaining a better understanding of the creative processes, you can fine-tune your creative skills. You can create a new healthy body when you know you can.

Since most humans currently incarnated on Earth at this time are spiritually aware of the opportunities available, it would be helpful to "wake up" and become sensitive to what is happening around you. Be consciously observant of everything, and then maximize your energy availability.

One key is to share your Love and live more fully, touch, hug (minimum 6 people & two trees per day), laugh more, forgive more, be joyful and activate your ecstatic state of being to remain healthy and happy. A second key is to implement non-resistance, non-judgment, and non-attachment. These patterns will not only lighten the physical, mental and emotional load, but also assist us in understanding and activating your multidimensional consciousness through gaining an understanding of your unseen "Light Body."

Some may ask why humanity is currently living in the "End Times" when a dramatic "Shift" is to occur. The answer to that question relates to the cyclic nature of the galaxy. The Milky-Way galaxy spins with all component parts moving together all rotating at the same speed, like a giant spinning wheel with massive arms extending millions of miles out into space. Within the center of this galaxy, there is what many have termed the "Great Central Sun." Within the region of "The Great Central Sun," there is polarity.

In all of physics, there is always polarity from the smallest particles to the largest Universe. Matter is one polarity and antimatter is the other. This polarity creates a push and pull that holds all component parts of creation together. Within the center of the Milky-Way Galaxy, science sees a giant black hole. Within that hole is an inter-dimensional force that is not gravity, it is a force beyond the concepts of three-dimensional science and is within the realm of quantum consciousness, or what some call spirituality. The center of the Milky-Way Galaxy has consciousness. There is intelligence there. That intelligence is timeless and lacks any semblance of space. Within the unseen spiritual realm, there is no time and no space. All occurs now in the same space. If you are interested in moving from one location to another -- you are there with a thought and no time has elapsed.

The concepts of time and space are third dimension illusion specifically created for their value within the Creator School called Earth. As the Earth moves into the fourth and fifth dimensional states of consciousness, you can anticipate events and changes that have never happened upon the Earth before. Time and space will be no more. The predictions of Nostradamus, the Bible, Edgar Cayce, and a coming Armageddon involving Islam may fail to happen because of the mass shift in human consciousness. The changing consciousness is constantly creating a new reality. No one, not even God/Goddess knows what will happen in the future.

To complete our lessons here in "Creator School" and graduate requires several shifts in consciousness. The most significant is to develop our multidimensional consciousness. That is, learn how to shift our consciousnesses to the higher dimensions, those above the third and fourth DMC levels while residing in a low frequency physical body. To make that shift involves remembering and understanding your signed contracts. Once we remember our contracts, our tasks and responsibilities in each life, then we have a greater potential of graduating from these lower dimensional challenges. As with any school, success requires hard work, patience, persistence, and a large measure of dedication. To accomplish this task will require that you clear out your dysfunctional features. Once you recognize what those many dysfunctions are, then you can ask your High Self to seek out spiritual help to remove those dysfunctional roadblocks.

Why develop spiritually? How does one develop spiritually? A reminder, the main reason most individual Souls came to Earth school was for Soul development, a spiritual process. Thus, humans could benefit by asking and answering the question: What value is the present design of religious, economic, political, and/or various social beliefs? When you contemplate the answer to that question, you will need to understand that the third dimensional state of consciousness is based on a pattern of duality – good and bad, right and wrong, and Love and hate.

These social patterns are obviously part of Earth School. Thus, the next question is, "What lessons have you learned from attachment to these social patterns and beliefs?" Is it possible that these class questions help us realize that there are very few accurate sources of reality on Earth?

We came to Earth as advanced spiritual beings, created perfect. If that's true, where did the imperfections come from? We individually and collectively created them and we can also un-create them. Again, we have to ask the question, why did we create them?

As society evolves, it becomes obvious that these old outdated social systems are in need of being upgraded to a loving Service To Others orientated society. Our immediate task may be to eliminate all the selfishness and let's get on with creating a "New Earth." It's somewhat late in the game to revise all of these old outdated social systems. Let us concentrate on projecting our thoughts to what we would like to have on the "New Earth."

Important Questions Humanity is Facing

Ever since humans came to Earth, they have been faced with many questions such as -- Who am I? Where did I come from? Why am I here on Earth? How long do I have to stay here? What's this mess all about? When do I get to leave? In addition, humans frequently ask many more similar questions. For example -- Where did the Universe come from? Why does the Universe appear so intelligently designed? Why am I here at this current time? Is there free will to make my own decisions? What are my options concerning possible futures? Where am I supposed to go from here? Is there a Creator or God/Goddess whose consciousness brought all of this into being? If there was a conscious thought that contributed to the creations, then where did that consciousness originate? Then obviously, what is consciousness?

Following are some additional questions that have been voiced by those who have read the book "You Can Avoid Physical Death," by Robert E. Pettit. Obviously there are thousands of additional questions that could be asked, many of which we have difficulty answering.

Consider the following questions and come up with your own answers. Your answers may be more attuned to your beliefs and reality. However, at least consider some of these questions and my High Self's answers, as you prepare for your future.

Question 1: What difference will it make in my life if I continue to read this book and prepare for the future? Secondly -- Should I prepare for my future or just follow the crowd?

Answer: If you are interested in the future of planet Earth and your life then this book may be very helpful for you. Some of the questions discussed in this book are partially answered. You have a personal responsibility to come up with similar questions and their answers. .

Question 2: Dr. Pettit if what you outline within this book is correct – then "why haven't all of these anticipated events been reported within the communication media."

Answer: Those in control of the communication media do not want you to know about these upcoming events. Their objective is to keep you ignorant so that you are more easily controlled. If you were aware of coming events you could better plan for your future and the controllers would lose one of their prize slaves. Once you realize there are additional questions you need to ask, then you have a basis for meeting your individual needs and learning how to prepare for your future. If you are interested in graduating from Earth School then one preparatory procedure is shift your consciousness so that you are ready for ascension. If you are concerned about family members and friends who appear to be unprepared, then you will have to be careful not to interfere with their pathway and contract. There is no way I know how to step into someone else's shoes and live his or her life. If you are concerned about others, then prepare yourself and be an example to them.

Question 3: How can I help others without interfering with their chosen path?

Answer: As just mentioned, prepare yourself as an example others can follow. Prepare fifth density Light Body and yourself for ascending to the "New Earth" as soon as possible. Then as others ask for your opinion or need your help, you can make suggestions. Then they could confer with

21

others to obtain a second opinion. Then they will be faced with making their own decisions.

Question 4: How can I utilize my consciousness to create the most efficient vehicle for following the evolutionary pathway designed for all humans?

Answer: Connect with your High Self to receive instructions, activate your "Light Body," and prepare for "The Shift," coming in the very near future. Study a multitude of books and other sources of information outlined on the internet and use discernment to make the most appropriate decision.

Question 5: How can I deal with upcoming events without moving into or becoming trapped in a state of fear?

Answer: There is nothing to fear but fear itself. Love cancels out all hate and fear. Live from the heart with Love. Light Body awakening and activation will help you avoid fear.

Question 6: Will the series of events scheduled to occur starting in 2012 benefit my future life?

Answer: Yes. They will benefit your future in ways that are difficult to imagine. A whole New Earth awaits your arrival. The rapidly changing events taking place on Earth indicate that there is a need to "Wake Up" and realize that the third dimension Earth we have become familiar with for several thousand years is coming to an end. In the very near future, the third dimension Earth will cease supporting humans. Humanity over the centuries has damaged the soil, air, and water so severely that climatic conditions will cease to support plant growth that humans and animals have so long depended upon. In addition to these environmental changes the traditional third dimension social patterns in economics, politics, education, religion, social behavior, technology, and various duality concepts will have to change to vibrate at higher frequencies. Most of these social patterns have been manipulated with the use of low frequency patterns, for the benefit of the controllers. Thus, the higher frequency changes arriving on Earth from the Great Central Sun and Photon Belt will assist Earth and all of its inhabitants to shift their consciousness to third dimension duality consciousness into fifth dimension unity consciousness.

Assuming this is an accurate summary of upcoming events, the question stated again is. How can I avoid all fear? Each individual person needs to answer that question and make adequate shifts in consciousness to prevent all forms of fear. Keep in mind that FEAR can be defined as "Forgetting Every Available Resource." It is essential that in place of any form of fear, you put in place LOVE. .

Question 7: Should I be concerned about others who appear to know nothing about the coming shift of the ages?

Answer: A careful analysis of human consciousness currently residing on Earth indicates that a majority of humans will choose at the Soul level and/or conscious level to leave their physical bodies on Earth. They would rather die than let go of their fears, preconceived ideologies and personal agendas. They have decided they have little **interest** in going through the necessary disciplinary steps to achieve graduation and ascension status. These souls will have another opportunity to make a choice while in spirit beyond the veil. Following death on the other side, or during some future life upon another low frequency planet, they will again have a decision to make about whether to graduate and ascend.

Some individuals place their faith in science to help guide their future. If that is your situation then please ask the following question:

Question 8: How much faith should I place on the results of the many different scientific experimental results people talk about?

Answer: When you closely examine a series of scientific documents, you will discover that each discovery is followed by another discovery that replaces the previous conclusions. Apparently, science progresses in small steps in their search to discover a portion of reality.

Keep in mind that most of these experiments were designed and carried out by individual scientists and technicians who had a stake in the experiments outcome. Consequently, the experimental results were largely determined by the experimenters (scientists and technicians) consciousness, those who conducted the experiments. Their "thought forms" produced an energy pattern that shifted the experiment to their anticipated conscious outcome. What you think you create.

Some other important questions relate to our "High Self."

23

Question 9: What is my "Higher Self" or ""High Self?"

Answer: Your "Higher Self" is you, the real you, your total Soul consciousness. The spirit part of you that is living here on Earth is a projection of the consciousness of your "Higher Self." The "High Self" is the more complete you, the one that is not frustrated by the veil that separates you from the spirit world -- when you incarnated within a physical body. Your "High Self" has a copy of your Earthly contract, your plan. The "High Self" knows everything about you. The High Self knows all of your thoughts, goals, intentions, and your feelings. There is no-thing that can be hidden from your "Higher Self."

Question 10: Where is my" Higher Self" or "High Self?"

Answer: Your "Higher Self" remains within the spiritual realm on the other side of the veil. A region in creation some would call the "ethers." You always have access to your "Higher Self." Your "High Self" is always with you.

Question 11: What is the role of my "Higher Self" or "High Self?"

Answer: Your "High Self" has the responsibility to watch over you while you are incarnated on Earth or anywhere else within the Universe. Your "High Self" knows where you are supposed to be and when. Before you incarnated your "High Self" arranged a meeting to help set up your plans for your future life incarnated within a physical body. You can contact your "High Self" to ask for spiritual help. Your "High Self" has access to many advanced spiritual beings with all types of skills.

Question 12: How do I connect with my "Higher Self" or "High Self?"

Answer: First, always know you are connected. Then attempt to talk with your "High Self." The "High Self" may sound different to different persons. It may sound like the "Still Small Voice Within" that comes in the form of thoughts. You may prefer to call the messages from "High Self" your intuition. When listening to your "High Self" make sure the thoughts you are hearing are not coming from your ego self. Several individuals have asked their "High Self" to type out the answers to a question while using the keyboard of the computer. Some may be able to visualize their "High Self" in the form of a Spirit that comes to visit them in time of need.

The speaking of your "High Self" may come through your imagination. All efforts to contact your "High Self" may take time. Just have patience and continue to know it is possible to communicate with your "High Self."

As you continue to read and integrate the thoughts throughout the book, additional questions will arise. As you seek out answers to those questions always, use discernment in choosing the correct answer. Confer with your God/Goddess within or High Self Spiritual Council for their insights. In all cases, make sure that the help from your High Self correlates with your understanding of reality. Keep in mind the importance of making wise choices for your future. If for any reason you lack trust in your High Self check out the answers to other questions by choosing books and certain web sites in which spiritual concepts can be verified by your still small voices within. That voice is most likely the God/Goddess within that is a major part of your spiritual reality and has your best interest in mind. That other voice may be your ego -- putting up a fight to stay in control.

Speeding Up of Time – The Effects

Many people are not aware of the many changes taking place around them each day. However, most people sense that there is less time to complete the many tasks they would like to have time to complete. Each day when you wake up and go about your daily activities, it appears that every activity you engage in take longer to complete. Thus, it appears that time is speeding up.

If you ask the question of others, do you think time is speeding up? The frequent answer is, yes, it is as if I just got out of bed this morning and before I know it, I am ready to go to bed again. Where did the day go?

Clock time, that low frequency measuring procedure for third dimension humans, was created to help us schedule various tasks in a sequential pattern of movement. Time we sense within our bodies is different. This time is more related to the rhythms and cycles held within our conscious and subconscious bodies. Such time is changing because the reference points used to calculate our activities are changing. Clock time remains the same. What is changing is our perception of the changes in the weakening magnetic fields surrounding the Earth and the increased Light energy coming to Earth from other regions of the Universe.

Preparation time is short, since as of January 2010 there is less than three years until December 2012, a mid-point during "The Shift." That is when some believe the null zone (intense band of photons) of the "Photon Belt" is scheduled to affect Earth with three days of darkness. Remember the null zone will absorb all electromagnetic energies including light and electrical energies to create darkness.

With the arrival of the photon belt, a multitude of new energy patterns will arrive on Earth. One change that everyone is aware of is that time appears to be collapsing. Although the internal sensation inside the human energy systems indicates that time is going faster, actually time is collapsing into a single moment of Present Time, NOW.

As the Light frequencies increase, the magnetic field of the planet is decreasing. This collapse of the magnetic field affects our physical, mental, emotional, and spirituals body's perception of events, one of which is time. The collapse of the magnetic field, which is tied to human consciousness, is caused in part by the passage of Light through the Earth's magnetic field. Since our sensing systems are tied to the magnetic field, they are also altered. Installation of the Mer-Ka-Ba tetrahedron can help provide protection from the collapse of the magnetic field since the Mer-Ka-Ba creates its own magnetic field.

As the Solar system moves further into the "Photon Belt," the Light frequencies increase and the magnetic fields around us decrease. As a result, our physical, mental, emotional, and spiritual body's perception of all events are altered. That is, as these new waves of Light pass through us and with the collapse of the Earth's magnetic field, our magnetic field within collapses. As a result, our sensing systems will have to change and our communication pattern will of necessity change.

For example, if you have walked to work every day over the same path for many years, your body would have developed a sense of how long it takes to reach your destination. However, as time collapses you have less time to walk that same distance to work. What is happening is that your internal sensing system associated with your bodies is telling you that time is going faster because you had to hurry to get to work at the same time you used in the past? Although your watch recorded the same time, you sensed that it took longer.

As these higher frequency light waves are arriving on Earth, our internal rhythms are aligning up so that we can eventually align to a singular flow of consciousness in the Present "Now" Time. This alignment occurs because in reality the only place we actually exist is in the Present "Now" Time. Clock time may appear to be real however, it is actually an illusion we created within the third Dimension. Spiritually speaking, time and space are both illusions that we will better understand as we evolve to the higher dimensions and higher densities.

Our heartbeat, biorhythms, and pulses within the meridian system have always been synchronized with the frequency of the Earth, called the Schumann resonance. As the Schumann resonance goes up within the Earth, these body functions change to match that of the Earth.

Our memories, thoughts, emotions, and beliefs that were developed and utilized at the lower frequencies are fading away. The old patterns we have become so used to will not be able to function at the higher frequencies. That is, as the Earth's frequency increases and the magnetic field decreases, we are losing our old memories, beliefs, emotions, and thoughts that helped us maneuver through the lower third Dimension Earth. The Earth is moving to a fourth Dimensional state of Consciousness or fourth Density and our bodies are attempting to adjust to those new energy patterns. You cannot take your old arguments, embarrassing moment, and painful experiences stored unconsciously within your memory to the new fourth Dimension Earth. Those old patterns have nothing to do with who you are becoming.

The task of adjusting to all of the new energies arriving on Earth may not be easy. However, you have been given a choice to strive to make the needed changes, evolve, and move along in Consciousness to the new fourth and fifth Dimension Earth. There are other third Dimensional options, which are available and will be discussed later.

New waves of light are arriving on Earth for the expressed purpose of clearing away all old behavior patterns, false beliefs, discordant programs, negative emotions, and other patterns that we have accumulated. These must be released and cleared away. During our many experiences within the third dimension, we believed what other people told us, what we read, and what we experienced in school, church, and heard on the radio or television. We thought that these beliefs were equated to truth and believed that they made up the real world. We gave our power away to those who controlled our lives. These patterns had value during these lower frequency third Dimension experiences and lessons. However, the Earth is moving to a higher frequency where these patterns will have very limited value.

Currently we are at a point in our evolvement where we need to and must take our power back. We will need to remember who we really are and who we are NOT. No longer do we need to be controlled by others. Those manipulative control patterns will be replaced by new more accurate high frequency patterns that are in harmony with the higher Dimensions and Densities. All of these old third Dimension duality concepts must be removed to make room for the new more exciting behavior patterns,

In order to carry out our tasks within the higher frequencies we must develop new patterns of behavior. These new patterns will be based on the concepts of Love and Oneness, frequently called Unity or Christ Consciousness. In addition, these patterns will be based on the concept that everything that happens is actually occurring "NOW." There will be no past or future to consider as our bodies evolve to the higher states of Dimensional Consciousness and Higher Densities. There will be no need to think of the past or plan for the future. Your reality will be created each "NOW" moment. Thus, what you think "NOW" will be what you experience.

As these experiences described above take place within your life, do not be alarmed. You are not the only one on Earth having these experiences. You still have all of your mental and emotional capabilities. These experiences are not related to any sickness or lack within your energy system. There is nothing broken; it is simply that who we are NOT and never were is beginning to fall away.

As each human awakens to what is happening on Earth each one should strive to seek their own truth and walk in their own unique path. An awakened individual is realizing there is much more to who they are. Much more than what the outside world has led them to believe. As we each look within, we begin to understand that we are multidimensional, spiritual beings, capable of aligning our consciousness to the higher frequencies. Your truth can help create joy, happiness, success, health, and at the same time adds simplicity to your life.

Shifting From Third to Fifth Dimension

In the past, only a few souls experienced the Spiritual truths now available upon planet Earth. Because of your reading this material and wanting to live in a more pleasant way of life, a new reality is emerging. The old is fading away and the new is ready for the asking. Together all of these changes make up "The Shift" from one low third Dimensional state of Consciousness to either the fourth Dimensional state of Consciousness or the fifth Dimensional state of Consciousness. The other choice is to remain within the third Dimensional state of Consciousness and vacate the Earth. There will be no third Dimensional Consciousness remaining as a favorable environment for survival. Third Dimensional Mother Earth will initiate a cleanup process that will take many centuries to complete.

Each of these Dimensions or Densities relate to different vibrational frequencies. As you know, everything is energy and all thought forms including each form of matter and antimatter vibrate at specific frequencies. All thoughts created anywhere in the Universe have an individual frequency and influence everyone upon the planet.

For example, the higher Love frequency has specific energy properties that are quite different from the lower Fear frequency. When thought forms of Love are projected out to any target, they influence everything. The same is true of negative thoughts. Everyone else senses all thoughts, positive or negative that may be projected to a specific target. Those "thought forms" not only change the features of their target but are also projected out into all of creation and have an infinite influence.

As humans make the choice to move out of the third Dimension frequencies and move to the fourth Dimension frequencies, they will have made a shift in Consciousness. Likewise, as we move out of the fourth Dimension into the fifth Dimension we have again changed frequency. These different Dimensions are not places. They are vibratory levels of Consciousness. The new Earth (Heaven on Earth) may appear to be a new place. However, it's most important feature is that it resides within a different state of dimensional consciousness (DMC).

Humans have been living within the third and fourth Dimensions for the past 60 years. In fact, most humans have lived simultaneously within these two Dimensions many times before. Each Dimension has different frequency characteristics. As we describe the differences between these three dimensions hopefully you will better understand what choices are available for you during "The Shift."

The reincarnation cycle where the human Soul has continued to incarnate upon low-density planets, for over seventy-five-thousand years is ending. Planet Earth has been given permission to shift to the fourth density and later on to the fifth density. For those souls who are interested and have prepared to graduate and ascend to a new parallel reality, "New Earth" is forming right here within a higher density and higher state of dimensional consciousness (DMC). The drama and old play is ending. It is time to prepare for the new fifth dimension Earth and a lengthy life span that each Soul will determine by their belief. The false belief that the human body must die through various means needs to be cleared from one's consciousness. The human body was designed to live for thousands of years when one takes care of their energy various bodies. The Creators of this Universe have provided for another option that is available when our spirit has made the decision to vacate the physical Earth. That new option is to obtain a new physical body and take it with you to the fifth density and fifth state of dimensional consciousness (DMC).

There are fast-track procedures available for help in preparing for graduation and ascension available. That help is only provided when an individual asks for help from other parts of one's reality such as their High Self and God/Goddess within and High Self . The asking must be associated with a faith, belief, and knowing that such assistance will be forthcoming. A limiting belief system creates a blocking energy.

There are a multitude of preparation procedures for graduation and ascension from the third dimension Earth. Many of these procedures have been available and you have been working on them for many lifetimes. Several of these procedures take many life times to complete effectively. One very important preparation procedure that will be discussed in **Section V** is Light Body Awakening. Make sure you complete the series of twelve steps outlined on Light Body Awakening. If you have waited until this point in history to complete your preparation for graduation and ascension, it is time to start your "Light Body Awakening" procedures – "NOW."

After an individual Soul develops their spiritual capabilities and thus meets all of the requirements for graduation, they can qualify to pass through a portal or dimensional doorway to the next higher density and/or state of consciousness. There will be an inspector at the portal to check your credentials. So be prepared before you approach the portal.

The next opportunity to become involved in mass graduation and ascension will occur between 2010 and 2015 with the peak experience to take place on December 21, 2012. However, keep in mind that individual graduation and ascension can occur at any time.

One tragic behavior, we humans (supposedly with some intelligence) allow greedy financial managers to extract the very lifeblood (oil) from Earth. This practice must be stopped for Earth's survival. Many other sources of free energy have been proven many times over. Tesla long ago patented an automobile engine that obtains free energy from the atmosphere. Why has it been kept off the market? Could it be because of greed and the realization, by our controllers, that they would have to relinquish some of their power over us?

What should we do to solve this situation? Will it help to "Wake Up" and observe what's happening? To "wake up" implies seeing what you are doing to yourself, other people, animals, plants, and all of creation. Are you constantly sending Love to all parts of Creation? Observe your self-centered destructive behavior patterns: For example living off others labors, holding on to false beliefs that make you right and others wrong, and knowing the answers all the time. We should be careful in judging those "others" - the "non-believers." Some will say, "let me tell you the truth" or "unless you believe like me you are going to hell." Each of us needs to consider letting go through non-attachment. We all know so little, so let's release those old false beliefs and replace them with new accurate beliefs that assist our graduation and ascension.

Section II. Cyclic Nature of Creation

Milky Way Galaxy and Cyclic Events on Earth

The question that one should strive to resolve is how the cyclic nature of the Universe affects my life here on planet Earth. First, we must make an effort to understand that everything throughout the Universe is energy and that energy is cyclic in nature and spirals back upon itself in varying repeatable patterns. For example, the milky-way galaxy travels around the great central sun called Alcyone, every 26,000 years. .

However, the Milky Way Galaxy, Solar System, and planet Earth exhibit specific rotational patterns and influence the third dimension events anticipated at the end of the coming cycle. The 75,000, 50,000, 25,000, and 12,500 years cycles are ending around the month of December 2012. The collective consciousness on Earth is insufficiently strong to alter this galactic pattern. Therefore, we should accept the fact that we have come to the end of a galactic cycle and need to prepare for the predicted changes.

Some may ask why do we need to know anything about the Milky Way Galaxy? How does the Milky Way Galaxy relate to changes taking place on Earth and "The Shift" and approach of December 2012? With all of the interest about 2012, one thing that's true is there will be a galactic alignment during that time frame.

An advanced race called the Mayans predicted this galactic alignment. They were not in the business of fortune telling or prophesying. They accurately predicted there would be a galactic alignment in 2012 when the December solstice sun aligns with the galactic equator. This galactic alignment is not only an accurate prediction but has been proven scientifically. Thus, there is no question as to the accuracy about a significant event occurring in 2012.

As 2012 approaches, a majority of the population on Earth have become aware of the rapidly changing climatic and geophysical conditions that are affecting all aspects of human activities. A similar sequence of events has happened at least four times in the history of the Earth, according to many ancient tribes and Extraterrestrial records.

The most recent galactic alignment occurred 25,000 years ago and helped bring about the submergence of Atlantis into the Atlantic Ocean.

At that time and during the previous alignments, a majority of the human population perished during a series of physical Earth changes. Available information indicates that these Earth changes have been caused by a reversal of the North and South poles, and a misuse of energy that resulted in dramatic earthquakes, floods, and volcanic activity. These events created climatic changes that limited the production of food for lengthy periods.

This 25,000 year repeating cyclic changes occur in response to the location of the solar system and Earth in relation to the Milky Way Galaxy. The Milky Way Galaxy, Solar System, and planet Earth exhibit specific rotational patterns that influence the third dimension events experienced at the end of each cycle. In round numbers, these changes have occurred in the past at the end of 75,000, 50,000, 25,000, and 12,500 years. The current 25,000-year cycle, that began when Atlantis collapsed, will end during the month of December 2012.

Our solar system is located at the far edge of the Milky Way Galaxy, in a band of white light that can be observed across the sky on a clear night. The Milky Way Galaxy is a massive spiraling (pinwheel shaped) collection of 300 to 400 billion stars (suns) most of which are invisible from Earth. This Milky Way Galaxy is very large, about 120,000 light years across and 7,000 light years thick. Estimates are that this Galaxy is over 13 billion years old. Since no space craft has ever gone outside the Galaxy, it has been impossible to obtain pictures of this Galaxy. Thus, our concepts of the Galaxy are based on the photographs of other Galaxies with similar structural features.

There are billions of Universes and billions of Galaxies in each Universe, each with its own structural features. Galaxies tend to form in groups where a few have the pinwheel shape. The spiraling pinwheel shaped galaxies have many arms that extend far out into space. The arms are named after the constellations that reside within that arm. Our solar system is located within one of the minor galaxy arms called "Orion Spur." It is far from the center of the Galaxy, out near the very edge.

That arm called the "Orion Spur" is part of the constellation called the Pleiades, also known by the ancients as the "Seven Sisters." Our solar system orbits around the Pleiadian constellation's central sun, called "Alcyone." It takes approximately 25,000 years to make one complete orbit around the Pleiades. Alcyone has a dramatic affect on the planets within our solar system.

The central hub of the saucer shaped Milky Way Galaxy has a huge bright bulge, visible from Earth. That bulge, called the Galactic Center, is within the flat portion of the Galaxy, called the galactic equator, and is where the December solstice sun will align in 2012. Each time our solar system has aligned with the galactic equator, in the past, all planets have been affected. There have been significant changes in the energetic patterns on Earth. Apparently, these energies originated from the galactic equator and the great Central Sun "Alcyone." These different energetic patterns influence all parts of the solar system. The energetic patterns from the galactic equator and Great Central Sun in combination with the energies of the "Photon Belt" help bring about the cyclic changes that occur every 25,000 years. These astronomical events are established cyclic patterns that cannot be influenced by the collective consciousness of the inhabiting spirits.

The question that one should strive to resolve is how does the cyclic nature of the Universe affect my life here on planet Earth? First, we must make an effort to understand that everything throughout the Universe is energy and that energy is cyclic in nature. Consequently, everything in the Universe spirals back upon itself in varying repeatable patterns. For example, the Solar System rotates around the great central sun called Alcyone, every 26,000 years.

As a result, due to the cyclic nature of events within the Universe and Milky Way Galaxy the Solar System, planet Earth, and all living forms on the planet are going through a frequency and phase shift. By the year 2012, the Earth will experience a Galactic Alignment with the energy plane of the Milky Way Galaxy, a solar eclipse, and a Venus transit across the sun. As a result, everything on Earth will change or go through that which has been called "The Shift of The Ages." This "Shift" in frequency has taken on many terms, the most descriptive being "The Shift," "The End Times," "The Rapture," "The End of The Age," and/or "The Shift of The Ages." Humans will greatly benefit in terms of their understanding of reality, once they understand something about where they live.

Photon Belt and Two Thousand Year Light Cycle

The first known accurate description of the energy pattern called the "Photon Belt" was published within the book "You Are Becoming a Galactic Human" by Virginia Essene and Sheldon Nidle" in 1994. This message originated from the Sirians and Council of Ascended Masters. The Galactic Federation of Planets sanctioned Washta to explain what Earth humans can anticipate as they pass through the Photon Belt. The upcoming event that will be initiated in 2012 will have both physical and spiritual characteristics. Robert Pettit recommends anyone interested in graduating and ascending to the New Earth study the book "You Are Becoming a Galactic Human," carefully.

From a scientific perspective, the initial discovery of the "Photon Belt" occurred in1961. Satellite instrumentation discovered an unusual nebula phenomenon in the Pleiades Constellation that consisted of a vast cloud-like mass of energy. Because of its anomalous properties, it was called the Golden Nebula. Then in the 1980's astronomers discovered and announced that our solar system was about to enter a unique electromagnetic zone. This announcement was not made public, rather suppressed by various governments throughout the world, purposely, to keep that information from the human population. Again, an attempt designed to limit spiritual development.

What is the cloud-like mass that was called the Golden Nebula or electromagnetic field? As the Solar System orbits the Great Central Sun of Pleiades, (Alcyone) it periodically passes through this massive cloud of energy now known to be composed of photons. A photon is released following the collision of anti-proton and a proton. The photon represents a quantum of light that appears as a form of radiation; however, a photon has no physical mass or "zero rest mass."

This multiple band of different light (photons) patterns has a doughnut shape through which our solar system periodically passes. It passes through this light band (Photon Belt) twice every 25,920 years. The solar system remains within the Photon Belt for 2,160 years. This period is called the "Light Period." The Light Period is followed by a "Dark Period" of 10.800 years. Within one 25,920 cycle around the Great Central Sun (Alcyone) the Earth experiences two Light Periods and two Dark Periods.

During the positive half of each twenty-five-thousand-year cycle, called the Golden Ages, humans have expanded their consciousness and experienced unlimited possibilities. 'The Fall" of mankind, sometimes referred to in the Bible as an event where Eve consumed an apple, was about partaking of the tree of good and evil. Thus, "The Fall" was about a compromise in values associated with the higher levels of consciousness that had previously been established. "The Fall" was created by humanity's desire to experience polarity (duality) at the lower dimensions. Humans chose to separate from God/Goddess. Thus, "The Fall" in consciousness created a rift in the perfection that had existed previously. As the "The Fall" proceeded, during the 26,000-year dark cycles, humanity gradually descended into the rift of duality. Now, after these many years and many incarnations on Earth we have come to an end of that dark cycle. Since the majority of humans have very limited memory of their past lives, because we agreed to forget at the time of "The Fall," we are now faced with an awakening (remembering) with the arrival of the "Photon Belt."

As mentioned, consciously, you are unaware of the thousands of years you have been on Earth in many different bodies. This means that the real you, not the conscious one residing here on Earth at this time, still possesses the knowledge of all those past lives. We all have the potential to resurrect that knowledge into our current awareness. As you let go of the erroneous and distorted false beliefs and illusions that have limited you for thousands of years, you can begin to remember the great and marvelous being that you are. As you remember those portions of incarnations experienced during the higher states of dimensional consciousness, you can manifest them and bring them back into your physical life on the New Earth. The movement into the "Photon Belt" and the two thousand years of Light will assist you in remembering.

Recent information indicates that this "Photon Belt" phenomenon is also linked to the energetic features of the galactic alignment (convergence). That is, the convergence is the end of a stellar activation cycle that is in progress now. Keep in mind that the galactic alignment and the rotation of the Solar System around the Great Central Sun are two separate events, obviously interconnected.

The arrival of the Photon Belt will shift the solar system into a higher dimension that is from the third dimension into the fifth dimension.

Through a series of events, this will allow the solar system to move to a new position in space, closer to the Sirius star system. This shift in position of the solar system, as it becomes closer to Sirius, is exciting. Once located within the new position, Earth will go through many significant changes.

This massive "Photon Belt" contains a multitude of electromagnetic frequencies within the visible region and beyond. That is, the 'Photon Belt" contains a wide variety of high frequency energies within the invisible spectrum. For example, there are significant levels of ultra violet (UV) and x-ray frequencies. Because of specific holes of the protective ozone layer, surrounding Earth, dangerous ultra violet radiation is entering Earth's atmosphere. Science is struggling to determine the causes and possible effects on life on Earth. However, it is well established that an increase in ultra violet radiation can interfere with many living systems on Earth. For example, increased exposure to ultra violet light in humans causes a lowering of the immune system, skin cancer, and cataracts. With crop plants an increase in UV radiation results in lowered production. In the Antarctica, below an ozone hole, the growth of phytoplankton has been reduced to where some penguins have difficulty finding sufficient food. Much of the thinning of the ozone layer is related to changing climatic conditions.

The main body of the Photon Belt consists of three major sectors, the null zone entrance, main photon Belt, and the null zone exit. The null zone is an intense concentration of photons that capture all electromagnetic radiation. Upon entering this zone, all light and electrical energies will be neutralized (inactivated). All electrical devices such as those used in our homes, transportation devices, lighting, factories, etc, will malfunction.

This brief period, during which established life style patterns change, has been called the "three days of darkness," however, the projected time within the null zone is 5 to 6 days. There will be no need to try to use a flashlight during the dark days, because it will not work. Obviously, with the loss of the heating effect of the sun it will become cold. The length of this period is yet to be determined and depends upon the support received from Extraterrestrial groups monitoring these changing conditions. They are working to reduce the adverse affects of many upcoming events.

During this period, called "The Shift of The Ages" individual humans who have prepared to ascend will have their bodies altered through a process related to "Light Body Awakening," discussed in **Section V**. The later stages of "Light Body Awakening," during passage through the null zone will cause an effect similar to putting ones hand in an electrical outlet. This sudden shock will last about a tenth of a second, thus will be over before one really notices it has occurred. At present, most researchers have evidence that humans have the experience of three different types of bodies.

1. The first type of body appears to be a relatively solid mass that humans presently inhabit within the third dimension.

2. The second type vibrates at a higher frequency, still has some mass, but is less dense. This body has the capability to move through a solid three-dimensional wall.

3. The third type has no physical mass at all. This body has been called a spiritual body.

Upon exiting the null zone entrance to the "Photon Belt," you will enter a period of extreme light and your body will shift to the second type. When you have passed through the null zone without fear, you will have taken on the second type of body that is essentially a fifth dimensional body. The Christian bible and other documents have described this event as "When one is changed to immortality in the twinkling of an eye." Some refer to entering the "Photon Belt" as passing into a period of eternal light.

The photon belt will supply sufficient photon (light) energy that humanity can abandon the fossil-fueled industrial age. Photon energy will supply all of humanities energy needs. Humans will take in a very limited amount of food. The human body will largely survive by taking in photon energy. This is why it is currently important to practice "prana" life force breathing, as described within the book "You Can Avoid Physical Death" by Robert Pettit.

The present dilemma that many humans are faced with is the urgency of preparing for these dramatically changing events. There is a need to rapidly clear all previous inaccurate belief systems and rapidly accept new ones. Generally, such changes take considerable time, in fact for some many life times. However, everyone who is now just "waking up" to what is happening, third dimensional time is in short supply. Time is collapsing and December 2012 is fast approaching. All of your options and choice are being compressed into a series of paradigm shifts that our present generation of scientific and spiritual leaders are urging everyone interested to address. Over two-thirds of the humans on Earth appear to be unable to make meaningful shifts in consciousness to accept these new incoming energies from the Galactic Alignment, Great Central Sun Alcyone, and Photon Belt.

A New Earth is being created right here that promises a bright future for spiritual evolution. There is an urgent need for those who understand what is happening to come forth and help Earth's population prepare for the future. Part of the problem many humans have is that they are unable or unwilling to take the time to understand the full meaning of their predicament. Many humans within the traditional occupations, such as education, religion, politics, marketing, manufacturing, farming, finance, etc. still attempt to advocate and promote worn out techniques that no longer serve the interest of humanity. Especially the needs of the many new more advanced Souls arriving on Earth, who need to have available a new social systems for their own well-being.

All traditional conservative approaches to the anticipated changes during "The Shift," that is scheduled to occur in 2012, have been designed to slow an individual's spiritual progress. The controllers continue to promote the fear of change through various forms of propaganda. They also use judgmental techniques to create the presence of enemies. They need enemies to help maintain control of the population and their well-established industrial war machine. These judgmental conservatives not only threaten our way of life on third dimension Earth but they also threaten the survival of third density Earth itself.

One of the most important benefits of these coming changes brought about by entrance into the Photon Belt is the opportunity to become a member of the Galactic Federation of Planets. In so doing, we will rightfully take our place as an active associated member of the spiritually evolved entities that make up a large population of the Milky Way Galaxy. We then will have help and access of advanced technologies beyond anyone's imagination. With help from many different Extraterrestrial groups that make up the Intergalactic Federation of Planets we will access to the true history of planet Earth. Much of our history has been lost, either destroyed, or manipulated to where it is almost impossible to make sense of what has happened. We all choose go through "The Fall" and experience these third dimension duality conditions.

There is one potential danger that the Extraterrestrials have been carefully monitoring for many years -- as they catalog all nuclear materials on Earth. There is a potential activation of those nuclear materials by the intense photon energy present within the null zone. During the three-day dark period, the atmosphere becomes compressed and all materials become denser. In fact, your body will become so dense it will feel bloated. The increased pressures could also set off a nuclear chain-reaction of the radioactive materials within all of the stored nuclear devices. Such a chain-reaction would set off a firestorm from all of the explosions. Therefore, add your request for support from the Intergalactic Federation of Planets to come with special landing and technical trained personnel to alleviate this potential danger.

If these concepts about the arrival of the Photon Belt are new to you, several websites can help you understand. Obviously, there are websites purposely trying to create confusion about the "Photon Belt" by stating that the whole idea lacks scientific support, thus should be ignored. Since when does scientific evidence make anything more accurate? Scientists do not have all of the answers to what is really taking place anywhere in the Universe. They are trying to understand, just as everyone else. They have limited knowledge just as the rest of humanity.

One helpful thought form sequence that could help facilitate your graduation and ascension is to become aware of what affect the energy form the galactic alignment and photon belt has upon the features of your Deoxy-ribonucleic-acids (DNA). A DNA molecule is like a program-able piece of computer hardware. The torsion waves of light coming from the Great Central Sun Alcyone and the Photon Belt manifest as hyper-dimensional light could restructure the DNA of all living systems upon planet Earth. Therefore, to take advantage of these incoming energies make sure you DNA and RNA have been upgraded to receive these new high frequency energies. With an upgrade in your DNA from the two strands to twelve strands your energy system will have difficulty accepting the new high frequency energies. There are many resources to help you work with making the appropriate DNA changes.

40

Section III. Oversouls and Human Soul

Features of an Oversoul and Human Soul

Keep in mind as we delve into the discussion of the humans Soul, that spirit body and Soul body are two distinct aspects of human reality. The term "Spirit" is that part of you that is undifferentiated and totally connected to Source (God/Goddess, ALL THAT IS). The Soul is that differentiated part of Spirit that experiences through your physical body. The Soul is that evolutionary component part of the individual that evolves up through the various densities, dimensions, coordinates communications, and is the power source for all life and related functions carried out by our many other bodies. The spirit is that component that is connected to Source energy and thus the energetic force that holds together all the various individual bodies and individual dimensional features that make up the one's multidimensional reality.

The human Soul is one of the most magnificent creations ever conceived by the CREATORS. What is even more wonderful is that each human and animal on Earth has a Soul. The Soul lacks physicality thus cannot be observed with physical eyes or any electronic detective apparatus. However, the Soul can be observed with spiritual vision. Those with keen physic vision have been able to detect a complex sacred geometric form that changes shape as the Soul evolves. The Soul exhibits a crystalline like form in combination with other associated geometric patterns with extending branches.. The Soul shape within the more spiritually developed individuals gradually takes on a golden egg shape. One of your most important tasks on Earth is to take care of your Soul. Lack of care and handling of the Soul can cause a vast number of imbalances in various body systems, especially within the mental, emotional, and spiritual bodies. Imbalances within these bodies indirectly influence the physical body's health.

There is a crisis brewing on Earth in terms of the evolution of Souls currently residing here. This crisis influences all of our bodies including the physical, etheric, mental, emotional, and spiritual ones. Because of this crisis, a growing number of human spirits are electing not to evolve and go into the Light. Decades of war, famine, drought, economic calamity, political unrest, and multitudes of challenging incarnations (within the lower densities) have led to the creation of billions of unsettled human spirits. A majority of these humans, over five billion, have evidently made the choice to remain attached to a third-fourth dimensional world rather than graduate and move on to the higher frequency ones.

One of the main reasons they are choosing to remain trapped within a lower density is because they do not understand the physical death state or the true condition of their Soul. Furthermore, they do not understand the necessary steps that they must now take to release themselves from their present condition or in many cases their current entrapment. In short, they do not know what to do next so they return to that which is familiar. All compiling evidence indicates that from 75 to 80% of the 7.5 billion humans now on Earth will remain attached to the lessons within the lower densities. That means about twenty to twenty-five percent are considering graduation and ascension to the "New Earth."

Dr. Mitchell Gibson (M.D.), who has conducted a series of workshops on the human Soul, addresses these challenges through his presentation of spiritual and religious educational materials. Concepts and enlightening information presented in his workshops have been designed to assist each individual in breaking away from existing attachments to these lower densities. For additional information on Dr. Mitchell Gibson's Soul workshops and related topics go to www.tybro.com.

In addition, there are an increasing number of books and websites designed to help those who choose to evolve spiritually. For example, the web site www.salrachele.com provides channeled materials from the Founders, twelfth dimensional (density) entities. Upon careful examination of these channelings and the associated book, I believe that these advanced entities have a very important message for humanity in this Now Time. The Founders have channeled through Sal Rachele of Sedona Arizona an important series of messages that are summarized within the book "Earth Changes and 2012.".

The Founders messages have arrived at the end of this current 26,000-year cosmic galactic cycle when humans are faced with a multitude of new challenges. Their messages are designed to assist humanity in understanding the many different changes currently taking place. Their guidelines and suggested help is primarily directed towards those Souls

42

who have chosen to become actively involved in the current ongoing "harvest" or "graduation" and "ascension" process.

Outlined in the following pages is a summarized discussion of the "Living Human Soul." This summarization is but a brief review of the nature and importance of the human Soul and the challenge we each have in taking care of our Souls. Throughout all of creation, one of the main objectives of the Creators has been to develop an energy system (Soul) that could accurately record the activities of humans and assist them through their sojourns throughout the Universe.

The human Soul has a dramatic effect on everything humans do while evolving up through the twelve densities and related twelve levels of dimensional consciousness. The Soul's structural features and related capabilities can be correlated with each individual's spiritual and evolutionary sojourns on various planets throughout the created Universes.

Our beginning challenge is to attempt to understand where our sovereign (supreme) Oversoul was created. The channelings from the Founders indicate that the GOD/GODDESS and associated Creators have brought into some form, everything throughout the Universe. These creations also include individual Oversouls and/or Soul fragments, one of which inhabits every human present on Earth. The original old Souls and those that continue to come into existence were all created to be extensions of (ALL THAT IS). As a result HE/SHE (GOD/GODDESS) instilled in every Spirit and Soul the desire to explore and come to understand all of the many creations. Thereby each spirit was to experience the many "CREATORS" AND "THEIR CREATIONS," more intimately.

The Founders indicate that the creative process-taking place between the first and seventh densities can be partially described. However, the languages present upon Earth are inadequate to describe the activities taking place within the eighth through twelfth densities. Because of these language limitations, many details about higher densities are very difficult to describe. The challenge is to describe these details in terms that are understandable by low-density humans. Therefore, we will have to wait until we evolve to the higher densities to understand many aspects of spiritual evolution above the sixth to seventh densities

Souls generally emerged within the various Universes in waves of creation. The first individual spirits with Souls, in this Omniverse (all Universes combined within this sector) were individualized billions of years ago. They were created as twelfth Density beings, at what has been termed the point of conception. These original Souls, from the twelfth density, have been called the "Ancient Ones," because of their origin.

During the conception of the Omniverse, these original Oversouls had a blueprint, a part of the Divine Plan that was encoded within all twelve potential densities and consciousnesses. These many different all-encompassing encodements are a component part of your Soul. That is, you have encoded within your Soul an aspect of self that is energetically represented within all component connections to all twelve densities and dimensional states of creation. As a result, each created Soul has a potential to experience all twelve densities sometime in their evolutionary journey, indicating that you truly are multidimensional.

Following creation, each Soul had a multitude of choices to make. Many Souls chose to lower their vibration in order to first explore the "outer" higher density worlds of Creation. The outer worlds include those Densities between the eighth and twelfth. Thus, shortly after their creation these Souls came down in frequency and started their journey at the seventh Density. From that point, they gradually worked their way back up to the twelfth Density.

The seventh density is that density of the Oversoul. When a part of your Soul (a fragment) came to Earth and inhabited a physical body it continued to vibrate at the seventh density frequency. Your purpose of coming down from the seventh density was to experience firsthand the nature (characteristics) of the lower realms of creation. While within your low frequency third density physical body, you have had an opportunity to experience the first density through sixth density component parts (duplicate selves) of yourself. Each time a part of your Oversoul has incarnated on some low frequency planet, you should have gained additional insights about creation. Those insights you continually gain will be sensed by the Godhead. That sensing process on the part of the GODHEAD (ALL THAT IS) can then provide more understanding of all creations, including those creations of all the Creator Gods. Thus, your insights about creation influence all of creation.

Most Oversoul or Soul component parts on Earth have emerged from the ninth, eighth, or seventh density Master Oversouls or Oversoul in pairs of 12. Normally the Master Oversouls and/or Oversouls divide into pairs of six Souls. Generally, one Soul of each pair (a total of six) comes

44

into an Earthly embodiment while the other six remain in the seventh density states or higher.

The six Souls that remain within the higher densities will be guiding the six that incarnated within the lower densities or lower dimensions. Their objective of remaining in the higher densities is for helping to make the task of evolving back up to the seventh density more pleasant or less traumatic. By helping, the incarnated Soul there is less stress and sacrifice by the planet bound Soul component or fragment as it proceeds through various chosen lessons. These lessons have repeatedly been outlined within a series of contracts. Before each incarnation on a low frequency planet, the Spirit and Soul develop a contract with guidance from their spiritual assistants. That lifelong contract, is then used by the Spirit as a guiding roadmap for the current incarnation.

In rare instances, two sovereign Souls come directly from the Godhead (twelfth density) down through densities eight through eleven. When these Sovereign Souls arrive on Earth or arrive on another planet, they are called "twin souls" or "twin flames." The Sovereign Soul members, who in a sense could be called a Soul family, are likened unto a husband and wife. This is the closest energy bond (connection) that exists between Souls within a Soul family. These twin Souls or twin flames move into the seventh density and simultaneously maintain a higher density emergence or connection with the Godhead.

These characteristics relate to the multidimensionality and unlimited potential of incarnating Sovereign Souls. A very small minority of Sovereign Souls are currently residing somewhere on planet Earth. A majority of all Souls within human bodies on Earth are Oversoul fragments, as opposed to Master Oversoul segments. That is, most Souls incarnated on Earth originated from their seventh density Oversoul. This highly important topic, concerning the fragmentation of the Oversoul and Soul fragments, will be discussed in more detail later.

When twin Souls or twin flames are present on Earth, (a very rare occasion) upon close examination it will be discovered that an addiction can develop between these two Souls, either or both ways. An addiction means that these two Souls are strongly attracted towards each other. They also have a tendency to become excessively dependent upon each other. This factor alone may account for the very small number of twin flames (twin Souls) present on Earth. That addiction would slow individual spiritual development. To avoid this possibility, generally when twin flames are released as individual Souls, one of them almost always goes to the lower densities alone in order that the higher density one may be a lifeline to the lower density one. If they were to both go into the lower densities together, it might be difficult for them to evolve from these lower densities individually. That difficulty could stem from a codependency created during that incarnation. Thus, each individual Soul would find it difficult to return up through the higher density sequence and evolve.

This lack of ability to break out of an attachment to the lower density has been a problem for many Souls. The challenge to release one's attachments to the lower densities not only occurs on Earth but on all low-density planets. This is especially a challenge when pairs of Souls come into a lower density vibration at the same time. More often than not, they both become stuck in the lower density and dimension. Frequently they need special spiritual help so they can continue their spiritual evolution.

You may be capable of visualizing a similar situation with two twins (two individuals) that simultaneously became stuck in quicksand. When both twins jump into quicksand and become stuck together (within a lower density) special efforts are required to rescue them. For either one to proceed on their spiritual path, outside help will be required. If one Soul had stayed on shore holding a rope attached to the one who was stuck, the likelihood of both Souls progressing (more efficiently), would have been greatly enhanced.

There may be some other form of spiritual help for Souls stuck within the lower densities. For example, each of these twin Souls could call upon their individual spirit guides. However, it is far easier for the twin flame, of an Earthly Soul, to be guiding from the higher realms rather than making a request for another Soul or Soul fragment to come in and help at the lower densities.

In chapter 5 of the book "Earth Changes and 2012" by Sal Rachele, on page 138 the following question was asked: *Can there be more than one twin Soul for an incarnated Soul?* The answer was Yes and No. Theoretically, there is only one parent fragmented piece that is twin to the parent-fragmented piece of an incarnated Soul. However, because Souls can fragment any number of times, it is possible that one or both parent-fragmented pieces of a twin Soul pair can go through additional fragmentation. When this takes place, there can be multiple fragmented pieces of the pair either in the astral and/or etheric realms. In addition, some fragments will proceed to the physical realms of planets for embodiment. Although this is not a common situation, sometimes several twin Souls originate from a parent fragment.

There have been reported instances where twin souls have incarnated on Earth at the same time. However, when someone believes he or she has found their twin it is more likely that, (1) they sense the presence of a Soul family member that has been mistaken for a twin or (2) the individual is having an encounter with a fragment of the twin flame parent. With the latter situation, the parent of the twin flame has further fragmented and is now in embodiment upon the Earth as a unit of multiple Soul fragmentation, each fragment inhabiting a physical body. Theoretically, there could be six fragments of a twin flame on Earth and six in the seventh density or higher, all connected to the parent pieces of the Oversoul, of the twin Soul. These Soul fragments when considered together, make up a Soul family.

Another important concept that frequently arises is, what types of Souls may be called "Soul mates?" Soul mates according to the Founders should more accurately be called "parallel Souls." These Souls have a similar path of evolution. Such combinations that make up parallel Souls could occur even though those Soul fragments do not belong to the same parent Soul. These "Soul mates" are simply Soul family members who may be fragments from the same original Oversoul parent within the higher (seventh, eighth, or ninth) densities.

Soul family members can extend out from the parent several levels deep. For example, if a Soul family member was one of the original twelve that came out of the same Oversoul, you have a primary Soul family member. When two of those who incarnate upon the Earth (out of the six that incarnated) meet, you have a rare experience and feel an instant kinship with that individual. You may think of this situation as a Soul mate type of relationship between the two of you. When this happens, the relationship may be very difficult because you each came upon the Earth plane for very different reasons and each Soul fragment has a distinctly different contract. Thus before these two Soul fragments agreed to incarnate on Earth they set up distinct contracts. These contracts have taken each one down different time lines and into quite different experiences.

It may be more common for you to meet and bond with Souls from your extended Soul family, those multiple Souls that came out of the same eight to ninth density Master Oversoul, or the Oversoul of your Oversoul. As you approach the next several paragraphs -- slow down your speed reading procedure and follow closely a series of possible events concerning Soul families.

The number of Souls within a Soul Family can vary. A partial explanation of why this is possible relates to the fragmentation or subdivisions of the Master Oversoul and Oversoul. One possibility is that the twelve individual Souls that came out of your ninth density Master Oversoul are individual Sovereign Souls. These Souls have gone through a process of Soul division (multiplication) as opposed to Soul fragmentation. These twelve Sovereign Souls (beings) have now become twelve individual eighth density Sovereign Oversouls. An eighth density Sovereign Oversoul can now multiply by a process of Soul division with each creating twelve additional seventh density Sovereign Souls. Now you have 144 extended Sovereign Soul family members that originated from your original ninth density master Oversoul. This pattern of Master Soul multiplication has been considered a two level deep process. This process is different from Soul fragmentation.

When half of these 144 Sovereign Souls from the seventh density incarnate upon Earth, you have 72 Sovereign Soul family members potentially living somewhere upon the planet. Remember the other 72 Sovereign Souls remained within the seventh density to assist those Souls who have incarnated on Earth. When you meet one of these Soul family members you may think you have found a Soul mate. In actuality, you may have met one of these 72-Soul family members that have incarnated on Earth at the same time you did. Once you meet, there is a feeling of closeness indicating you have had a close relationship to that individual somewhere. That closeness is primarily due to the basic inherited energy patterns obtained from the ninth density master Oversoul from which all-72 Sovereign Souls originated.

There is also the possibility that each of the 144 Sovereign Souls present within the seventh density make a decision to incarnate within the astral or etheric plane of Earth, as opposed to the physical plane. The potential now exist to have a three level deep Soul family. Remember each of the Sovereign Souls within the astral or etheric plane of the

48

seventh density lack the ability to multiply. For a seventh density Sovereign Soul to make a decision to incarnate within one of the lower densities, a process of fragmentation is required. The seventh density Sovereign Soul lacks the capability to duplicate itself.

Let us assume that each of these Sovereign Souls made a decision to transfer to the astral plane of a planet. While within the astral plane, each of these 144 Sovereign Souls can each fragment into twelve additional Souls. Now you have 12 X 144 or 1,728 individual Soul's fragments that make up the Soul family that originated from the ninth density Master Oversoul.

Some individuals reading the above paragraphs may have had difficulty following this sequence of possibilities. If so, go back and carefully study each step in the sequence of Soul division, and Soul fragment migration. Knowing how the process proceeds provides you with a better understanding of your history and the current number of your parallel lives residing on other planets in the Universe. Yes, it is important to know about your parallel lives on other planets, they have direct effect on you. In a sense, they are a part of your reality.

Your Soul fragment arrived on Earth following one of the above processes. In addition, remember you now have a basis on which to determine how many potential parallel lives you may have residing somewhere else within this vast Universe. Realize also there are millions of inhabitable planets within this Universe alone. In addition, there are millions of Universes. These parallel lives, that number 12, 144, or 1,728 individual Souls, came into reality through one of these sequential creation patterns. Within each category, all Soul family members are interconnected.

The Soul family can share many experiences through a process of "bleed through." For example, one of your parallel lives on another planet may be having a great time on vacation enjoying all the exciting sights. Simultaneously you have an urge to take a vacation and enjoy similar experiences. From a less than desirable viewpoint, you can also share various imbalances. If one of your lives had an accident and broke a leg, by the process of bleed through your leg could experience the pain of that broken leg. This situation is a challenge for the medical profession because of their lack of training about parallel lives and bleeds through energy transfer. All component parts of creation are connected; however, the connections within a Soul family are stronger.

One way of looking at these potential events is to think of a Soul tree, a procedure used when developing a genealogical tree of your family history. For an understanding of a Soul tree, the Founders used an example, (starting on page 140 of the book "Earth Changes and 2012"). They chose to follow the Soul evolvement of the Egyptian priestess known as Isis currently an eighth density Soul on the planet Sirius. Isis was very influential in the history of Egypt 8,000 years ago. Several of Isis's seventh density Souls had incarnated on Earth during the Egyptian era.

The entity Isis, currently vibrating in the eight density (Master Oversoul or Angelic Level) has divided twice and so there are 144 Sovereign Souls of Isis. Of those 144, half of them, or 72 could be now residing upon an Earth like planet and 72 will have remained within the higher densities.

Just for this discussion, let us say that you currently are one of the 72 Sovereign Souls of the entity previously known as Isis in Egypt. Then as you progress up the evolutionary path from fourth density to seventh density, somewhere along the way, you could meet one of your other 143 Soul family members. When this happens, you <u>will not</u> have the opportunity to reunite with these divisions of your original Sovereign Soul. You will retain your individualized status and the other Soul family members you meet will continue to be individual entities. You began as a Sovereign Soul as compared to having a beginning as a Soul fragment.

Keep in mind that each of these 144-soul family members were Sovereign Souls, not fragments from a seventh density Soul. To understand why you will not integrate we need to consider a distinct difference between Soul fragmentation within the seventh density and Soul division within the eighth and ninth densities. Multiplication of a Sovereign Soul that is residing above the seventh density keeps its individuality.

It may help to go back and consider when you were a parent Soul, a sovereign being or Oversoul within the seventh density. Remember at this level before any part of you incarnated, your parent Oversoul divided into twelve Soul fragments. These fragments were essentially pieces of your original Sovereign Soul (an individual being). When you came to Earth, your Soul was actually one twelfth of your original Sovereign Soul.

Eventually these twelve fragments will become integrated back into your parent Soul. Apparently this is a requirement before you qualify for evolution up through densities eight through twelve. Souls that have evolved above the seventh density do not fragment rather they divide into individual Sovereign Souls.

Thus, in this example, where we are using an eight density Soul known as Isis, we realize that we are dealing with a different situation or sequence of events, as compared to an Oversoul who has fragmented while within the seventh density. When Isis had evolved to the eighth density her Soul had gone through a process of multiplication or what may be considered two Soul divisions to create 144 Sovereign Souls. This process of Soul division is like giving birth. The Soul Isis has given birth to additional Sovereign Souls that can reside within and between densities eight through twelve. Here a Sovereign Soul has an option to divide (give birth) and become multiples of twelve.

I repeat for emphasis, since Isis has evolved to the eighth density, her Soul can divide again with the results of (12 X 12) for the creation of 144 individual Sovereign Souls. All of these individual Sovereign Souls are component parts of Isis. These 144 are actually individual Sovereign Souls since that process involves a multiplication (duplication) procedure. The duplication process takes place for Souls above the seventh density. These 144 Sovereign Souls of Isis have become what are known as a "Clustered Soul." This would be somewhat like a family of 144 individuals, each independent, thus INCAPABLE of integrating back into one.

A majority of all Souls incarnated upon the Earth plane are fragments of their Oversoul that previously resided within the seventh density, before fragmentation. In order for your seventh density Oversoul to evolve up through densities 8 through 12, these fragments will need to be integrated (brought together) to form a Sovereign Soul. When your 12, 144, or 1,728 Soul fragments become integrated back into Sovereign Souls then you regain your Oversoul status.

This Oversoul status is a very important requirement for continued ascension above the sixth to seventh density. All of your Oversoul fragments must be integrated back into the same seventh density Oversoul body for your continued evolution into the eight density. Once the Oversoul fragments become integrated then you have opened up a pathway to evolve through the eighth to twelfth densities. These higher densities have been called the "collectively consciousness realms" by some higher spirits. Also, these higher densities between the eighth to the twelfth are strictly a spirit realm. Within this realm, there is no distinct individuality and each entity or group of entities lack a physical or mechanical device for movement. Travel occurs by thought.

A good example of Soul integration that recently took place on Earth involved a close relationship between two light workers who assisted each other in their teaching activities. A male individual became acquainted with a female light worker and offered to assist her in her work. He appeared to be very spiritually minded and talented so she gradually accepted his offer. By mutual agreement, he would frequently merge into her embodiment during a workshop and share his insights. Gradually as a team, they became skilled teachers while working together. That relationship continued for 20 years. One day the male light worker came to his female coworker and indicated he would no longer be able to assist her in the ways (techniques) that they had developed together. Her emotional reaction was, of course, intense. She felt a tremendous loss — as though her closest and dearest friend was going to "die." He indicated that the reason for his departure was that he would be merging into her embodiment along with her. On the one hand, she felt elation that his love and wisdom would now become a part of "her." As the situation turned out, he was one of the fragmented Souls of her Oversoul Cluster. It was time for them to integrate into a combined embodiment in preparation for their future graduation and ascension process.

A relatively rare event like this can happen here on the Earth plane; two Soul fragments from the same Oversoul become aware of each other and join their efforts in Service to Others while in embodiment. When the appropriate time comes, these two previously independent Souls rejoin back into the same Oversoul (their original) to continue their spiritual evolution.

The process of spiritual evolution through and within densities eight through twelve is much more complex than the abbreviate discussion above. The Source known as the Founders is apparently aware of these complexities but is unable to find the words within our current languages on Earth to describe them. This is especially true of events taking place within the higher densities. As we evolve from the fourth density up through the fifth to seventh densities, we will obviously have expanded our conscious awareness. As a result, we should be better able to understand the evolutionary activities within the "Collective Consciousness Realms."

When you have decided to cease your activities within the lower densities (first through the seventh) and you have integrated your Soul fragments, you will then apparently be prepared to work through the densities known as the "Collectively Consciousness Realms" (eighth density through the twelfth density). The lengthy process of evolving through all twelve densities, in terms of illusionary Earth time, is incomprehensible. However, if you consider these events within or from a spiritual perspective of "no time" the process of evolving back towards the Godhead is all happening "NOW."

Once your Soul reaches the tenth density it will became a Creator God and when at the eleventh density a Universal God. Although you are evolving back to become like the twelfth density Godhead, in actuality when you reach that density you have finalized your capabilities as a Creator and Universal God. You then have the potential to create like your Creator Godhead. Not only will you have an opportunity to create other Universes and Oversouls but you can also travel and have unlimited experiences within many different Universes. You will never stop learning throughout eternity. Growing, evolving, and changing with understanding is the driving force throughout the multitude of Universes, collectively called the Omniverse or Multiverse.

Not all Souls have been created at the Godhead level (twelfth density). Other Soul waves can come into creation at a lower frequency known as the seventh Density. Most human Soul fragments on Earth originated from a seventh Density Oversoul during a wave of creation that was brought into being by a Creator God. That Creator God is the result of the sequence of evolutionary steps where a Sovereign Soul created an Oversoul who had evolved back to the twelfth density to become a "Creator God" or Universal God." These evolved Creator Gods now have an option or choice to create new Universes and new Sovereign Souls.

Some evidence indicates that such creations are brought about by a collective effort of several Creators working together. Once your Oversoul unit (Sovereign Soul) has evolved back to twelfth density and you become a Creator God, your group Sovereign Soul will need to make a lengthy review of existing creations and Universes before becoming involved in these complex creations. Your Sovereign Soul will need to create a detailed plan of your proposed new creations or new Universes. Those plans will then be submitted to a highly skilled "Creative Review Committee." If your proposal is uniquely different from all existing creations or other Universes, and approval would have value for evolving entities, you may receive approval. Once the committee approves, the "Sovereign Souls" proposal, then procedures can be implemented for creating their joint proposal. A similar group of Creators was assembled, developed a proposal, had it approved, and then created the "One Universe," with all of its galaxies and solar systems, where we now reside.

We humans on planet Earth have difficulty understanding these creative processes. However, we can say that there have been many waves of Souls that have been created with countless variations in the creative patterns. All of these Souls are component parts of GOD (ALL THAT IS). Some Souls emerged as solitary sparks of light while others came in groups of three, four, six, and twelve-point clusters. In some cases, Souls have been created in large clusters that segregated into smaller units as they descended down into the lower Densities. Somewhat similar to the process described above, however some processes take new unique variations.

As these Souls descended, many chose different densities to gain new experiences. Some went from the twelfth Density down to the third Density while others chose those Densities between the seventh and third. As they evolved back to the twelfth Density, they report to their "Creator GOD" about their experiences. As these Sovereign Souls arrived back, they did not meld into the "Creator God" and disappear. Instead, the process can be likened to the children that humans give birth to on Earth. Children do not climb back into the mother's womb once they mature, but become like their parents. In many cases, they evolve beyond the capabilities of their parents.

Thus as each Soul evolves back to the twelfth Density that Soul becomes a Creator God that originally came out of the Godhead, went into the seventh Density, experienced those Densities below the seventh Density then evolved back up through the eighth, ninth , tenth, eleventh, and into the twelfth Density Godhead realm.

Historical records indicate that these Creator Gods, the group that created this "One Universe" had their proposal rejected during their initial proposals. The Higher Spiritual Council, that approves Universal proposals, requested that the Creator Gods modify their proposal because of the excessive negativity that was proposed. Thus, they came back with a proposal with less negativity. The final approval for the Creator Gods proposal came after several trial proposals had been rejected.

In essence, it does not matter whether your One Universe, galaxy, or planet Earth was created directly by ALL THAT IS (Father/Mother GOD) or a group of "Creator Gods." That is not important, because the concept of belief prevails. Whatever fits your belief is quite adequate for the "Now," experience. Those beliefs will constantly change, somewhat. All existing evidence indicates that many of the densities between levels one through six have been brought into existence by the Creator Gods. These Advanced Souls have completed their evolution up to the twelfth Density and now have the opportunity to carry out their creative skills learned through eons of experiences in the lower densities. These Creator Gods now also have the opportunity to create new Souls within their Created Universe. Those words typed above contain the thoughts that my "Spiritual Team" believed would be important for your consideration. Go beyond the words, connect with your High Self and feel the thoughts they are trying to convey.

To give a theoretical example of the potential these Creator Gods have, consider the following scenario. If there were ten billion Souls that evolved back to the twelfth Density to become Creator Gods or Universal Gods, then they each will have similar capabilities. Let's say each Creator God or Universal God created an additional ten billion Universes. Then each of these Universes would or could contain Souls created by each individual Creator God. Thus, each individual Soul on Earth and on millions of other planets are potential Creator Gods. The point is that the potential of the infinite creation plan that you and I are a part of is way beyond the imagination of any creation incarnated on a planet. Even the Creator Gods form groups so they can share their knowledge and thus determine how to continue the creative processes.

There is accumulating information that there is currently an infinite number of Universes. Certain groups of Universes could be united in some format to make up what has been termed the Omniverse. Then groups of Omniverse could be grouped together to make up various Multiverses.

Spirit indicates that the above description of the potentials of an advanced Soul who has evolved to twelfth Density and reached Creator status has been presented in a very simplified format. The complete explanation would be so complex none of us would understand. Although the subject is very complex, it provides interesting speculation, to the current understanding of third-fourth dimensional consciousness. It rapidly becomes evident that we are very limited in knowing how our future has been charted. We do know that as we evolve, greater understanding will become available. Eventually we will know about all of these un-imaginable Creations, including more about our potential future.

The "Founders" make a very important point concerning multidimensionality and the individual Soul's capability to function within various densities. The Founders have evolved to the twelfth density and have apparently received an assignment where they can remain "there" to carry out their assignment. As Founders with Creator status, they should be able to do anything that is conceivable. However, in order to do that, they must maintain their twelfth density vibration. Like all component parts of creation, they are faced with the Universal Law of Attraction.

That law states that "Like Attracts Like." Thus, what you focus upon you become. Where you place your dominant thought energy is the level at which you vibrate. Therefore, if you are focusing on twelfth density, you will eventually vibrate at twelfth density. Likewise, if you lower your focus to one of the lower densities, you will start to vibrate at that lower density. Once you lower your density, you will be unable to carry out the many things that were potential capabilities at the higher dimensions. The densification process alters one's capabilities. Because when you densify much of your memory has been cleared, your intellectual capabilities reduced, and your level of awareness will lack sufficient insight to make wise decisions. You have "fallen" in your consciousness abilities. You would have difficultly remembering who you are, just as most humans on Earth have forgotten who they are.

Keep in mind that each human on Earth has many multidimensional aspects that vibrate within many different densities. You have selves that vibrate within the higher densities that you will become familiar with as you evolve. Within the higher dimensions, you will not only meet many other aspects of yourself, but you will also be able to manipulate time energy speeding it up or slowing it down.

56

Within the third dimensions, your life is greatly influence by time and your ability to speed it up or slow it down -- is limited. That pattern drastically changes when your consciousness shifts to the fifth dimension and higher. As mentioned, within these higher states of consciousness, you will be able to manipulate time. Also, please recall that the law of attraction is very important, because of the potential it has for assisting you in carrying out your contract. Your thoughts can help create the dimensional state of consciousness you desire. Visualize and create the thought of existing within the fifth density and opportunities will open up to help you move your density and consciousness into that frequency range. The law of attraction will add to your creation, making it more complete.

A majority of Souls on Earth originated from the seventh Density. As a seventh density Soul, you existed as a component part of an eight density Oversoul. In order for you to experience third and fourth Density, you had to bring a part of your Oversoul and seventh Density awareness down to these lower densities. Even though the seventh density Soul has a fourth density self and can access that self, the fourth density self does not easily maintain a level of awareness while experiencing the lower density worlds. As you incarnate within the lower density, a part of your Oversoul (an individualized Soul) remains within the seventh Density. Refer back to the beginning listing of densities and note that the Soul vibrates within the sixth density and the Oversoul vibrates within the seventh density.

Keep in mind you are multidimensional. Your mineral components vibrate at first density, your molecular components from plants vibrate at second density, and some of your energy bodies vibrate at third density. Your overall human form is located within the fourth density and your Light Body (when activated) will vibrate within the fifth density. As you contemplate your multidimensionality, think about the density of your various body parts. We have discovered in the Subtle Energy Research program that those body parts that are weakened vibrate at lower frequencies (lower densities). At these lower densities, the body part has restricted function efficiencies. Lower density correlates with slowed activities. These slowed activities have implications concerning the repair of weakened body parts. This understanding (feature) should help you phrase a question when considering the challenge to "Ask and

Receive." Unless you know the question, how can you ask and how can you receive. Ask to raise the weakened body part and utilize adamantine particles, commanded by Love. These particles are the building blocks of creation. Jesus in the book "Love Without End" by Glenda Green, describes how the sharing of adamantine particles can be considered the breath of life. On page 108, Jesus states:

There is an ongoing exchange of these particles throughout existence. They not only comprise organic life, but also the planet, the wind, and every substance that is. -- Inhaling and exhaling, these particles bring vital balance and connections to life. In the presence of Love a natural rebalance occurs. This is how the laying on of hands can help to restore health to another. Such is the power of healing touch or even a hug."

Now Spirit says, stay tuned to what you are about to read, read slowly, and ask for an explanation from High Self. Your developing fifth density Light Body is an etheric crystal Light Body form that employs silicon as its basic element, instead of carbon. In order to vibrate at the fifth density one of the criteria is to have your carbon-based body transmuted into a silicon-based Crystal Light body. To accomplish this change, the DNA codes will need to be upgraded and activated. Then your highest frequency component part (your Soul) can become luminescent and vibrate more effective at sixth density. When this takes place, that part of your reality that remains with the Oversoul, vibrates at the seventh density. The seventh density form often appears as a collective Soul Cluster (of Oversouls) that is made up of all your Soul fragments (individual Souls) that have incarnated within many different realms and/or on different planets. As your Soul and Oversoul evolve back up through the lower densities to the higher densities, each of your Soul fragments join each other. This process is called Soul fragment integration, resulting in the formation of "Oversoul Clusters." Once this process is completed, the Oversoul Cluster is generally described as a single being composed of many sub-beings or individual Soul components that have become ONE.

Those Souls in the higher densities (above the seventh) do not easily materialize, that is, take on a physical form and walk upon the earth as eighth, ninth, tenth, eleventh or twelfth density entities (beings). It would be very difficult, or in reality impossible, to do that within the current universal design pattern. If such efforts were made to incarnate at a lower density, the higher density being would most likely become caught (trapped) in the lower density incarnation. This is why these advanced spiritual entities do not walk the streets. They teach classes here on Earth directly from their consciousness. In reality, there is no need to create a physical body on Earth, just to deliver their messages. The Arc Angels, Ascended Masters, Extraterrestrials, etc. all communicate with lower density beings (third, fourth and fifth density) through telepathy and channeling.

Soul Evolution and What You Can Anticipate

The lower six levels of creation (densities from one through six) are governed by free will. That is, each individual Soul has choices and/or decisions to make constantly. The sixth density Soul from the seventh density Oversoul, has the ability (within the Creator school known as Earth) to create their own individual worlds within. As you evolve up through the fifth, sixth, and seventh densities you also have the opportunity to explore all of the outer world creations brought into existence by various Souls who have gone before you.

We have been given the ability to explore the six lower density levels of Creation. That is, you have freedom to explore those dimensions that are governed by free will. In order for your Soul to explore these lower densities of Creation you have had to begin your incarnations within the lower densities where you had many different and difficult challenges. These challenges were associated with the choices associated with inhabiting an animalistic body. That choice to take on an animalistic body was allowed so that the spirit and Soul could have individual separation. In addition, that separation allowed for self-expression. This activity has exposed you to the third density where you have become handicapped.

In order to proceed to evolve spiritually up through the various densities we were given the ability to use a fragment of our Oversoul, the individuated Soul to reincarnate repeatedly. Each time you have incarnated upon a low frequency planet you were required to develop individual contracts while in spirit form. The ultimate goal of those contracts was to help us remember and gain an understanding in the Creator School called Earth. This process of coming up with a contract each incarnation and repeating this process until you have sufficient understanding of the various densities, has continued for thousands of years. Assuming you have now evolved beyond this repeating pattern in your evolutionary path, you now have a choice to change that pattern.

When Soul fragments come back into another physical body from the astral plane or above, such as, from the seventh density, they frequently come back into the same genetic family and/or ethnic group repeatedly. Under these conditions, the rate of evolution is in part dependent upon group consciousness. Only after a majority of the group has evolved sufficiently, will the individual fragmented Soul have an opportunity to evolve. You may have observed these group features in individual families. When an individual Soul has evolved to a specific level, it may then join another group that has evolved further up the scale of densities. In many cases, the DNA of the group has a profound influence on evolutionary progress.

From the third density body you can create a fourth density body that has increased psychic and intuitive functions, those that are more developed. With focus, you can accelerate your rate of evolvement into the fourth density. Then with the various techniques outlined in the book "You Can Avoid Physical Death', and within this book about ascension, you can prepare your fifth dimensional Crystal Light Body for graduation and ascension to the "New Earth.".

The human body has all the functions of the animal plus additional attributes. The humanoid form began over 100 million years ago in the constellation known as Lyra/Vega. The Creator Gods with help from the Founders were commissioned with the job of forming a cellular structure that would be able to experience the various worlds of creation with maximum effectiveness. Certain functions are present within the human structure to help you interface with your fourth, fifth, and sixth density Soul and with your seventh density Oversoul. Your brain and heart function to assist in that process. All human brains were initially given a massive capacity in order to help you keep in touch with other component parts of your energy systems. The capabilities of the brain and its associated sensing systems have also been designed to help you recover from "The Fall." That is, recover from the process of densification where you moved from the seventh density (Garden of Eden) down to the third density of planet Earth.

Once a planet evolves, or possibly, when a planet returns to third density, it is capable of receiving human Souls in their third density physical bodies. Some human Souls may choose to fragment a portion of themselves in the form of minerals and/or plants residing in first and second densities in order to have those experiences. This process is complicated, thus it is rare. However, the process of evolving from the first to the second density and from second density to the third density is different compared to the shift from third density to fourth density and on to fifth density.

Some individuals have asked the question, can an animal come back as a human or can a human come back as an animal within the third density. The answer to that question is yes but not through the traditional process of reincarnation.

Those evolutionary steps, when shifting (evolving) from first and second density require a specific unit of spirit energy. That unit of spirit energy must become available and intense enough to facilitate the required shift from first to second density. This procedure rarely occurs because most of the time when a Soul has decided to explore first and second density, it does not continue to go back and explore those realms repeatedly. That is, if your Soul has had the experience of living as a cat, once you have evolved to take on a third density physical (higher level) animalistic body, you do not incarnate back to become a cat. You may search out more information about that procedure -- if you have a keen interest.

Keep in mind that spirit and Soul are two distinct aspects of reality. The Soul is that evolutionary component part of the individual that evolves through the various densities. The spirit is that component part of creation that holds together all the various individual components that make up the individual reality. Recall that each choice to become involved within a density is for the learning experience. That is, the various experiences are to help you to remember who you are and why you have chosen various densities as tools for expanding your consciousness.

At this time, Earth is moving from third density status to fourth density status quite rapidly. Many observing from "afar -- off planet" believe events are speeding up so that by 2011 Earth will essentially vibrate within the fourth density. It will have completed that shift by approximately 2030, on the current time line as mandated by the cyclic nature of reality and the consciousness of humanity.

In the future Souls who wish to experience a third density planet will look elsewhere. Those Souls who wish to experience a fourth density planet moving to a fifth density can choose to come to the New Earth. A third density human biological entity essentially takes on an animal like form. That is, the third density humans consciousness is animalistic in nature, although the physical form is a bit more refined compared to most animals upon planet Earth. The consciousness of a third density human is primarily evolving according to the ideas of procreation, survival, instinct, and related animalistic behavior patterns. The mind of a third density human is not fully developed, although it can function well enough to create some semblance of civilized behavior. A fourth density human being has a Soul that is inhabiting an animalistic human form, however has evolved to where it is aware of itself as consciousness, realizes it's creative potential, and realizes that consciousness creates its perception of reality. As a result, the fourth density human becomes a conscious creator walking on the Earth plane. Because the third and fourth densities have similarities, the fourth density human is capable of interacting with third density humans as well as with other third density animals such as dogs, cats, sheep and cows. These animals have evolved to the higher third density; this is not true of many animals.

Eventually Earth will become a fifth density planet, sometime in the near future. The exact time is unknown, because those who plan to ascend are creating the New Earth. Thus -- no accurate date as to when it will reach fifth density is known. It is quite evident Earth will not become fifth density in December 2012.

However, many humans currently have an opportunity to take on fifth density etheric Light Body and have the capability to live on a fourth density Earth. While there, you can explore other fifth density worlds and bring back information to help create fifth density Earth. You can also choose to remain confined to fourth density Earth, as a fifth density being, for an extended time and assist in its evolution to fifth density. In addition, if you were to discard your physical fourth density body you should have an option to incarnate upon another fourth density planet. Most fourth density humans will stay upon the fourth density Earth. You can also move off the reincarnation spiral and proceed onto the ascension spiral.

Those humans who have chosen to remain upon a third density planet will be leaving to a more suitable planet, as one of their choices.

Once you reach fifth density you no longer have to discard your physical biological entity, you can simply modify it directly by thought so that it can perceive fifth and sixth density levels and to a limited extent seventh density happenings. Within the fifth density, you will have taken on Light Body status. This Light Body is less dense, more sturdy, with an ability to maintain itself indefinitely, within the time stream of the lower worlds. Your fifth density vehicle is capable of exploring fourth density and to some extent third density without having to go through the physical death experience.

The wheel of reincarnation was essentially a teaching device within third and fourth density. Within the fifth density, your physical vehicle is no longer subject to the law of entropy, or the previously experienced decay cycle. Thus, there is no experience of sickness or disease within the fifth density. Also, realize that within the fifth density you can easily travel from one location to another without the aid of any mechanical device. Your thoughts will carry you to your chosen destination.

One of your main future objectives is to return to the seventh density from which you fell. After "The Fall," when we all forgot who we were, we each purposely (by choice) became attached (some became trapped) within the lower third - fourth densities.

As a fifth density being you can interact with fourth density worlds and Souls, but in most cases, your communication with third density world or Souls will be very limited. Your vibratory rate will be so high that a third density individual will be unable to visualize your presence and communicate verbally because of your inability to move air sufficient to make distinct sounds that can be picked up by third density hearing mechanisms. That is the third density human will have difficulty perceiving and comprehending the communication attempts of a fifth density entity. When and if a third density human has developed some telepathic skills, some communication may be possible.

The fifth density entity is also faced with the challenge of exercising caution about consciously focusing on the lower third and fourth densities. It is uncommon for a fifth density human to reincarnate into a third density world however, it can happen. This could happen when an attempt is made to be of assistance to lower frequency Souls. It is possible to shift your consciousness to that lower density, however when you do you can be pulled backward dimensionally. That process can also pull your density backward. As a result, the fifth density entity can easily become "trapped" in the third density reality.

Earth is going through an exceptional transition where the process has been changed — compared to the normal sequence of events for planetary evolution. Because Earth is moving to fourth density with humans on board many Souls are coming from the higher densities to assist in Earth's evolutionary activities. Many new Souls with features of the higher densities have been incarnating on Earth for several years. These new souls, called Indigo, Crystal, Rainbow and Dragon children have capabilities beyond those of their parents. They know that Earth is about to move into fourth density, and want to be a part of that experience. These spiritually more advanced beings (Souls) have volunteered to come to Earth now and assist Souls struggling to understand what is happening and to help them shift into fourth and fifth densities. The ongoing process they are assisting with -- is helping awaken the consciousness within those humans who have an interest in graduating from third-fourth density Earth up to fifth density Earth right here 'Now." Together all of these Souls are helping create "Heaven on Earth."

We humans on Earth are also in the process of finding our way back to the level of the seventh density Oversoul. Once you have learned all you need to know about the fifth and sixth densities you will be proceeding to find your way back to the seventh density. Here you will have a choice to go out and explore again the lower densities, continue on your evolutionary spiral up to twelfth density, or choose other alternatives.

One alternative is to divert your Soul along the evolutionary path and become a spirit guide or angel. These entities are eighth density, thus a portion of your multidimensionality would be involved in choosing this alternative. To become a spirit guide or angel you will be required to take a portion of your Soul energy (an eight-density fragment) or sometimes called a disembodied spirit form, to manifest as a guide or angel.

The idea that a Soul must keep incarnating repeatedly in order to learn a lesson is not a very accurate concept. Most Souls do not want to abandon the contract they agreed to before coming to Earth. They would prefer to complete their contractual lessons before moving on to the higher densities. To abandon many lifetimes of effort would defeat the original purpose for that Soul having arrived on Earth during this incarnation. Therefore, exercise extreme caution when attempting to understand another individuals' chosen path or their need to complete his or her previously agreed contract.

An individual's basic reason for coming to Earth will generally be beyond your understanding no matter how skilled you think you are. It may appear that a Soul is "trapped" on the wheel of karma. From a broader perspective, that Soul is not trapped. It has chosen to continue its lessons and thereby keep incarnating until the Soul feels complete and ready to proceed toward other opportunities. Many Souls have not gathered all the Soul experiences they desire to have when they voluntarily chose to come back to re-experience and continue their lessons within the lower densities. Thus in all situations, cease to place any type of judgment concerning the spiritual status of any individual Soul. Everyone has chosen a preferred path or time line for his or her evolutionary experiences. We are to honor and respect their choice. If they seek your help in understanding various choices (available to them), then you may confer with their High Self to make sure that you are not interfering with their contract and chosen lessons. Once approved by their High Self then you can offer the insights that were provided to you by their High Self.

Consequences of Soul Fragmentation

There is also another reason Souls may stay within the lower densities upon the wheel of reincarnation. The reason many Souls are not ready to evolve to the higher densities is that their Soul has become fragmented (damaged). If a Soul has been fragmented into pieces, and parts of the Soul have incarnated on many different planets, then those scattered pieces need to be recovered and returned to their source Soul. When many Soul fragments are missing, that incomplete Soul may lack sufficient energy to change consciously. Therefore, the Soul will have difficulty moving up through the evolutionary spiral toward graduation and ascension. This is more of a challenge when starting from the lower densities. When a Soul comes to you for help exercise caution unless you have the capabilities to determine the degree to which their Soul is intact. That is, if you have the love and understanding plus the skills to seek spiritual help then exercise caution. With permission, you may inquire of their High Self if all of their Soul fragments are present and the extent to which they can efficiently function -- as a unit. Before attempting to help someone else make sure your Soul is intact.

The next obvious question is -- How can I determine if my Soul is complete and functionally efficient? Your feelings are the first place to begin to ascertain the answer to that question. How do you feel physically, mentally, emotionally, and spiritually? Do you struggle in any one of these areas? If you feel like you are having difficulty on some days for no apparent reason, one possibility is, you may have parts of your soul missing. If you constantly feel tired, that may indicate some parts of your Soul are missing. When several facets are missing, you may detect a significant lack of energy. With less energy, it is difficult to keep various body parts functioning at or within their potential optimum capability. If you have a tendency to become mentally or emotionally upset, again this is a sign that you may be missing soul fragments (facets).

The subject of Soul fragmentation is highly important for all humans. This one factor can be the trigger for a multitude of imbalances within a majority of our energy bodies. To evolve your Soul spiritually it is highly desirable to make sure your Soul is in good working order and capable of carrying out its many responsibilities. This task requires some knowledge of the features of the Oversoul, the Soul, and its known capabilities.

The most effective procedure and most accurate technique for measuring the status of any body system, including the Soul, is through accurate pendulum dowsing. Only use pendulum dowsing when you or another skilled dowser has proven the dowsing is 100 % accurate. It would be a waste of time and dangerous to attempt to pendulum dowse and end up obtaining inaccurate readings. Such readings could cause more harm than good when they were used as a basis for your attempt to solve a serious challenge.

Let's briefly review to set the stage for the subject of Soul fragmentation. A complete Sovereign Soul is born from a parent aspect of GOD. A "Soul fragment" is a piece of a Soul that is not, in and of itself, a sovereign independent being. Realize that in order for you to incarnate upon planet Earth your Oversoul fragmented into twelve separate units, one of which is now a key part of you on Earth. Other fragments of your

Soul reside in other bodies somewhere within the Universe on other planets or in other densities as parallel realities or parallel lives. Thus, keep in mind that any Soul fragment is a part of some Oversoul.

Repeat — a Soul fragment is created with the desire of the Sovereign Soul (Oversoul) to experience the lower density worlds; the objective is for that Oversoul component to have specific experiences within the lower densities. The process of fragmentation may be voluntary or involuntary, depending on the Soul's level of consciousness. Some Soul fragments and/or pieces may be quite large, some of which, because of their size are called parent Soul fragments. Others fragments may be very small. Regardless of the size of the missing fragments, when a fragment is missing that Soul is incomplete and is limited in its ability to evolve.

Your Soul has some properties, like those of a quartz crystal -- with many facets all connected when completely intact. A complete Soul with all its fragments (facets) that is incarnated upon the Earth plane should contain 617 facets. Each individual facet is arranged in a desirable configuration. In addition, each Soul facet should be integrated and aligned with all other facets, for functional efficiency. As the Soul fragments each component part remains as a part of the one united aspect of God as designed in its original format and recorded experiences. Even after the Soul fragments have been gathered up, cleansed, and integrated within the original Sovereign Soul (Oversoul) there still remains the possibility at some future "Now" time in the evolutionary sequence, that Oversoul will again fragment in order to have some new exciting experiences.

Recall that the Old Souls came into being via individualization through division from the twelfth density Godhead. Once created these Souls spiral from the twelfth density to the seventh density and then evolve back to the twelfth density. Other complex events take place within those densities between the eight to twelfth densities that are difficult to comprehend. Thus, we will have to concentrate on what happens to a seventh density Soul, as it incarnates within the densities from the third through the sixth densities.

The seventh density Soul has several ways it can fragment. When a Soul from the seventh density incarnates within a lower density it only takes a small part of its total reality with it. The parent Oversoul remains within the seventh density. The fragment separates itself out from the parent through a process similar to physical cell division.

A seventh density Soul could fragment itself and manufacture a sixth density Light Body in order to experience a sixth density world. In fact, the parent Soul can fragment many different times and experience several sixth density worlds. When the Soul decides to come into fifth density, additional fragments can still become a possibility. Thus, the parent Soul could have several fragments within the fifth density also. Each of those pieces could have a primary fragment in sixth density, which in turn has the parent Soul fragment in seventh density Oversoul. The fifth density fragments, in turn, can create a densification that allows the Soul fragment to enter into a fifth density Light Body in order to experience fifth dimensional worlds. The process of creating (manufacturing) a fifth density Light Body is more involved compared to creating a higher frequency sixth density Soul fragment that creates a Light Body.

As a Soul desires to step itself down from fifth density into fourth density, a different process ensues that involves an incarnation into a body with a genetic imprint. That imprint becomes an embryo and fetus, capable of housing an incoming fifth density Soul fragment. The Soul fragment densifies itself by coming into the womb of another Soul (a humanoid mother) and that Soul fragment then comes with the fetus through the birth canal as an incarnated Soul. That incoming Soul has many Soul family members somewhere in the Universe, all of which have their origin within the seventh density Oversoul.

When a Soul desires to experience third density coming from the seventh density there are four levels of fragmentation involved before the Soul is able to come into third density. All of the fragments within the fourth, fifth, and sixth densities are considered a part of the Soul linage, or in other words part of the Soul family, of that third density entity.

Old mature Souls normally divide into twelve individual parent Souls, which in turn fragment into additional Soul fragments in order to experience the realms below the seventh density. Those human Souls on Earth within fourth density could have twelve fragmented pieces of their Soul incarnating into a third density being at any given time. Remember that these Soul fragmentations generally take place within the astral realms of the higher densities. These fragmentations do not originate from the offspring of an individual third density Soul.

When a Soul fragment enters the physical body in the third dimension, it goes through its lifetime as a Soul incarnated into a human biological organism, the physical body. If the Soul has not evolved sufficiently to be able to move directly into the next dimension it has several other choices. That Soul may go back up the evolutionary spiral through ascension. The Soul could choose to discard the body at the end of that lifetime and become a disincarnate. Here the Soul will remain within the astral or etheric realms until it can re-enter another physical body. The Soul fragment may be capable of going up one density or more, depending on its spiritual status. Sometimes the more advanced Souls can go all the way back up to the seventh density in-between incarnations. All of these possibilities (and more) are determined at the individual Soul's spiritual level, based upon the internal conscious awareness and/or the awareness of that Soul's journey. That awareness will influence the Soul's decisions and choices about what it needs to learn for future new "Now" evolutionary purposes. Make sure you connect with your High Self to know of your preferred path.

If the Soul stays at the same relative level as to which it left when existing in the physical body, it will enter one or more of the twelve levels of the astral plane. The astral realms consist of twelve sub-planes, each with distinctive features. The lower sub-planes you would describe as grotesque, dark and scary, and the higher ones you would describe as quite pleasant and beautiful.

That Soul fragment, that recently left a physical body, can briefly wonder around in the astral plane however, it does not generally remain within the astral plane for lengthy periods. A review of the Souls Akashic records may help determine its future path or time line. If the lifetime previously experienced has been quite traumatic, the Soul fragment may wonder around within the astral realm and attempt to attach itself to various Souls incarnated on Earth. In those cases, you have what has been termed a disincarnate spirit, ghost, astral entity, or orb just wondering around, as if it is lost. These entities have been reported to be capable of attaching themselves to an incarnated Soul in a process called possession. Such possession can be partial or total.

Keep in mind that the wandering Soul fragment is still a part of a higher order of fragments that will eventually go back up to the parent Soul, so it is not truly lost. That Soul fragment does contain several energy imprints accumulated in its Soul experiences (journey) through many incarnations. When the disincarnate Soul fragment attaches to an incarnated Soul, the associated imprints can be downloaded into the incarnated individual, causing various types of imbalances.

In many cases when an individual passes from the physical body, there is a possibility that the Soul can lose some of its facets. These lost Soul facets contain some of the imbalanced energies that were a part of the individual when they were alive. Thus, the attaching Soul facets from the disincarnate now have a direct effect on the incarnated Soul, the one that picked these facets up.

Eventually all Souls who have chosen to come down to the lower densities to experience various forms of duality come to a point where their awareness is such that they no longer wish to keep reincarnating into physical bodies. At this time, the decision is made to shift consciousness to a higher level of self-expression within the fourth, fifth, sixth, and seventh densities. When a Soul reaches the fifth density, they often experience a reuniting with some of their Soul family members (Oversoul fragments) or higher density Soul fragments (pieces) of their parent Soul.

When these fragment or pieces of the parent Soul are reuniting and coming together, that process has been called Soul integration. It will become important for each Soul to become aware of its fragmentation and make concerted efforts to carry out procedures to promote Soul integration.

To complete the discussion about Soul fragmentation, we need to discuss another form of Soul fragmentation commonly occurring within the third and fourth densities. Many have heard of leaving your Soul somewhere with an employer or a previous lover. It has been well established that after you have worked for an employer within a certain building for a given time period, a fragment of your Soul can be dislodged and entrapped in that building. Sometimes that entrapment relates to another employee who has dislodged a part of your Soul. Even when you get up out of a chair, where you have been seated for some time, a Kirlian photograph will reveal that a part of your Soul energy still remains within that chair. This phenomenon is similar to an energetic bed pattern where most sensitive individuals can detect a part of your Soul present in the bed after you have got up, dressed and gone about your daily tasks.

After awhile that separated soul energy dissipates (where it had became attached) and returns to your physical body to re-attach to the original Soul unit. However, this dissipation and return to the parent Soul does not always occur immediately. When there is emotional energy attached to a place, individual, or event, a part of your Soul can remain lodged within that location for varying times.

If you become attached to another person through sexual activity, a part of your Soul (a fragment) remains with that sexual partner. You could have a multitude of Soul fragments attached to many different partners, places, associates, friends, and various events.

Soul fragments can also be stolen from your parent soul and hidden for devious purposes. It is entirely possible that after you have lived a productive life on Earth, at the end of that life you will have a large number of Soul fragments (facets) missing. That is, during your incarnation you have failed to make a conscious effort to collect those missing fragments, clean them up, and have them reinstalled within the most appropriate part of your ongoing Soul maintenance program.

The extent to which you have taken care of your Soul directly relates to your overall well being, health, and ability to obtain a new physical body for ascension to the new Earth. Unless some efforts are made to recover missing Soul fragments, your Soul may be severely limited in its functional capabilities. Especially this is true when a large percent of your Soul is missing. So many humans appear to be very unaware that parts of their Soul are missing and do not realize the importance of keeping their Soul together. If you have Soul fragments scattered in many different locations, how can you hope to stay healthy and evolve spiritually?

Also, keep in mind that as you go through life you will meet some aggressive individuals. These aggressive individuals may be very possessive and dominating. Frequently they have the capability of taking pieces of your Soul and keeping them for various purposes. You all have heard of energy sappers, energy vampires, and energy snatchers. These individuals have learned how to take energy fragments from other Souls and hide them within themselves, by placing them in their aura. One purpose for this procedure is based on the concept that by having that additional Soul energy (from some other Soul) it will give them more power for their chosen purposes. For example, more power to manipulate and control others.

Such an activity is generally counterproductive because of the incompatibility of someone else's Soul fragment. When you carefully observe these individuals, you will detect a high degree of confusion. Such confusion is more dramatic when two or three Souls inhabit the same physical body. Each one takes turns trying to express itself and you may have difficulty knowing which Soul is communicating with you.

Another way Soul fragments (facets) can end up in undesirable locations occurs within an individual family. Family members sometimes exchange Soul fragments because of emotional ties. Such exchanges are again counterproductive because of fragment incompatibility. In addition, a dominating member of the family may accumulate fragments from several members of the family, as a control mechanism. These power hungry individuals are primarily guided by the philosophy of "Service To Self," with minimal regard about the damage they cause to others.

There are many other ways that Soul facets (fragments) can be confiscated. For example, the Soul can be damaged during traumatic experiences that take place during surgery or dental work. Soul fragments can enter various astral realms for various reasons brought about by various forms of trauma or specific challenging experiences. Some individuals have the capability to take some of your Soul facets and hide them somewhere on Earth, for example within a tree or large rock.

The medical procedures of organ transplants and blood transfusions are other methods whereby Soul fragments can be transferred between individual humans. Remember that when a body organ has been present within that body for a long time that organ takes on the vibration of the Soul within the donor's body. When that organ is transferred to a recipient, a part of the Soul essence (a connected fragment) in the organ is transferred to the recipient. There are methods for clearing these fragments before making the organ transfer. These clearing methods should be used before all transplant operations.

Another example of Soul fragment transfer can be illustrated by blood transfusions. When an individual gives blood, many different energy patterns are present within the blood. Then when a donor receives that blood, those energy patterns (within that donor's blood) are transferred to

72

the recipient. Those energy patterns generally are not compatible with the recipient. Thus, they can interfere with the integrity of the consciousness -- in one or both Souls. Usually, only a small amount of the donor's Soul energy is lost and transferred to the recipient in the blood, however it does not take much to make a difference. Again, some effort should be made to clear any carry over Soul energy during blood transfusions or any other medical procedure.

Souls can fragment involuntarily because of their structural designs. The human Soul is an energy unit made up of various projections such as facets, cords, filaments, and fiber like structures that extend out from the Soul. Some of these connecting units bring in spiritual energy that helps maintain healthy body functions. Spiritual energy (from SOURCE) flows though these connecting units to an individual's Soul crystal foundation. Just as the branches of a tree can break off, the connecting units extending out from the Soul central matrix can also break away. When these branches break off they are free to become attached to another Soul. For many reasons, some individual Soul's can function like a sponge or magnet attracting many of these dislodged fragments.

The ability to attract the dislodged fragments of other Souls will depend on several factors. For example, the psychological stability and/or the general state of consciousness of all individuals involved. When this transfer takes place, the consciousness of the new parent Soul is changed (altered) in many different ways. Various types of energy patterns embedded within the Soul fragments, those that were part of the parent Soul, now become attached to another Soul. The Soul that has these new attached fragments now has to deal with conflicting energies from another person. When this takes place all kinds of imbalances can occur. In some cases, these imbalances may become very serious and even severe.

When an excessive number of these fragments (from another soul) become attached to the body of the recipient Soul, it can become overwhelmed. This can result in severe mental problem for the recipient Soul. All of these attached fragments from other Souls bring with them mental and emotional challenges previously associated with the donor. Dr. Mitchell Gibson (MD) has stated in his workshops that many individual physiological challenges can be traced back to the Soul's structure. Likewise, the Soul who has lost these important Soul appendages can also experience difficulties. As parts of their Soul become dislodged, a part of

73

their reality is missing. Have you heard the statements, "They are not all there?" Alternatively, "That person is missing some of their marbles."

The dislodged Soul fragments attempt to find any Soul that is open or has an affinity for their energy patterns. Like attracts like could play an important energy affiliation when a Soul fragment is attempting to locate a host. A fragment with limited intelligence, true of many fragments, will seek out an individual with limited intelligence. Keep in mind that many Soul fragments from other Souls, because of their size, have a limited level of intelligence. As a result, their ability to use wise judgment within a future host is very limited. That poor judgment can mingle and mix with the host mental abilities. These individuals are frequently emotionally disturbed, tired, and generally sickly. Attempts to use traditional psychological procedures have difficulty resolving these causes. Upon close examination, many of these individuals have been discovered to be loaded down with various Soul fragments from other individuals.

In other cases, these weakened individuals have lost a large percentage of their Soul. Our subtle energy research indicates this is a very serious challenge that is seldom addressed by any individual health care professional who claims to be of Service To Others. Many health care professionals treat symptoms rather than treating causes. It is much easier to treat symptoms compared to determining causes and then knowing how to correct the causes.

One effective method is to ask their High Self what the status of an individual's Soul is and what caused the damage. Their High Self knows all about the Soul's status. Once you ask you must be capable of hearing what their High Self communicates. Because of the complex subject of human Soul fragmentation, the procedures required to discover where the lost Soul parts are located will require spiritual assistance. Also, the complex procedures required for cleaning, reinstalling, and aligning those fragments will also require the help of skilled spiritual Soul technicians.

Retrieving Lost Soul Fragments and/or Facets

Soul energy, like all other energies, can never be destroyed, only changed in form. However, Souls with certain structural features can fragment many times. In fact, some Souls have fragmented into thousands of pieces like shattered glass. In those cases, it may be difficult for the individual Soul to gather its fragments without skilled spiritual assistance. On a planet like Earth where Souls have been incarnating for thousands of lifetimes, many souls appear to be powerless in their attempt to control their lives. Such Souls have become so fragmented they have very little energy remaining and thus are unable to create meaningful life experiences except on a very rudimentary level.

Dr. Mitchell Gibson discusses, within his workshops, that a majority of human mental and emotional challenges frequently can be correlated with lost Soul fragments or the taking on of Soul facets from other Souls. Because of the serious nature of this Soul fragmentation challenge several meditation and healing techniques have been developed to help an individual retrieve their Soul fragments. In addition, techniques for working with the spiritual realm are available to help retrieve, clean up, and reinstall missing Soul fragments.

If you have an idea about where or who has taken some of your Soul fragments or you have some of their fragments, then you need to take action. Sometimes you can intuitively know that an individual Soul, one who has caused you to experience anger, pain, or sadness, has some parts of your Soul. When this occurs, you can ask for forgiveness for all individuals, regardless of who they are.

The now famous phrase is "I'm Sorry – Please Forgive Me -- Thank You – I Love You," is almost miraculous in the power it has to bring many aspects of the human personality back into balance. As you ask for forgiveness, that mental process assists in removing another's fragments from anyone's auric field. Those Soul fragments that have been holding on to you have sensed they must leave to facilitate that forgiveness. How do you know when there is a need to clear the Soul of some fragments? When you have difficulty releasing some negative emotions this could be an indication that someone else's Soul fragments are helping hold those emotions within your energy bodies.

Soul fragments can also affect the physical health of an individual. Just recently, I received a Telephone call of someone who was having difficulty recovering from pneumonia. The High Self of the individual with pneumonia indicated that the disease was held in place by fragments of a Soul that had died of pneumonia. By removing these Soul fragments, the pneumonia energy was re-patterned.

When you intuitively realize that you may have given some of your Soul fragments away then again you can also ask for forgiveness. Those fragments need to be located with the help of your High Self. Then have them cleaned, and reinstalled in their proper position. Remember that through the process of forgiveness you can remove and/or recover Soul fragments and have them returned to their original Soul site.

It is very important to avoid becoming a "psychic sponge" by picking up Soul fragments that are laying or drifting around. Soul fragments, either originating from the living or deceased (disincarnate) frequently seek out those who are open to picking them up. When you have difficulty thinking for yourself or have difficulty making decision (experience brain fog) you could have picked up Soul fragments that are interfering with your mental and emotional capabilities.

Some other proven techniques for removing or retrieving soul fragments include hypnotherapy, psychotherapy, biofeedback, meditation, rebirthing, spiritual response therapy, sweeping the auric field with specific energies, advanced reiki, radionics, and many other related healing, clearing, and balancing procedures. Once you have gone through the process of recovering your Soul fragments or the removal of someone else's fragments you will sense a difference. Normally, you will gradually have an increase in your physical, mental and emotional energies.

In meditation, using the concept of asking and receiving, you can ask your High Self Spiritual Council and/or spirit guides to find the most appropriate spiritual team to clear your energy bodies, hologram, aura, chakras, meridians, grids, and all interfering energy patterns. Ask that all Soul fragments be cleaned up, returned, and integrated within the Soul from which they originated. Once reinserted within the original Soul, ask that their High-Self Spiritual Council synchronize and harmonize all Soul fragments (facets) for maximum functional efficiency.

Likewise, request that your High Self Spiritual Council recover all of your missing Soul facets from all locations throughout any portion of this and other Universes. You can ask that they search the Omniverse, Multiverse, or all known Universes for any Soul facets that may have been lost during any incarnation or spiritual sojourn throughout all "Now Times."

Detailed studies of individual Souls, reveals that missing Soul fragments (or facets) may have been stolen or detached and left anywhere within all different parts of creation. It would be impossible for you to know how those Soul fragments became detached or even where they are. However, your High Self knows everything about your many sojourns and incarnations. Thus, one of the most logical approaches to solving your challenge of restructuring your Soul is to request help from your High Self Spiritual Council. Most High Selves will consider your request as a high priority and take quick action to be of assistance.

The loss of Soul fragments (facets) or the attachment of unwanted Soul fragments should be considered a high priority in any effort to bring balance to an individual's life. You may be surprised to discover that one of your major causes for a multitude of challenges can be traced back to a damaged Soul.

The Founders indicate that there are many humans on Earth, who have left fragments of their Soul at previous incarnation sites. Frequent loss could have occurred during any past, present or future incarnations, including fragments of the Soul left on other planets during their incarnations. Because most Souls have incarnated thousands of times at a multitude of locations it is humanly impossible to detect all of those sites. When you realize that you may have left parts of your Soul, one of your first tasks is to determine current degree of damage. If you are familiar with some of your past and future lives, you may remember specific physical, mental, or emotional trauma. Sometimes those experiences surface to be cleared during this lifetime. Check to determine the extent to which these experiences may have damaged your Soul.

Therefore, make sure all Souls fragments or facets are present and work in harmony. As noted throughout this book the most efficient method is to use accurate pendulum dowsing. Once you have verified that you have a damaged Soul, the repair of your Soul should receive high priority. The structural integrity of your Soul influences every known feature of your well being here on Earth. Once the damage is known, one can then seek spiritual assistance to rectify the damage.

Realize that you can have considerable Soul damage without the appearance of obvious symptoms of any kind in any of your twenty plus bodies. Remember, there is a constant need to keep your Soul intact. You have very limited capabilities to know exactly when Soul damage could occur.

Within the subtle energy research program, we have discovered that a majority (55%) of humans Souls currently incarnated in physical bodies on Earth have significant Soul damage. There is a very high probability that you, the reader, has inadvertently left parts of your Soul somewhere or have picked up parts of someone else's Soul. Anytime an individual human body (with a Soul) resides for any length of time within a given location, there is the possibility of leaving part of their Soul at that location. Likewise, anytime you travel around or communicate with others there is a possibility of picking up a part of their Soul.

For example, when you go to a restaurant and set in a chair that contains a part of the previous individual's (the one who set in that chair) Soul's fragments you can take some of those fragments home with you. We have discovered that individuals, who travel and sleep in motels, pick up soul fragments. Those fragments are frequently left in the bed where someone else has sleep. Everyone leaves an energetic bed pattern where they slept. Portions of those bed patterns can contain Soul fragments. Keep in mind that the bed pattern energy, can felt by psychic individuals and can be measured.

Disincarnate Soul fragments that have been disconnected from their "parent Soul" are quite frequently found somewhere on Earth. The process of fragment disconnect can occur throughout one's lifetime but is more apt to occur when the Spirit leaves their body following death. Parts of the soul become dislodged in association with physical death for a host of reasons. Many disincarnates are unaware that when they physically died, the parts of their Soul and/or Soul fragments they picked up while incarnated, have been dislodged. Sometimes the missing Soul fragments of other Souls attached to the deceased can be taken with that Soul as it moves beyond the veil into the etheric realms. Those missing soul fragments now reside somewhere beyond the veil, within a vibrational level of the astral realm.

Some facets may currently reside within another density or dimension below the seventh density. In fact, detached Soul facets can be found most anywhere humans have incarnated, traveled, or experienced any component part of their evolutionary Soul journey.

Another feature of these displaced Soul fragments is related to the subject of what many call implants and imprints. For example, many humans have picked up what have been termed implants or imprints during one of their incarnations somewhere else within the Universe. You can carry those implants or imprints in your etheric body from one lifetime to another. Again, to facilitate your graduation and ascension process it will be very helpful to remove all implants (etheric or physical structures with attached cords) and imprints (thought forms).

Many humans would be surprised to know how frequently both implants and imprints are present somewhere in their bodies. Remember that implants with attached cords can be used to manipulate a physical person's behavior and energy level from a distance. These implants and imprints are continually utilized by individuals whose objective is to control and manipulate others. Also, those who desire to control others can take parts of your Souls when they believe that process can give them more power and lower your power.

Incarnated humans can also pick up Soul fragments left behind by some other Soul. As a result, they can be carried with that individual into future incarnations. Everyone is aware of what has been termed a haunted house or place where evidence indicates the presence of soul fragments that may have been associated with an individual who previously lived there. Even though there is not a physical entity present, there are signs of human-like behavior. There are instances where large numbers of Soul fragments (ghosts) have been discovered within a given location. Souls previously living within the area have obviously left some of their Soul fragments behind when their spirits left the physical body.

Our etheric bodies can contain Soul fragments, implants, imprints (thought forms) and various crystallized energy patterns frequently deposited during traumatic events or separations during previous lifetimes. Many of the traumatic events that took place between Souls during a previous incarnation are still very active because they occur in the current NOW time. Sometimes during your review between lives this experience will surface and during your upcoming incarnation you will set up a situation where you will be able to clear these attached energies.

When you discover some Soul fragments of someone who has passed over, that is they left parts of their soul on the lower densities, you have an opportunity to assist that parent Soul. You may request that qualified spiritual helpers locate those fragments, clean them up, and return them to the parent Soul.

You may be advised by spirit that it will be difficult to locate the parent Soul. You can still be of assistance by requesting that those detached Soul facets be collected and sent to the light for recycling. Many of the fragments will depart when that request made. It is always helpful for you to focus on an attitude of love and Service To Others. That's always true when doing Soul work such as attempting to help lost detached Soul fragments find their preferred location.

This means to avoid all forms of judgment, regardless of the situations involved. That is there is no value or need for concern about what caused the fragment detachment. In addition, it is not your responsibility to determine who or what was at fault. In reality there are no faults; everything is in Divine order. Avoid trying to analyze the situation and just accept that a need currently exists and you have become aware of that need. You were alert enough to discover the need and because you cared enough to be of assistance -- that challenge will be resolved as a result your efforts.

Free will, as we currently know understand "it," is a difficult concept to comprehend. With free will choice there is also the factor of curiosity, the choice to become curious. Many Souls like to explore or be curious and adventurous. Because of their excessive curiosity, they may get themselves into a great deal of trouble. They can become involved in events that are totally out of their ability to control. When this happens, it is often very difficult for them to extricate themselves from a situation where they have become energetically trapped. That entrapment could have an adverse affect on the individual's Soul.

Again, when you become aware of an individual who is having difficulty experiencing an event that is beyond their ability to understand and you have been asked to assist, exercise extreme caution. They may have become entrapped within a very complex situation. In these situations considerable spiritual assistance may be required. Obviously, you do not have to respond to every request. As you remain receptive, you will have many other opportunities to be of Service To Others. That is, you have an opportunity to help others out of their self-imposed entrapment when they request help and you do not interfere with their contracts.

In terms of recovering your missing Soul fragments, you can ask your High Self Spiritual Council for assistance in locating those missing fragments and have them brought back. Alternatively, if your High Self

Spiritual Council lacks that ability, ask them to find the appropriate spirit team that can respond to your request. I, again emphasize the following point. Once you're missing Soul fragments have been returned they will need to be cleansed and reinserted within the proper position of your Soul, then integrated, and brought into harmony with your other Soul facets. It is important to keep all component parts of your Soul working as a team.

In closing this discussion about the Retrieval of Soul Fragments, you may need to be reminded that humans on Earth are now living during the end of a cyclic period when mass ascension becomes available. It will be highly desirable as you prepare for graduation and ascension that you bring all structural components of your Soul back together as soon as possible.

As a reminder, a new special dispensation has been made available to those interested in completing their current incarnation here within the third to fourth densities of the old Earth. This special dispensation is known as a "spiritual transcendence." The newly developed spiritual program (approved by the Creators) is designed to help you prepare for graduation and ascension as soon as possible. It would be highly advantageous for you to confer with your High Self to make sure that you are preparing for and on the new time line, established by the Creators.

Each Soul upon Earth now has an option to choose the path of spiritual transcendence. This dispensation replaces the old path of cause and effect, which is sometimes referred to as a karmic path (the old time line). The old path frequently required many lifetimes where efforts were made to balance out an adverse experience (karma) by reincarnating back on Earth to make amends. In order to complete this evolutionary cycle on time, at the end of the age between 2012 and 2030, there is a need to contact your spiritual assistants to accelerate the healing processes in all of your energy bodies. The window of opportunity for requesting this assistance will only be open until the end of this current galactic cycle. Each Soul will be required to make its own choice as to whether to take advantage of the opportunities now offered to incarnated Souls. May your choice assist your Soul evolution and may that choice assist you along your new path, new time track, and new time line towards that "special spiritual transcendence" that is in your future NOW.

Role of Your Higher Self on Earth

The Higher Self is who you truly are. As you ride around in your physical body you are living an illusion, only pretending to be a third-fourth dimensional being, That's because you want to experience the dualistic (negative and positive) features of your journey, here on Earth. The lower self is an illusion you have created for the learning purposes. Your Higher Self has no concept of the negative and positive, and it does not want to play within that arena or in that game. Yes, it knows what you are doing here on Earth and what lessons you plan to complete. As a result, your High Self will offer assistance and guidance when you make that request. Restated, your conscious mental effort is required to establish communication with your High Self.

When you have a conversation within your mind you quite frequently are speaking with either your Higher Self or your ego. Make sure you separate the mind chatter from the messages of your High Self. Through practice, you can constantly communicate with your Higher Self to help you complete your daily journey here on Earth. The most important part of that journey is moving from fear into love. As a major part of that responsibility, you are required to take control of your emotional and physical body as means of experiencing ecstasy, joy, peace, health, and well-being.

In order to communicate with your Higher Self you must be truthful. When you proceed down a blind path, following a pattern that does not involve the High Self, the High Self is very aware of your activities. Because of its desire to assist you with your challenges on Earth, and you fail to accept its wisdom, it can shut down, actually stop communicating completely. That is, quite frequently you may discover that the Higher Self chooses what it wants to communicate rather than what you are expecting. When this happens, you may need assistance as soon as possible. Life on Earth without High Self support is difficult.

Your Higher Self is much smarter than your lower self is. Very much more intelligent compared to your ego. Therefore, to communicate you must give it a reason to respond to your current challenges. In addition, it will be very important to trust your Higher Self because it knows what is best for your journey within the lower densities. You can continually have a dialogue with your Higher Self. However, when you

82

request help you must listen to the proposed solution. When the proposal is given, it is best to write the answer down for future reference. Consistently ignoring the suggestions given by your High Self can cause some additional challenges for your incarnation on Earth. Thus, it pays to pay attention.

When and if you become interested in becoming a channel of spiritual information it is best to start by communicating with your Higher Self. When you communicate with your Higher Self you quite frequently, sense a far off feeling like that which is sensed within a dream. When you have become skilled at communicating with your Higher Self, then you can branch out and channel your angels, guides, extraterrestrials, a tree, whales, the Earth, and all other component parts of creation.

One approach in communicating with your Higher Self is to set aside times to go into meditation. The Higher Self will point out areas within your consciousness that need to be fine tuned to help you realize that the journey from fear to love is the most important part of your life on Earth. Your High Self is there to outline techniques that can help you overcome all fear.

Make sure that you know what the term "Fear" means. All negative emotions can be lumped together under the term Fear. All forms of negativity such as stress, depression, tension, anxiety, worry, fright, jealousy, grief, etc. are all fear related. Remember, stated again, the only thing to fear is fear. Once this task is accomplished, you will know that nothing outside, in the world beyond can harm you. You are safe -- there is nothing to fear. You will be in Love with ALL THAT IS. Making that accomplishment, of living with Love, is one of the major reason for creating the illusion (misguided belief) that you are a physical body. That physical body and ego have helped create many of the lessons here within "Earth School." I repeat again, "your key lesson on Earth is to overcome fear with love." This point is stated over and over several times elsewhere within this book because of how important overcoming fear is.

Realize that all fear related emotions are frequently stored within various locations inside the physical body. When that negative energy builds up in a body part, watch out for some related imbalances for you to overcome. Each stored emotion can be correlated with a specific disease symptom. Review the book, "Emotions Buried Alive Never Die" by Karol K. Truman and related books on storing emotions and their related symptoms. Then clear out all stored negative emotions. You may already know that a majority of all imbalances in the body are related to some negative emotion. If that concept is new to you, now is the time to beef up your understanding of how important it is for you to take total control of your emotions. When you sense an emotion building up ask the question, what value will I gain by amplifying this emotion?

Throughout the process of creating, you will learn that there are seven to twelve levels of truth. Re-stated, there are twelve levels of consciousness within the third dimension. Within each level of truth, there are four more levels of understanding or a total of twenty-eight levels. Master Kirael in the article published within the October 2009 issue of the "Sedona Journal" gives an example of this concept.

Quoting: *"Spiritual alchemy has four levels of mastery, black, white, red, and gold. Within each of those levels of color are seven other levels of color, each representing a different truth or a different consciousness."* Master Kirael goes on to state: *"With respect to channeling, when you reach the level of truth for what I call mediumship, this third dimension journey will disappear."*

To obtain real guidance we need to go outside the third Dimension realm. Keep in mind that this third Dimension experience is ending here on Earth. Earth is rapidly completing its transition into the fourth Dimension. You can use your meditation and channeling talents to obtain reliable information for the next step in your journey to the New Earth. When you come into frequent communication with your Higher Self, you can do automatic writing, channeling, or mediumship to obtain the keys to your spiritual evolution within this "Now" moment. Sometimes you will need to get out of your physical body to get a clear view and answer. That is when you for sure need guidance from your High Self. The point is that you must not limit your communications with only your High Self. There will be an unlimited number of other spiritual sources for finding accurate information. One such source is 'Universal Consciousness" the Source I constantly approach when using accurate pendulum dowsing.

If everyone would perfect their channeling and mediumship skills, there would be nobody seeking out others for guidance because everyone would know everything -- before it was said. You also would not be within third Dimension consciousness. As a channel or medium, you can go to the fifth, sixth, seventh densities, and beyond to obtain helpful spiritual insights of truth. Many individuals are fearful of channeling and mediumship. They may need assistance in gaining heir self-confidence become skilled at communicating with their High Self before attempting any channeling. When you feel a need to become a channel of Higher Spiritual Truths, go to your Higher Self first. When in contact, ask for assistance in accomplishing that goal. You can go anywhere when you become skilled at communicating with your Higher Self. Until you perfect your channeling skills, I recommend a subscription to the Sedona Journal of Emergence, a monthly publication of some of the most accurate channels within the United States. These messages can help you keep up with the rapidly changing events on Earth every month.

Let us consider an example of how important it is to be in contact with your Higher Self. There will soon come a time here on the old Earth when we move into a very dense portion of the photon belt. When this occurs the photon particles will be so dense (termed the "Null Zone") that it will become completely dark. For many this could be a frightening experience. To accept this experience without any form of fear and maintain a state of Love, can be facilitated by receiving moment-by-moment guidance from your Higher Self. That part of you that remained on the other side of the veil is there for a very specific purpose. That Soul fragment (portion of the Oversoul) remained within the higher frequency spiritual realm of the sixth to eights DMC to assist those parts of your reality that have incarnated on Earth. Your High Self knows these will be challenging times, when you have limited understanding of why various events are raking place. Trust your High Self to help you remain positive -- as you realize that all experiences are in Divine order.

Section IV. Density States of Creation

Consequence of a Creative Consciousness

As we approach the subject of density or also the concept that everything has been created from light, then we need to determine what force was involved in bringing forth various creations. Then we of necessity will need to explore some concepts about how the many different Universes came into existence. One possibility is that the Universe is a consequence of a colossal consciousness nonphysical independent atemporal reality, (CREATOR OR CREATORS -- GOD/GODDESS). That consciousness provided the foundation (thoughts) for the formation of all dimensional creations and the creation of a human spirit capable of sensing those creations.

We then ask what are all of these creations composed of, how do they differ, and why did they come into existence? Let's assume that all creations exist as a multitude of imaginary concepts (thought forms) designed as tools for use during our participation within the Universal school of creation. Currently many of our lessons occur within the Universal classroom we choose, called "Planet Earth."

Then the Universe we are familiar with, from a third dimension perspective is an imaginary concept created by an atemporal consciousness. Realize also, that the third dimensional consciousness that senses the illusionary Universe is also illusionary. In reality all creations that have ever been created by that same atemporal consciousness are illusionary. If this reasoning is correct than the only part of creation that is not illusionary is the atemporal reality that created everything. Also, we can further state that if all creations came from an atemporal conscious reality then all of those creation must have some form of consciousness.

We are well aware that we can communicate with other human consciousness and thereby learn. Likewise, we should also be capable of communicating with all other conscious creations as an aid in our evolution. Consider the possibility that every creation is here to assist our Spirit in learning about each creation -- to help humans to become creators. Therefore, we can learn (gain knowledge) from all other creations by communicating with them. All major component parts of creation have some form of consciousness. As you become aware of their levels of understanding, you may learn by communicating with any created form. For example, as you become intuitive you can communicate with a tree, dog, whale, rock, and a sparrow. You can even channel any component part of creation by going within. Using you intuitively listening skills you can record those messages and share them with others.

Metaphysical Concepts and Creations

To describe any of the creations brought into being through conscious effort there is a need to consider metaphysical concepts. The field of metaphysics is a philosophical branch of science that deals with first principles. For example, the principles of being, knowing, substance, cause, identity, time, and space. By focusing in on these concepts, one may be able to explain how all creations came into existence.

Previously existing theories in physics have failed to consider that these creations are related to a colossal consciousness. It is impossible to define existence without the concept of consciousness. One could state that existence is best defined in terms of how it is related to consciousness. Then we again ask the important question, "What is this colossal consciousness?"

It is impossible to imagine a state where nothing exists. Why is that true? Because, for an existence to comprehend that there is an existence present, an existence must be present to sense its presence. Therefore, existence exists necessarily, even if nothing else exists. If anything at all exists, then existence has to exist.

Keep in mind that paradoxes are inherent in reality because reality is self-referential. For example, what philosophers call paradoxes, logicians may call contradictions. What theologians may call mysteries, physicists may call them dualities. It is humanly impossible to resolve all of these ambiguities. However, each discipline has at its disposal some insights to help resolve some ambiguities. We will need to consider a few more paradoxes, brought about through attempting to correlate (tie together) metaphysical concepts, existing philosophies and scientific understandings.

Densities in Relation to Frequencies

Densities are discrete vibratory levels within the frequency spectrum of Creation. Generally, densities are divided into harmonics or octaves. That is, we can arbitrarily assign density levels to various vibratory frequencies in the Universe. By separating different frequency ranges into densities this procedure can help spirits (entities) have terms for communicating with the third-fourth density realm. These patterned descriptions of various densities can help you and me to have terms to understand and communicate more efficiently with others entities anywhere in the Universe. Once communication is set up with thought forms, each human can gain an understanding of how the Universe is designed and/or constructed. To illustrate this communication concept we can arbitrarily assign a number to a color of the light spectrum. For example, if yellow equals third density, then orange would be second density, and green the fourth density.

Another example would be to assign an actual frequency to a density. First density could be assigned to lie within a range of from 100 to 1,000 Hz (cycles per second), Second density would cover the range between 1.000 Hz and 5.000 Hz and third density between 1,000 Hz and 10,000 Hz. From this example, you can note that densities do not have to be linear, but can be logarithmic.

The main attribute of a density is its harmonic relationship to other densities. In the television episode of "Star Trek," (in part originating from off-planet) reference is made to warp factors when describing the speed of an Intergalactic vehicle. Warp speeds are speeds faster than light, using a scale of 1 to 10 where a warp speed of 10 corresponds to an infinite velocity. Whereas speeds below warp one, use fractional values. Intergalactic vehicles speed, from a third-fourth perspective, generally depends upon interstellar conditions and quantum drag. Consequently, various sensing equipment, computer technology with various formulas are required to calculate required speeds to reach a destination safely. Also, consider traveling in the absence of time and space within the fifth DMC as you contemplate your future travels. Each warp factor can be related to a density, the higher the warp factor, the lower the density.

In quantum physics there is the concept of parallel time frames. Each time frame is accessed by achieving speeds that are harmonics of the speed of light. While it may be difficult to conceive of exceeding the speed of light, it is possible to conceive of dialing up various harmonics of the speed of light. In Einstein's equation $E=mc^2$ where c^2 is a harmonic of the speed of light. In this example, c^2 could be second density and c^3, third density, etc.

In this discussion, we will use density to illustrate some differences related to the progression of various life forms along an evolutionary (frequency) scale. The higher the vibration of a given life form, the lower its density is.

You will note that each density corresponds to a dimensional state of consciousness with the same number. However, the dimensional states of consciousness more accurately depict activities within the world of consciousness. We can also state that the conscious activities humans engage in during different states of consciousness (first, second, third, fourth, fifth, sixth, seventh) do overlap each other and we are dependent on that fact for our survival. The overlapping features of dimensional states of consciousness are the features of our multidimensionality. In contrast, when we consider different densities that make up our reality -- they do not overlap like state of dimensional consciousness overlap.

In **section VII**, we will discuss some features of the twelve different states of Dimensional Consciousness. You will remember that we defined levels of consciousness as follows: To become very conscious means to be continually aware mentally and emotionally alert to all of your conscious, subconscious, and superconscious activities. Those activities include events on the physical Earth and various activities beyond the veil as you leave your body in dreams or astral travel within the Spiritual realm. These sensing activities should involve using all of your outer and Inner sensing systems as they relate to the conscious, subconscious, and superconscious mental states. By utilizing all of your energy systems, you can become more conscious of all aspects of life. To accomplish this task will require that you become aware at all times.

To help in your ascension process while residing upon the Earth plane, make a concerted effort to notice how conscious events unfold around you during every "Now" moment. To notice, means listening to the God/Goddess within and your High Self to answer any question that would be of assistance in helping you follow closely within your chosen path (time line). With a higher level of consciousness, it becomes possible to be aware of every event your outer and inner sensing systems can perceive much more quickly and accurately. These levels of awareness then can be recorded in your conscious and subconscious minds. These sensing data can also be recorded within your Akashic records for eternal referencing.

One helpful approach to understanding how changing frequencies alters our sensing capabilities is to classify these levels of creation into densities, each having a different vibrational frequency range. The Densities of creation can be arbitrarily arranged as a function of the frequencies of the Light Spectrum as follows:

Twelve Density States of Creation

First - Minerals (Rocks and Soil)
Second - Plants and Microbes
Third - Lower Human (Animals)
Fourth - Higher Frequency Humans
Fifth - Light Body Status Human
Sixth - Soul Body
Seventh - Oversoul Body
Eighth - Angel Realm
Ninth - Archangel Realm
Tenth - Creator God Realm
Eleventh - Universal God Realm
Twelfth - Godhead – Founders
When you consider various densities of an entities status (frequency), they do not overlap.

First Density: Minerals (Rocks and Soil)

The vibratory level of this kingdom is very dense, but has its own level life force and consciousness. In fact, this is the density of consciousness, where the minerals and water learned from fire and wind the awareness of being. Here the spiraling energy, a characteristic of light, gives these minerals and water a desire to strive in a type of awareness to manifest in second density. You can communicate with this kingdom in a rudimentary fashion. Everyone is aware that many individuals have communicated with their pet-rock or a crystal. This density is the first stage of evolution within the creation of a manifest Universe. The mineral kingdom consists of all known elements within the Universe. Each element has a specific vibratory frequency, atomic number, and isotopic designation that differentiate the characteristics of each individual component.

Second Density: Microbes and Plants

This kingdom is more organized than the mineral kingdom. However, it still has limited ability to move as evidenced with the microbes. Plants move as they strive towards receiving light. In each case, these second density entities strive for growth. Members of this kingdom have reproductive systems and can photosynthesize (capture light energy from the sun). Plants also have an awareness to survive, however their perceptions are rather limited. That is, they are aware of events taking place within their environment, can sense each other, and can sense the feelings of the members of the animal kingdom. They do store within their consciousness events taking place within their environment. Those who are sensitive to receiving or picking up thoughts can recover this information. For example, a tree records all events that have occurred within its vicinity from when it began growth. By quietly listening (within) to the tree, you can learn a lot about its history.

The second density strives towards third density because of its interest of obtaining self-consciousness and self-awareness.

Third Density: Animals and Lower Humans

The animals and "lower" level human beings reside within this kingdom with a mind/body complex where the first evidence of spirit becomes evident. Third density humans are experiencing the animal kingdom in humanoid bodies. Contrary to popular belief, animals have the same abilities as third density humans. For example, animals have the instinct to survive, reproduce, and care for their young, as well as rudimentary awareness.

As we contemplate densities, we should also consider how dimensional states of consciousness relate to densities. Let us briefly differentiate between third density and third dimensional states of consciousness. Obviously, the third dimensional state of consciousness includes the plants and mineral kingdoms. In contrast, the third density specifically refers to animals and "lower" humans. "Lower" here refers only to the frequency of the entity and is in no way a judgment for or against any creation. In other words, a third density human is just as Divine as any fourth density human. A majority of humans (approximately 75 to 80%) have purposely chosen to incarnate within third density frequencies (bodies) for the experiences provided.

Anyone who would have a tendency to judge themselves superior to a rock in the first density is displaying a serious level of ignorance about the overall features of the "Creations." Relatively speaking the rock is equal to the human making the judgment. Some of the most aware or advanced souls within the Universe have chosen to purposely experience third density because of the many challenges at these lower frequencies. Those choices were not made with the idea of becoming inferior. Those challenges have been taken on within the lower density because of the learning experiences available.

The directive "judge not least ye be judged," indicates that all is one and thus none is superior because they all exist within a density or dimensional state of consciousness where nothing is defined as being higher or lower in superiority. The higher or lower aspects relates to frequency, not superiority or inferiority. Each density and each dimensional state of consciousness, just is, what it is.

Many humans apparently prefer third density because of the urges associated with survival capabilities and the sexual urges they enjoy. However, many third density humans have the belief they are victims. Consequently, they would like to alleviate the pain and separation. Thus, they have a tendency to want to escape from the chaos, challenges, and confusion. Many humans attempt to escape by becoming religious, take on specific "false" beliefs and ideologies, and other social movements for peace of mind. Others attempt to escape via self-punishment with drugs, excess sex, and many other "pleasurable" habitual tendencies. Why are these human escape characteristics frequently observed?

Because, many humans who have attempted to escape from reality on Earth, have very specific needs. Frequently, they have difficulty thinking for themselves. We frequently note they have damaged Souls. They fail to realize that by shifting to a higher state of dimensional consciousness (fourth to fifth) they could move out of (away from) these less than desirable challenges and in a sense escape.

Third density humans are very frequently ruled by culture beliefs, previous life experiences, and biases. These individuals are easily programmed to behave as their controllers ("masters") have dictated. Once they have given their power away and are programmed by societal dogmas (doctrines) they have become trapped.

To survive they revert to operating on automatic pilot, repeating the same activities day after day. A repetitive robotic life style of awakening, going to work, coming home, eating, going to bed, and repeating the same cycle day after day is highly counterproductive. Some seek repetitive pleasures and a distorted concept of happiness to escape from the boredom of such a lifestyle. When someone is experiencing these behavior patterns there is a good indication that some outside consciousness has programmed them. You could believe your friend, when he states, "If you just have one more beer, you'll be happy."

Also currently a majority of humans on Earth appear to be "sitting on the fence" between third and fourth density. This means that a part of their being has evolved to fourth density but a large proportion remains centered within the third density. If you strongly desire to be in the fourth density or even shift to the fifth density, your best approach is to honor those aspects within the third density, then ask for spiritual assistance to shift to the higher density. As a result, you will discover that you will gradually increase your fourth to fifth density vibratory frequencies. To make that shift will also require many other criteria outlined in the book "You Can Avoid Physical Death."

To be completely free of the third density requires a willingness to clear out all third density false beliefs, fear related emotions, discordant programs, and self-centered ego guided behavior patterns. While living on a planet where 75 to 80% of the residents are in third density creates a strong force field in the aura of the planet that tends to pull down one's efforts to prepare to ascend. Many Souls did not consciously choose their beliefs; rather they took on the prevailing beliefs of their controllers (parents, schools, churches, television, etc.) or were unable to overcome mass consciousness, around them. It takes a strong disciplinary effort for an individual to "wake-up" and think for himself or herself. Once an individual "wakes up" and follows their internal guidance system (God-

Goddess within and High Self), they can break free from their entrapment and follow their own internal guidance systems. These disciplinary efforts to break free are more effective once you know whom you are, have consistently used discernment in your choices, and have removed all fear related negative emotions.

Fourth Density: Higher Frequency Humans

One of the major features of the fourth density is the change in the space/time continuum with a different vibrational configuration. This shift creates a scattering of thought as some humans shift and others remain within the third density. The present social complex is poorly designed to assist these changes towards fourth and fifth density. Consequently, those entities unable to grasp the importance of Love have to repeat the third density until they "get it." Here in fourth density the entry of Love or vibration of understanding is highly important and comes into consciousness.

The fourth density human are lighter and in general more loving than a third dimension human, with some exceptions. They also are slower to age, more creative, and more powerful. Fourth density humans are more aware that they create their own life experiences through their thoughts and belief systems. Fourth density humans also have awakened their psychic and intuitive capabilities. They frequently have enhanced imaginations and tap into the astral realms. Outwardly, they look very similar to third density humans, however intellectually they tend to be more mentally and emotionally refined. As a result, the fourth density human tends to draw specific experiences that enhance their rate of Soul growth.

The ego is still very much a part of the fourth density human. These entities are frequently very rugged individuals, free thinkers, and may become rebels and/or radicals that attempt to shake up the status quo. Although they may have superior creative ideals, they remain polarized against those with opposing viewpoints. These individuals organize protests, marches, and demonstrations in an attempt to shake up the status quo. To make a significant difference these individuals need to move into the fifth density, a step many are now making as they evolve spiritually. When an individual moves towards fourth density, the third eye opens and all sorts of entities become evident, many of which exist within the fabric of the ethers.

A majority of all fourth density humans use their abilities for the good of humanity. They focus on meditation, develop beliefs that are more positive, utilize affirmations, and are involved in reprogramming their consciousness. Remember duality still exists within the fourth density.

Negative fourth density humans use their abilities to control and manipulate others. They have perfected their ability as Soul snatchers. Many fourth density Souls throughout the Universe are technologically advanced and are capable of exerting a powerful influence on others. Some of these negative entities use their psychic and mental powers to control entire planets for ego purposes. These fourth density entities have the capability to mesmerize others with psychic phenomena while taking power from them. In most situations, their followers receive minimal returns for their subjugation.

To a fourth density being, the astral levels are often mistaken for the more heavenly realms because, through the power of thought and belief, the astral can be made to look any way you want it.
You could make it the way you believe heaven should exist based on your past beliefs. As a result, that is what you visualize and experience -- you could call heaven. That heavenly state would be more characteristic of the higher levels of the fourth density entity. The fourth density is the beginning evolutionary state that opens up a sequence of events leading to the concepts of graduation and/or "ascension."

Fifth Density: Light Body Status Humans

The fifth density is where many humans have dreamed of going during their many incarnations. Here the concepts of graduation and ascension have taken on real meaning. During the galactic cycle leading up to "The Shift" the Creators have granted a special dispensation to the more evolved fourth density humans. That dispensation will allow those more spiritually advanced individuals to access fifth density before they have completed self-mastery. Therefore, the current definition of fifth density humans has been sub-divided. There are now two categories: ascended beings and ascended masters. Ascended beings, by definition lack the qualifications to become ascended masters.

The process of ascension involves the building of your "Mer-Ka-Ba," its modifications, and "Crystal Light Body" activation, a process that involves the mutating (transformation) of your carbon-based life form to a silicon-based life form. The creating of the "Crystal Light Body" is a precursor or requirement for actual ascension. The procedures used to create the "Crystal Light Body" are a part of the concepts related to a "Quantum Shift" and will be outlined in Section V.

The Soul that has evolved beyond fourth density has no need to continue on the reincarnation cycle. This means the body's cellular structure has increased in frequency sufficient to the point where a fifth density individual becomes invisible to a third-fourth density (third-fourth dimensional state of consciousness) individual. For third density individuals the fifth density body is invisible. Fourth density individuals are generally visible to third density humans. For sensitive fourth density individuals (those with psychic capabilities) the fifth density body may appear as a luminescent mist or glow. Many third density individuals seldom pay much attention to fourth and fifth dimension individuals because their minds are constantly pre-occupied trying to survive or are involved in various repetitive self-serving pleasures.

As planet Earth shifts to fourth density, it is possible for fifth density (fifth dimensional conscious) individuals to incarnate on a fourth density planet. Remember the fifth density body is capable of flying through the air and can walk through walls. Thus the fifth densify individual can easily exist calmly within a more hostile lower level fourth density environment.

One of the primary procedures for achieving fifth density status involves knowing who you are, why you came to Earth, and most of all an opening of your heart to love yourself and others unconditionally. Love will lift your vibrations above the third-fourth density Earth and provide the foundation for creating a silicon based radiant, immortal, crystalline Light Body. The vibrational frequency of the fifth density Light Body status is etheric in design.

Sixth Density: The Soul Body

The sixth density vibrational frequency is a very important component part of one's multidimensional nature. The sixth density body is called the "Soul Body" or is also called the Higher Self. In addition to being able to fly about the Earth the "Soul Body" is capable of traveling throughout the Galaxy and Universe. This ascended form is no longer bound by Earthly space and can maneuver the corridors of time, (that is move forward and backward in time) and travel the highways of light. These capabilities allow the Soul to learn more about the many features of the Universe and integrate them into their consciousness expansion.

The sixth density is also the gateway to the angelic realms, which are a part of the celestial heavens. The celestial body, a component part of the vibrational frequencies of the sixth density is constantly changing in appearance. The appearance of that celestial body is determined by the consciousness of the spirit entity. As visualized by another fifth density human the entity may take on various forms that deviate from translucent, to brilliant, and can include a variety of changing hues and colors.

Everything within the sixth density is crystalline in character. This is where the causal and crystal worlds exist. One will also observe crystal temples, castles in the air, and many mythological creations as they become visible within these higher densities. The nature spirits, for example reside within these densities. For example, fairy entities such as devas (from the inner Earth) associated with each plant species, commonly function within the etheric realms of the fifth and sixth densities.

Beings that occupy a particular density can see visions from the next-higher density. To sixth density entities, the angels within the seventh density appear as great winged creatures that dazzle the skies with their brilliance.

Sixth density, being ethereal, is completely non-physical and is not subject to any of the physical laws of Earth. For example, there is a sixth density civilization (The Hathors) residing on Venus at the higher frequencies of the planet. To the third density human, the third density Venus is composed of poisonous gases and temperatures exceeding 600 degrees. Obviously, these environmental conditions are unsuitable for any third density life form.

Within the sixth density stratosphere of Venus, there are beautiful etheric cities. These cities have been termed "Holy Cities," They are beautiful crystal like cities that can be observed by those sensing systems that are characteristic of fifth and sixth density ascended beings. As you consciously evolve to the fifth DMC, you will have the capability to not only see these cities but also visit them.

Entities that have evolved to become a part of the sixth density (the level of the Soul) are the highest and purest evolutionary form, where individuality is maintained. Those entities residing here have stripped away all the previous experiences taken on while incarnating within the lower densities. As a result, because of these changes the sixth density Soul Body emerges as a spark of God, the basic unit of Creation. Within this density, each Soul is unique, and has its own "signature" (individual designation). The ego self (characteristic of the third density) is only an imperfect image of the real self or sixth density Soul. Thus, the Soul exists three levels above the Earthly designed third density ego self and its physical vehicle.

In a sense, the process of evolving sequentially ends when a being reaches sixth density Soul level, because at that point in your evolution time no longer exist. The Soul essence of the sixth density is eternal; it has always existed and always will. Consequently, an entity does not evolve into a Soul status, it simply returns to Soul awareness. Remember the Soul originated from the Oversoul that originated from the Godhead with a directive to descend into the lower densities. The objective was to evolve back to the seventh density of the Oversoul by going through all the learning experiences available in the second, third, fourth, and fifth "lower" densities.

An evolved Soul is one in which all of your lower bodies (physical, etheric, mental, emotional, intellectual, and psychic) have aligned themselves with the free Soul body (High Self) of the sixth density. Until this process is complete, the Soul body essentially remains "cut-off" from the rest of the being — not in truth, but in awareness. What is taking place relates to where you have focused your awareness. Where you focused your awareness is where you vibrate. Thus when you return to your free sixth density Soul, you will have realized the importance of focusing your awareness at the sixth density Soul level. In addition, you will realize the importance of your Soul's experiences and their influence on your evolution while incarnated on lower density planets like Earth. Once your consciousness has shifted to the sixth density you can, with assistance of your High Self, correlate the features of your Soul with the functional efficiency of all your lower bodies.

Currently it will be very helpful for you to understand that the functional features of the Soul influence the physical, etheric, mental, emotional, intellectual, and psychic bodies. That is, while you reside upon the third to fourth density Earth. The paradox is that these lower bodies determine the spiritual status of the Soul. In turn, as stated, the features of the Soul determine the status of the bodies. When you give careful attention to your lower bodies and your Souls status, you have come to understand what preparing for graduation and ascension is all about.

Seventh Density: The Oversoul Body

The seventh density is the beginning of an entirely different spiraling feature of Creation. The evolutionary process ascends up through the first six densities, becoming more and more refined as an individual progresses. In contrast, the higher densities (seven through twelve) become more and more joined together and invisible from the perspective of a third-fourth density entity.

Seventh density is that density state where true union between Souls occurs. Up until this point along the sequence of densities (gradually vibrating at the higher frequencies), any attempt for Souls to join with each other was counterproductive. Souls that attempt to join with another Soul (within the lower densities) will take on the essence of the attached Soul. These essences (energies) will cloud their aura, cause confusion, and slow spiritual progress. Taking on any Soul fragments of another at the lower densities can cause a multitude of challenges on Earth, especially with the mental and emotional bodies. To have a healthier more stable mental and emotional body you should avoid taking on Soul fragments from another Soul. When any fragments are detected, within any of your bodies, those fragments should be returned to their rightful owners as soon as possible.

The true joining (uniting) with another Soul can only occur after that individual Soul has been purified (cleared of adversities) and made complete within the lower densities. A complete Soul is one whose lower bodies (physical, etheric, mental, emotional, intellectual and physic) have been cleared of all foreign energies picked up within the lower densities. When all of these foreign energies have been cleared or stripped away, only the eternal, unchanging spirit eternal "Real Self," remains.

NOTE: Make sure you know what these adverse energies are, by name. I would estimate there are thousands to consider. It is very important to clear all adverse energies in preparation for graduation and ascension. Unless you know the names of thousands of such adversities, how will you know what to clear out and what to ask for, how can you ask and receive unless you know the question. Therefore, it is your responsibility to educate yourself about various adversities. Once these are recognized, there are spiritual assistants that can help remove large numbers of adversities simultaneously.

Once the clearings are complete and your Soul is intact, (relatively speaking) your "Real Self" will have qualified to return to the family of Souls (Oversoul) where true bonding can take place. The Oversoul is a group of Souls, or Soul family, comprised of individual Souls who have merged into a larger whole. The whole process is somewhat complex because of the history of each individual Soul. Most frequently, each Soul that fragmented from the Oversoul has evolved through many different incarnations on many different planets. During those experiences, a multitude of thought-forms have been recorded within each Soul's energetic makeup. Once they have reassembled within the original Oversoul, all of the joint experiences come together as an evolved Spiritual Being ready for the next exciting challenge.

In order to tie together the concepts of the Soul and the evolution of that Soul through the series of densities and states of dimensional consciousness, let us review a few key points about your Soul. Many of these were discussed in Section III, "Oversouls and Human Soul Evolution."

During physical death, the spirit rises out of the body. However, more is left behind than a physical empty shell. Although the body decomposes over time, much of the Soul essence that has not evolved sufficiently to ascend along with the spirit remains in the lower density planes of the astral dimension. These parts of the Soul essence have experiences separation and fragmentation from the higher spiritual essence. Those Soul fragments that became separated are now faced with their future. Remember a major part of the Soul has ascended into the next density and state of dimensional consciousness.

These separate pieces (fragments or facets) of one's Soul wander through the astral planes, appearing as ghosts, apparitions, poltergeists, astral entities, orbs, and other energy forms. The Soul fragments of the disincarnate, in their desire for unity and integration, feel lost. As a result, they seek out incarnate beings on some lower frequency planet to attach themselves. These fragments can actually cohabit with an incarnate where they can combine their energies with the incarnate. As a result, the soul energies of the disincarnate (fragments and facets) appear as intermingled mosaics of energies woven into the auric fields of the physically living incarnated entity. These attached Soul fragments cloud (distort) their host with the energies they have carried with them from their previous incarnations. Some clairvoyants have observed several layers of other Soul fragments distorting the essence of the host Soul's auric fields. From an emotional perspective, the attachment of these fragments can cause many challenges. Therefore, it is very important to remove all attaching fragments.

Not all of the soul's essences (fragments) that are attached to a person come from disincarnate entities. In many cases, other incarnated souls may be "corded" to another living human (incarnate) while both are still within the physical third-fourth density bodies. In other words, a "piece" (fragment or facet) of one soul has been dislodged (a fragment) and that fragment becomes attached to another soul. As mentioned in "Section II about the Oversoul and Human Soul Evolution," these processes can occur through the bonding experiences of various family members, through sexual union, and several other earthly activities.

When a person dies physically with these attached Soul fragments (facets), these fragments may enter into any number of dimensions (and time frames) depending on the Soul's level of consciousness at the time of death. That Soul has lost parts of its ideal structural makeup. When that Soul reincarnates, those Soul fragments that are left behind are unable to incarnate with the incoming Soul. Consequently, the incoming Soul could meet parts of itself in other people during this new incarnation (lifetime). This situation can occur when the incarnated Soul has sufficient awareness concerning its missing Soul fragments. That awareness could be sensed unconsciously or consciously. In other words, the incarnated Soul is aware of its Soul facets within another incarnated Soul currently residing on Earth.

Consequently, these facets and fragments could attract that individual to themselves unconsciously in an attempt to be joined back together. When this awareness is sufficiently strong and with spiritual assistance, it is possible to attract one's Soul fragments (facets) back. Once discovered and attracted, those returning Soul facets need to be cleared of all adverse energies and re-integrated within its original Soul structure.

The missing Soul facets may be strongly attached to another incarnated individual. Sometimes the original Soul may have to wait to recover its missing facets. They may be recovered when the individual Soul housing the fragments dies and the fragments (facets) are released to find their way "home." Since these Soul facets, those attached to another incarnate host, frequently remain corded with their original host body; then it may be possible to cut the cords and recover the missing facets.

There are many other aspects of Soul fragmentation, involving past lives, future lives and other dimensions. This becomes quite complex and difficult to understand using the terms available within current human languages. As you evolve and need additional information, just ask your High Self to seek out those thought forms that will be of assistance.

Within the seventh density, individual Souls first begin to bond as couples, or "twin flames." These twin Souls then seek out other twins from the same ray, or family tree. As each twin unites, these Souls form a cluster which fuses together into one Master Soul - called the "Oversoul."

As the Oversoul chooses to gain other levels of experience, individual Souls may again choose to go out to incarnate within the lower more dense levels of creation. These Souls may later re-merge to become a part of the Oversoul. These processes may continue for what could appear to a third fourth density incarnate, thousands of years. Time is not a factor for making this decision. There is no time within the higher densities. The flowing patterns towards Soul growth takes as long as the Oversoul believes there is a need to go through new growth experiences. Those choices have to be made to determine each experience that will be helpful in advancing the total understanding of the seventh density Oversoul.

Sometimes Souls from the same Oversoul meet on the Earth plane and recognize each other. Some form lifelong relationships as lovers, parents or friends. Remember that often several Soul family members, of the Oversoul family, will remain in the higher planes and assist another Soul who has chosen to incarnate on the physical Earth in one or more densities.

During these rapidly changing times (at the end of the current age) when mass ascension becomes a possibility, these twin Souls may have made an agreement before they incarnated to speed up the evolution of their Soul family. They become aware that the Earth bound Soul tends to evolve more easily if his or her twin flame is in the ascended state of consciousness helping the evolutionary process along. Only on rare occasions, do twin flames incarnate at the same time and meet in the Earth plane. If a Soul is not sufficiently evolved, such a meeting can be a distraction rather than a help. When twin flames do meet and become close, there is a tendency for them to develop a co-dependency or any other addictive relationships that can slow spiritual evolution.

Thus, keep in mind that a majority of the Souls on Earth came from the seventh density to incarnate within a physical body on the Earth plane. Moreover, as you spiritually evolve you return to your Oversoul until your group Soul makes the decision (votes) to proceed along the spiritual path towards eighth density.

Eight Density: Angelic Realm

The eight density is where the angels reside; it is also sometimes called the celestial heavens. Visionary artists have captured a glimpse of the color and vibrations of the angelic worlds. Although the angels have a fine, glorious vibration, they are considerably more dense, compared to the archangels within the ninth density.

As beings evolve higher and higher into the spiritual density (parallel Universes), words become more and more meaningless. The concepts of densities (levels) and dimensional states of consciousness become rather insignificant in the heavenly realms. In the heavenly realms everything just IS, there are no subdivisions. Within the vastness of IS-NESS, there is great variety and depth in knowing, much of which there are no words to describe. The angels soar through the celestial oceans, creating rainbows and dazzling pillars of light that are indescribable. Everything sparkles and shines with newness and there are an infinite number of activities or opportunities to participate in the eight density. Abundance is limitless and available instantly in any form imaginable.

As an entity (being) increases in vibration along the evolutionary pathway, it encounters more and more of the energies of the realm corresponding to that vibrational density of the angels. Angels, since they have evolved up through the lower seven densities have access to many levels and various dimensions simultaneously. They are capable of communicating with many humans simultaneously, all at once. They have the capability to create holographic images of themselves and thus can appear in different forms in many different places simultaneously. They also have the capability to create an aura of light wherever they go. Most of humanity at one time or another has felt their presence. Each individual human on Earth has a guardian angel. One of their assignments is to assist that individually incarnated spirit; inhabiting the body, for which they have been assigned. In other words, help the incarnated along his or her chosen path. One common form of assistance is providing warnings, to help you avoid some type of upcoming serious danger.

Fallen angels are those who have lowered their vibrations down from their previously established eight density vibrations. There are many reasons for this phenomenon. For example, some angels have never been in physical embodiment. As a result, they have a desire to gain experiences within the lower densities. Some of these fallen angels have become trapped in the lower third, fourth, and fifth densities. Frequently they forget their angelic origin. There are many well know examples of the challenges that fallen angels face within the lower dimensions. In fact you may at times have met a fallen angel who is unaware of their past.

Within the eight density of awareness and above, the concepts associated with the various Dimensional states of consciousness, begin to merge. Beyond the eighth and ninth density and related dimensional states of consciousness are the "Mansions Worlds." the dwelling places of the Eternal Ones. These are spiritual Light Beings who have merged with the Godhead.

Ninth Density: Archangel Realm

The ninth density is the vibration of the "Great Archangels." In a sense, the Archangels are to the angels what the Oversoul is to the Soul. Archangels are Beings of Light that encompass large areas of the Universe, much like Galaxies on the physical level. Many of the Archangels have been given names and labels throughout humanity's historical records.

These names, with a few exceptions end with the "el" suffix, when interpreted -- means "In God." The first half of the name indicates to humanity the archangel's specialties. Archangels are capable of being in many places within a single concept of a "time frame." Any time you are in need of assistance, you never have to feel that your personal challenge is not important enough to ask for Spiritual assistance from an Archangel. Once you have determined the most appropriate question and the Archangel to ask, just ask for assistance, any time day or night (24-7). In addition to the Archangels, remember to keep in touch with your guardian angel, your High Self, God/Goddess within, and a host of technical spiritual assistants such as the encodement technicians, spirit surgeons, and Creators of shields.

The most well known Archangels are Michael, Raphael, Gabriel, Uriel, Ariel, and Metatron. Less well known are the Archangels: Chamuel, Jophiel, Raguel, Azrael, Camael, Haniel, Jeremiel, Raziel, and Sandalphon. Obviously when the historical records are closely examined, you may discover hundreds of other less known Archangels that have been described and may be willing to assist you, when called upon. Many of these are still active. Several individuals have asked, how many Archangels actually exist at any "Now" moment? The answer to that question is difficult to find. No one seems to know how many are present and active. Some have theorized that these may be thousands of Archangels.

The first Archangel created by God, from a historical perspective, is believed to have been   Michael. Michael has the responsibility of protecting humanity physically, emotionally, and psychically. He also oversees the lightworker's life purposes. Michael carries a flaming sword that he uses to cut through attached etheric cords that could be harmful. Call upon Michael if you sense that you are under psychic attack or have an attached cord. Often times you will also discover that Michael has the capability to assist individuals overcome their addictions, helps those who suffer from nightmares, and relieve those with degenerative and related terminal illnesses.

Raphael specializes in healing humans and animals. You can call upon Raphael to heal body, mind, and spirit. You can also call upon Raphael in behalf of someone else; however, he cannot interfere with an individual's contract or free will. Raphael is very sweet, loving, kind, and gentle and you know that he is around when you see sparkles of green light. Raphael frequently works with Michael to remove disincarnate entities from humans and physical places on Earth. You can call upon Raphael when you are traveling to assist you in having a safe trip. You can also call upon Raphael to assist the medical practitioners in their efforts to speed the healing of your various ailments. Raphael not only deals with current challenges, but also has the capability to heal wounds from past lives.

The name of Archangel Gabriel means "The Strength of God" or Divine Strength." In the art and literature world, Gabriel is illustrated with female characteristics. Those who call upon her will find themselves pushed into action that leads to beneficial results. Contact Gabriel when you discover that your third eye is closed. Ask for help in restoring your spiritual vision. Once your third eye has opened, it will assist in developing your spiritual insight. The third eye opens up your spiritual vision and the channeling of prophecies related to the changes taking place throughout the Earth and beyond. She also helps anyone whose life purpose involves the arts or communication. You can call upon Gabriel if your body needs cleansing of toxins and negative imprints or negative thought forms.

Archangel Uriel is the wisest Archangel because of his intellectual information and capability to bring forth practical solutions and creative insights for humanity's challenges. Call upon Uriel and he will implant within your consciousness brilliant new ideas that help make your task easier. Uriel gives accurate predictions related to upcoming events on Earth. He is the Archangel that assists those who have gone through Earth changes in the past and more recently such as earthquakes, floods, hurricanes, firestorms, volcanic eruptions, tornados and other natural disasters.

The Archangel <u>Ariel</u> works closely with Raphael in healing activities of various animals. Ariel also works to protect plants, birds, and animals living within natural settings. Ariel oversees the nature spirits associated with plants and the nature Angels associated with water. He also has been associated with the function of the wind that blows across the Earth's surface. If you need help in healing an injured animal call upon Ariel. Archangel Ariel's book "What Is Lightbody" channeled by Tashira Tachi-ren is quite appropriate for your use in preparing for "The Shift" and graduation.

Metatron is one of a few Archangels whose name does not end in "el" and one of two known Archangels who were humans before becoming Angels. His human name on Earth was Enoch. On Earth, Enoch was a prophet and a scribe. He was also a scholar concerning heavenly secrets. At one time, Enoch was given wings and transformed into the great Archangel named Metatron. He is one of the most important Archangels in Western tradition because he represents the Angel of death, to whom God daily gives orders to which Souls will be leaving that day. Since Metatron excelled at his work, he has been assigned a similar job in the ninth DMC.

He has taken on the task to scribe the records of everything that happens on Earth and is the keeper of the Akashic records or "Book of Life" on each Soul. Since Metatron has access to your records, you can call upon him to help you understand your evolutionary status. In addition, he can assist you to know how to work with the Angelic realm and other spirit realms. He has a special place in the hearts of children, especially those who are spiritually gifted. He continues to lead children both on Earth and within the Spiritual realms. James Tyberonn channels Metatron with postings on www.Earth-Keeper.com

Tenth Density: Creator Gods

The Creator Gods are "Vast Spiritual Beings" who can create an entire Universe and whose light emulates the light of the Heavenly Father and Divine Mother. In historical religious literature, these Creator Gods, called the Ancient Ones or Paradise Sons, became involved in various creations. The Creator Gods are supreme rulers of the spiritual hierarchy, second in spiritual capabilities to the "Heavenly Father" and "Divine Mother."

Eleventh Density: Universal Gods

These highly evolved Gods are the Gods of Parallel Dimensions and many different types of Universes. Spirit indicates that these advanced creations exist beyond the spiritual hierarchy of this Universe. Humanity, up to this point in planetary evolution has a very limited understanding of their features and functions. Our primary understanding is that these members of the spiritual hierarchy have the capability to unite as One Universal God to initiate new creations. That not only have the capability to create new Universes but also all component parts of those Universes and spirits of various forms that will inhabit those Universes.

Twelfth Density: The Godhead – Founders

The twelfth density is the vibration of the Godhead, the Great Central Sun and the un-manifested aspects of the Heavenly Father and Divine Mother. The Great Central Sun is the Gateway to the "Unknown Void," sometimes called The Tao or the Great Mystery. The "Unknown Void" is also referred to by some entities as the Thirteenth Density. For an expanded understanding about other aspects of the densities "The Founders," located within the twelfth density, have recently provided some important insights about the coming events within the book "Earth Changes and 2012" by Sal Rachele.

Section V. Light Body Awakening Sequence

Note: The following discussion about Light Body Awakening is (in part) based on a discourse from Archangel Ariel channeled through Tashira Tachi-ren. These channelings have been published within the book "What Is Lightbody."

As you proceed through this section, keep in mind that everything within the Universe is composed of light. A plant exists because of its capability to take in sunlight and store that energy within a carbon bond. Humans consume plants in the form of Biophotons or quantum bundles of light energy. Every metabolic reaction in plants, animals, and humans is controlled by these biophotons. Thus as we consider Light Body Awakening, we are working with gaining an understanding of the science of Light or "Biophotonics," and the characteristics of fifth dimensional bodies. Check out the internet for more information about "Biophotonics."

Are You Ready For Light Body Awakening?

Your answers to the following questions can help you know if you are ready.

1. Have I been on a spiritual path for several years?
2. Am I aware that I am much more than just a physical body here on Earth?
3. Is my spiritual growth important to me in my daily activities?
4. Do I realize that I am a special creation with unlimited capabilities?
5. Am I aware that I have a Soul and High Self as very important parts of me?
6. Is finding and knowing my inner purpose very important to me?
7. Am I sufficiently open minded to consider that alternative thoughts can help me?
8. Do I trust my inner guidance (intuition) for help in solving daily challenges?
9. Have I developed a belief that I create my reality with my thoughts?
10. Am I setting aside time to pray, meditate, and communicate with my High Self
11. Have I learned to control my emotional body and Love myself?

12. Am I interested in knowing what subtle energies are and how to control them?
13. Do I believe with all of my being that I can have a joyful and abundant life now?
14. Have I an interest in expanding my state of consciousness for going to the "New Earth?"

If you answered yes to a majority of these questions then you are ready to proceed to request help in your "Light Body Awakening and Activation. You know within that you came to Earth for a purpose. In addition, you know you have an opportunity to learn more about spiritual energies and to understand how those energies can influence your daily activities. Therefore, seek out help through the internet, books, seminars, workshops, etc.

Definition of Light Body Awakening

In order for Souls to take on a physical body and incarnate upon a low frequency third dimension planet, they had to agree to lower a part of their frequency and densify -- become denser. Through a chronological sequence of several thousand years, a NOW time was reached where maximum separation and densification occurred. That densification cycle is ending.

Then as the planet Earth enters a new cyclic pattern, that density shift is reversing. Within this changing cycle -- the Universe, the solar system, and planet begins to reverse the densification process by increasing their frequency. As the frequency of everything increases, everything becomes less dense. In order for the creations upon planet Earth to survive, they must be synchronized with the new density (frequencies). Thus as the planet evolves from the third to the fourth and fifth densities, in order for humans to survive, they must shift to these higher frequency densities.

The individual separation process and recovery phase has been repeated many times on many planets throughout the Universe. As the planet and its inhabitants raise their frequency to ascension status, each inhabitant becomes less dense and therefore lighter in weight.

Recall that we are using an evolutionary based twelve-dimension model to describe these events. A majority of humans on Earth reside within third density. The fourth density consciousness is primarily emotionally based in the astral plane, where it resides. These two density planes, (third and fourth) make up the Lower Creation World; a state of being that involves the creation of an illusionary separation. The Lower Creation World is the only density state where souls can play the game of separation. You came to the Creator School called Earth to determine what it was like to manipulate matter, create illusions, instill pain and suffering -- all for the experience of what it feels like to create challenges and overcome them. Each challenging lesson is a means by which we can grow spiritually and create a God like Soul.

This game of separation at these lower density states has been in progress during the 10,800-year dark cycle. When we entered this dark cycle to come to "Earth Creator School" we were required to lose our memory and had our axiatonal lines connecting us to our Oversoul severed. At the same time, each incarnated Soul gave up eleven strands of their DNA and took on an animal like body for transportations. As a result, brain function was altered, genetic codes for aging were activated, and a death hormone was created to help terminate the physical body. The objective was to create conditions that would shorten each incarnation period. At the end of each incarnation the spirit returned beyond the veil to have its spiritual progress measured. Once various life experiences are reviewed and correlated with other incarnations, a new contract is prepared for the next incarnation. With a shortened life span it is possible to make more frequent reviews and thereby, accelerate one's spiritual evolution.

The physical body we agreed to take on has in several ways actually limited our spiritual capabilities. Some believe that if they did not have to spend so much time concerned about their physical body, they would not have to experience so many duality type lessons. Some are so upset by having to ride around in a physical body they have a tendency to concentrate on enjoying all of its sensational capabilities and/or they abuse it. For example, some individuals emphasize the pleasures of sex, the taste of food and drink, and a joy of accumulating things. Others dislike their physical body and as a result state the following, "I am not going to feed you." "I am not going to let you play." "I am not going to pay any attention to what you are telling me." "I am going to make you miserable by my attempt to escape through drugs and other abuses." I'll keep eating until I get fat.

The current opportunity to awaken our Light Body has come about because of the current passage of the Earth into and through the photon belt. The solar system and Earth have moved into a 2,160-year light cycle that began in 1987. At that time, the Earth first re-entered the photon belt containing new high frequency light energies from the Great Central Sun. These energies became available to help raise all of creation's frequencies so they could become less dense.

A shift that facilitates light body activation has been made possible by the light that has been coming into the planet by ever-increasing amounts for 20 years. This light is carrying information from the fifth dimension, the realm of love where our higher consciousness resides. This new light is helping to awaken your inner being to the love that makes up your higher consciousness. As a result, when you awaken to seek your full potential and remember who you really are and why you are on Earth now, you can evolve more rapidly. Little by little, this new light sparks threads of memory to surface. As a result, you experience the need within to awaken to your full potential. You can remember now that you understand the evolutionary path and can take advantage of the opportunity to shift to the higher states of dimensional consciousness and join the New Earth during "The Shift."

The energetic body that is capable of utilizing these new frequencies is the fifth dimension "Light Body." While upon the Earth plane this body has laid dormant for approximately 11,000 years, that is since the flood when Atlantis and Lemuria sank under the oceans. To prevent this fifth dimension body from being activated too early, before adequate preparations have been made, specific "crystal like" structures were installed to block many of these light energies within the Photon Belt. Those "crystal like" blocking structures are now being removed and/or cleared.

To regain your potential fifth dimension light body status, humans are required to activate their etheric holographic template and have the axiatonal lines reconnected. This connection will facilitate the energy flow through the axiatonal lines, assist in reactivating your DNA, reconnect the axiatonal meridian system, activate the axial circulatory system, and restructuring various spin points throughout all of your energy bodies. For these events to take place, the human energy system must become linked to the electromagnetic and subtle energy fields of the Earth. There are many new energy fields arriving on Earth to assist in making various cellular changes. These energy fields are all designed to help create your new bodies. You will be unable to take your old worn out body through the portals to the New Earth. The body you take with you, as you leave the Old Earth will need to be compatible with the New Earth's frequencies.

Chakra Function and Light Body Awakening

One other major shift that will be part of the Light Body Awakening, relates to the function of your chakras. Humans have a total of seven major chakras (plus the Alpha and Omega chakras) that exist multidimensionally. These seven major chakras starting at the base of the spine up to the top of the head are: base, spleen, naval, heart, throat, brow, and crown. Two additional very important chakras, the Alpha and Omega chakras, must become functional for Light Body activation. The Alpha chakra is located approximately eight inches above the crown and the Omega chakra is located approximately eight to twelve inches below the base of the spine. The Alpha chakra connects the lower bodies with its upper dimensional counterparts. The Omega chakra anchors the lower bodies across the holographic grid of various incarnations.

The activation of these new chakras relate to the ascension process. Two of these new chakras are connected to your etheric mind, the omni brain. Once these two chakras become activated, they will raise the brainpower from 10 percent up to 20 to 25 percent. To facilitate many of the requirements for Light Body Awakening additional energy must flow through the prana tube running down the center of the body. Once the Alpha and Omega chakras are open and operating correctly, you should experience a wave of Energy called the "Waves of Metatron." These magnetic, electric, and gravitational waves oscillate back and forth through the Alpha and Omega chakras. The new energy waves support the flow of prana through the prana tube and along with the "Waves of Metatron." Then the new energies coordinate the physical body's mutation to the pre-existing template of your immortal Body of Light.

In order to support changes in the physical body, new grids are laid down which connect the chakras directly to the spin points on the skin's surface. As a result these girds connect the chakras directly to the axiotonal lines (grid pattern) running across the body's surface. Because of these changes, the new chakras and new energy flow patterns assist the emotional, mental, and spiritual bodies to merge into one unified energy field. The unified energy field then connects to and receives energy from the Oversoul bodies.

As a result, the whole energy system becomes synchronized with Universal waves and pulses arriving from the Great Central Sun. Gradually these new energy flow patterns within and on the body, such as the new axial circulatory system, are continually recalibrated to optimize the flow of body fluids. Within the body new patterns of energy flow will be fine tuned to use adenosine tri-phosphate (ATP) and adenosine di-phosphate (ADP from biophotons.

As part of the transition to wholeness, the two hemispheres (right and left) of the brain merge. As this happens, you can move out of the local brain to the higher self and then on to the omni brain, called the "Universal Brain."

One method for amplifying one's brainpower is by prana breathing. During prana breathing, you bring prana energy through the crown chakra and into the pineal gland. The additional prana energy activates dormant brain stem cells. As you continue to use this exercise, your brain capacity will increase. If you feel a little off center or dizzy and have trouble remembering, after the activation, just realize that these feelings are just an indication that you are changing. Gradually these experiences will subside and your new capabilities become evident.

Once the stems cells of the brain have been activated with prana breathing and all major organs of the body that contain stem cells, can be activated. Thus by using prana breathing and working with your High Self you can activate those other stem cells throughout your body just waiting to be activated. The activating of the stem cells within all organs of the body will facilitate your creation of new body parts. Realize that you can activate the energetic characteristics (preferred functional activities) of any gland or organ by activating these resting stem cells therein.

Now that you understand a little more about the anticipated changing energy patterns, let us focus on the three new chakras. The three new chakras exhibit the colors gold, pearl and blue/green. The third new chakra to be activated is the gold chakra above the crown of your head that will be woven into the "omni brain." This new chakra can help optimize your communications with your High Self. As you summon your High Self for assistance, you may visualize a mist of golden light that flows into you. As this takes place listen with your feelings -- not your ears. You will feel thoughts coming through that relate to your request. You can continue to prana breathe to assist in this in-lightening experience. If you sense that you are becoming light headed, just relax and visualize moving these new prana energies down into your body.

The new pearl appearing chakra becomes active as a guidance system for all the new light frequencies entering your body. The observed pearl essence is your true spiritual essence. This essence represents who you truly are. You are a pearl appearing essence in reality. Remember the physical body is an illusion created by consciousness. You are not your body. Many are anticipating the return of the Masters such as Jesus, Buddha, and Lady Quan Yin. When they return they will not return in their physical bodies but in their etheric body of beautiful pearl essence.

The new blue/green chakra symbolizes the truth of all truths because of its design. This chakra opens up for the receipt of the highest possible truths. You can only use this blue/green chakra when your thoughts are in absolute truth. Any attempt to pass false information or a lie through the blue/green chakra will meet with failure. Also that thought will come out somewhere else within the body's energy system. When this happens you will know something is out of "kilter."

During the duality game of the third dimension, the structural features of the chakras were deliberately limited so that they could only transduce energy from the astral plane. In a sense, these chakras were sealed. As a result, the energy vortex associated with each chakra took on the shape of a cone. You will recall that the five central chakras had a cone opening projecting out towards the front of the body and another cone opening projecting toward the back. Where the narrow points of these two cones touch, inside the center of the body, a seal can form that closes the chakra down. These seals were purposely allowed to partially close down a chakra for safety purposes. They are partially sealed with mental and emotional "debris" accumulated as a residue from your duality lessons. That sealing" helped maintain the cone shaped configuration and helped regulate (limit) energy flow through the chakras.

However, realize that this clogging can become excessive. We frequently observe the crown and base chakras closed down. As the clogging proceeds, the speed of the chakra vortex spin slows down and may actually stop, closing down that chakra. As a result, the meridian system is starved for energy and when clogging becomes excessive, the overall results are various imbalances and sickness. When an extreme amount of chakra clogging occurs, death can result.

By gaining control of both the mental and emotional bodies the blocking debris fail to accumulate and can be cleared out. Currently in many humans on Earth, the functional efficiency of the chakra system is dramatically influenced by a lack of mental and emotional control.

As a part of the Light Body Activation process, the "seals" in the central points of the cone shaped vortexes must be cleared of all mental and emotional debris. The clearing process should proceed slowly. A rapid clearing could result in excessive energy flow and an overload of the energy circuits. Once the clearing is completed the spinning vortex changes to a spherical shape. This process allows the activated chakras to slowly open up and radiate energy in all directions. As a result the energy flow pattern becomes capable of transducing (receiving and converting) these new energies into useful frequencies.

Gradually as the body sheds accumulated debris, the spherical blueprint of the new chakra system makes it impossible for the debris to accumulate. These new sphere shaped energy vortexes gradually expand in size until all the chakras merge into one unified energy field. These changes are a component part of the ascension preparation activities. As the unification progresses eventually, all the lower chakras will be absorbed into the green heart chakra.

When this unified energy field has been created, your heart chakra will be your base chakra. Your new blue/green chakra and current throat chakra will join to become your "truth chakra." Once the "truth chakra" has become functional, you will need to exercise extreme caution when creating a thought. If you use your truth chakra to speak your truth, various events associated with that thought will be in truth and that truth will be projected outward. As a result, others with the ability to hear projected thought will sense that truth. Likewise, if you have created an untruth that will also be projected out and others will hear that untruth. To project an untruth has some very un-desirable consequences within the higher dimensional states of consciousness.

With the three new chakras, you will not hear with your physical ears. You will hear with your awareness just as if you listen to your High Self. When you sense untruths with your awareness, that is when anyone else communicates untruths towards you, immediately you will know because it will not resonate with your value system. That is, once these three new chakras have become activated and the unification of your previous chakras is complete, new behavior patterns will be required. You no longer have the option of manipulating duality concepts by utilizing both truths and untruths. Therefore, proceed slowly and give careful consideration to learn how these new chakras work. Misuse of these new chakras can cause you new challenges. Were you to create a thought form that contained an untruth it would damage your energy system.

Twelve Stages of Light Body Awakening

First, second, and third "Light Body Awakening" began in 1988 through 1989 when the entire crystalline structure of matter within all humans on Earth were activated. This was not an optional choice for everyone to have his or her crystalline structure altered. Many humans, who sensed these changes, have, since that initial activation event, left the Earth because they did not want to go through Light Body Awakening. They were not ready to experience the whole process during this lifetime. There emotional body was not strong enough. There High Self also realized that their consciousness was not prepared to avoid all possible fear related changes and other events leading up to and including "The Shift" in 2012 and beyond. Let's reemphasize the need to add Love to all of your energy systems and minds to neutralize hate and fear of any kind.

First Stage of Light Body Awakening appears as if a light bulb has gone on within your DNA and a still small voice within gives you the message, "It's time to cease the separation and density game, awaken your Light Body and let's go home." During that period, you were going through first stage Light Body Awakening there were genetic mutations taking place that could have caused many different physical body symptoms. Those symptoms varied depending on the individual's state of consciousness. Some experienced flu symptoms, some had headaches, and others had vomiting, diarrhea, rashes, muscle aches, and other similar symptoms. One dramatic evidence of this change occurred during March of 1988, when a flu epidemic affected millions on Earth.

This upgrade in the genetic makeup of human DNA has occurred many times in the history of the human race. Extraterrestrial genetic engineers have altered the Human DNA genome many times with the assistance of new energies flowing in during periodic galactic shifts. Bits and pieces of genetic encoding from 383 ascending planets, within the Universe, have been periodically assembled to create the human physical body. Many advanced Extraterrestrial biological engineers have periodically worked within different sectors of the Milky Way Galaxy to structure the human energy system. Those physical energy systems are biochemically guided from a multitude of genetic codes. Many of these genetic codes originated from many ascending planets. Their activation has been used to create all the organs, glands, tissues, liquids, and metabolic systems that help maintain the human physical body in its present form.

This first level of Light Body Awakening was designed to alter the way your physical body cells metabolize energy. After the awakening, human cells began to metabolize Light. This change has opened a completely new area of science called "Bio-photonics." Light is in part made of photons, the foundation for this new science.

Photons have always controlled all metabolic systems within living cells. Every second in an active cell there are over 100,000 chemical biophotonic reactions taking place. Those reactions can only proceed when they have been activated by a photon, with a certain frequency. Biophotons function in rhythmic patterns in a well-designed series of coherence light emission at the quantum level. The degree of coherence of these Biophtons can be correlated with the quality of biological systems. As scientists have known for many years, DNA molecules control a cell's metabolic processes. Scientists have now discovered that the genetic control process involves the flow of photons from the DNA to specific chemical reactions within the cells.

Recent discoveries reveal that the DNA molecule releases Biophotons to control cell metabolism. Varying emissions from the DNA are each directly tied to a specific biochemical reaction within the cell. Thus, the DNA controls metabolism through the process of releasing (emitting) Biophotons of different frequencies emissions.

Biophoton emissions can be measured to determine the quality of food, the health of an organism, a plant, and a body part. The emerging field of biophotonics is capable of measuring the emissions from various chemical molecules to determine their potential biochemical reactions. For example, measurements of Biophoton emissions can be correlated with the potential reactivity of specific chemical molecules. Measured readings can be obtained to indicate which molecules are toxic, mutagenic, or have antibiotic properties.

Biophotons (light particles of different frequencies) can function in many different ways. For example, cancer-causing chemicals can alter the body's Biophoton emissions. In contrast, a chemical extracted from mistletoe releases Biophotons that convert cancer cells back to normal cells. Within a living cell these Biophotons travel through microtubules to reach their destinations. Chemicals that interfere with normal healthy metabolism scramble the Biophotons limiting their ability to move through the microtubules.

The measure of how these changes have influenced human metabolism can be correlated with the measurement of high-energy phosphate bonds within the chemical composition of cells. Cell metabolism relies upon these high-energy phosphate bonds (adenosine triphosphate (ATP) and adenosine diphosphate (ADP) to supply energy to the metabolic system. Thus, a measure of the level of ATP and ADP within cells indicates how efficient the ongoing metabolic process is.

Before Light Body Activation, the cells took in food energy and converted that energy into the storage molecule ATP. This ATP originated from the action of the cell mitochondria where three phosphate molecules combine to store photon energy released during the metabolism of foods. Some of that ATP can lose one phosphate group to form ADP. As the ATP looses one phosphate molecule (atom) an energy bond is broken and that photon energy is released into the cell.

As Light Body awakening and activation proceeds, a series of latent DNA encodements light up (activate) and began to give instructions to the cells to recognize Light as a new energy source. At first when this change was recognized the cells did not know what to do with the information. However, the cells bathed in light began to fully absorb a new color of light and produce lots of ATP, in bursts. The cells had not yet absorbed enough light to stabilize the process and the ATP rapidly broke down to ADP. As a result, cellular metabolism speeded up rapidly. As this activity preceded many types of adverse energies (toxins, negative emotions, adverse thought forms) were released to create various symptoms in the body, such as the flue like symptoms.

Keep in mind that because of "The Fall" into third density, the brain function was separated into a duality mode of right and left-brain function, and nerve synapses within the brain were rewired. In addition, because of "The Fall" the pineal and pituitary glands were reduced in size. As a result, they have become less effective. Following first stage Light Body Activation, it has been discovered that brain chemistry has begun to change and new synapses (junctions between two nerve cells) have formed.

Second Stage of Light Body Awakening relates to the sixth-dimensional etheric blueprint. The awakening procedures begin to release some fourth dimensional structures, which tie the individual to other lifetimes. As these fourth dimensional structures become awakened, your emotional, mental, and spiritual bodies begin to change. Old useless programs begin to be released and/or are cleared to make way for all of the new programs. This series of changes can cause considerable tiredness. To avoid excess stress on various bodies, this stage of awakening is proceeding slowly. Many reading these words have completed stage two of Light Body Awakening.
Make use of accurate pendulum dowsing to monitor all of your Light Body Awakening events.

Third Stage Light Body Awakening was started within the bodies of those who were prepared in 1994. As these third level changes have proceeded, your physical sensing system has become more sensitized and thus strengthened. Although the senses have been strengthened, the specific sense, which is elevated in sensitivity, may vary with each individual. For some, the sense of smell has become enhanced. For others the sense of feel may be increased to where the chair they sit in becomes uncomfortable. Often in association with third stage Light Body

Activation, sexual activities become much more enjoyable. This change has been quite evident in the last several years. That is why sexual activity of young people has dramatically increased and a rise in pregnancies has resulted. The third stage activation has triggered many other physical body changes.

The axiotonal spin points on the body surface open to allow undifferentiated Light from the Oversoul to pour in. As a result, a fifth dimensional axial circulatory system has begun to form. This new system feeds energy along the axiotonal lines through the spin points, which in turn activates related spin points within every cell of the physical body. As a result, each cell within the body is exposed to new light frequencies. As the cells become accustomed to this change, increased light becomes usable energy and more ATP is produced, however less of it is converted to ADP. Simultaneously the energy flowing in through the spin points produces sound and light of different frequencies that are utilized by the dormant DNA encodements and ribonucleic acid (RNA). These genetic changes alter specific metabolic reactions.

Before Light Body Activation, the RNA was a one-way messenger to guide the cell as to what protein to synthesize. That one-way system was a closed system that ensured the termination of the physical body after a given period. Following Light Body activation, the RNA has become a two-way messenger system that changes cell metabolism. Consequently, the one-way system is gradually being closed down, as Light Body Activation proceeds. That change within the RNA messenger system and the related change in metabolism will help protect those individuals interested in spiritual ascension. Remember that those changes related to Light Body Activation will allow the human energy system to utilize more light (photons from the "Photon Belt") to maintain its many functional features.

In addition, this third level activation has created a "set point" which has connected many other planets in the galaxy energetically. Many of these third dimensional planets are simultaneously ascending to higher states of dimensional consciousness, just like Earth. When these shifts have been completed, there will be no more astral energy patterns (planes) on all these third dimensional planets will have ascended to fourth-fifth density. Also, those associated astral parallel realities (patterns) will change form.

Realize that it has taken billions of years for this Universe to create conditions for the densification and separation of entities into a duality configuration as a part of the grand experiment. That long-term experiment or "game" which began to be closed down (terminated) in 1988 is being revised (upgraded) in less than twenty years. That is, upon planet Earth the duality game will have been terminated and a new game will have begun at a much higher frequency, within the fifth density and fifth state of dimensional consciousness.

Never before within this Universe, that is, for over billions of years, has an opportunity of this magnitude been available to the Spirits created by ALL-THAT-IS (GOD/GODDESS) and a host of Creators. You have experienced a multitude of relationships and interrelationships as a student in Creator School on many different low frequency planets. As of 2012, that play (game) is over and you have an opportunity to return to the higher states of dimensional consciousness and set up a new play, a new game. A multitude of advanced Souls and Light Workers have incarnated on Earth to assist with the graduation and ascension process and in setting up the new play.

Your assistance is needed in this massive shift in consciousness. You have a choice, a very important choice to make. Therefore monitor your thoughts very carefully; those positive visionary "thought forms" will help create the "New Earth." Your other alternative is to ignore this opportunity and continue your duality game on another third density planet. It will be impossible for you to retain your current third-fourth density bodies designed for the low frequency and survive on a fourth-fifth density New Earth. Your body will be unable to tolerate those higher frequencies without significant physical damage. From a spiritual or scientific point of view, to think that your low frequency body could survive on a high frequency planet violates Universal Law.

Fourth Stage of Light Body Awakening triggers a massive change in brain chemistry and a change in the electromagnetic features of the brain. To assist these changes, regulator crystals are being installed within your etheric body. As a result, you may experience cluster headaches, chest pains, blurry vision, and hearing may become difficult. The two hemispheres of the brain have begun to fire across both hemispheres at the same time. If your body consciousness tries to stop this firing pattern, you feel yucky. Some have felt electrical energy flowing across their head, and down the spine. Also, you may experience non-linear thinking, switching to a now pattern with no concern for the future, which could become frightening at first.

The mental body begins to realize it is not running the show any longer. As a result, a degree of uncertainty sweeps in and your mental body has difficulty knowing what is real and unreal. You receive impulses or thoughts of what you should be doing. Then the mental body screams out "Wait a Minute." "What is happening here?" The mental body is trying to retain control even thought it knows that everything is changing. You begin to experience telepathy, clairvoyance, and channeling of spiritual entities. Once again, the mental body attempts to clamp down again and states, "All that stuff is illusion or you are delusionary, living in an imaginary world."

As you take control of that chattering mind and gain mental control of your ego, you can discover a purpose for the changes you are going through. Then assure the mental body all is in Divine order and we are on a journey together, a journey so wonderful you will be so happy when we arrive at our new destination.

Fifth Stage of Light Body Awakening is where the mental body says, "Maybe I should try to follow Spirit." "I am not sure it's going to work, but I might as well try and find out what will happen."

Once you experience the fifth stage "Light Body Awakening," your dreaming experiences gradually change and you begin to remember more of your dreams. Some experience "lucid dreaming" where the dreamtime becomes real, just like experiences you have in the physical awakened state. Some may feel like they are going crazy, again because of the non-linear events that occur all in the "NOW." Then again, the mental body screams out "Wait a minute; I can't control this pattern, What if this causes my body to experience death." Ask the mental body to relax. You could say to your mental body, "Let's just enjoy the trip."

A part of you is just like a child saying, "Yeah, we're going to the Light," and you experience joy and happiness. Then the old grumpy mental body jumps in and complains again. You are beginning to sense the two halves of yourself. You realize you are more than you thought you were. You are opening and closing to your new self. Your spirit is trying to get your mental body to surrender its control so you can become fully conscious of your multidimensionality and potential as you shift to the higher states of consciousness.

Sixth Stage of Light Body Awakening is where your spirit is guiding you to those who can help you understand what this process of Light Body Awakening involves. Books may come your way and your High Self begins to give you mental impressions of what will work best. Then opportunities to attend a workshop or group discussion become available. As you attend these gatherings, you will meet new individuals with related experiences that they are willing to share. This is a time to be open and at the same time use spiritual discernment to make sure the activity and the information received serves your best interest and can help you along your spiritual journey.

Often times when going through the sixth stage of Light Body Awakening you have experiences of things not being solid. In addition, you may have some items around your residence that just disappear, for no apparent reason. You look down at your hand and it appears other than solid, as if it is unable to sense what it is touching. Then you may observe a series of events in one big picture. The mental body is now functioning much differently, and the changes can become frightening. This is the time to clear away fear by implanting love for yourself and at the same time realize that these changes are for my highest and best good.

Some humans who have progressed to sixth stage Light Body Awakening find these new experiences very uncomfortable. They may ask themselves: "Do I want to continue with this program?" "Do I want to be here?" or "What have I got myself into and what's the best way out?"

When these thoughts come up the best approach is to ask your High Self for assistance in choosing the most appropriate path for my own spiritual evolution. Your High Self may indicate that you should hang in there and work through the challenges of change. Many have heard the High Self whisper loud and clear, "You have come this far -- now is not the time to give up."

Quite frequently, when you reach this stage of Light Body Awakening you can find someone to assist you in working through the challenges. If you can survive the fifth and sixth levels, you are home free and can make it the rest of the way.

Be kind to yourself while you are going through stage six of Light Body Awakening, because this is where your identity comes into question. Your friends may begin to leave you because you are odd or weird. You may lose your job and have financial challenges. When this happens, find new friends and a new job that is more fun and fulfilling. Remember the fifth dimensional state of consciousness is where Unity (Christ) consciousness becomes the prime pattern of existence. Here Love will become the most important motivating factor in your life.

However, your High Self could also indicate that you are not ready to graduate and ascend to the higher sates of dimensional consciousness. Then you can opt out, choose death, and thereafter look for another third dimensional planet to continue your lessons. There will always be another opportunity somewhere in the future to graduate and ascend from the lower densities. After all, all created spirits are eternal and endless.

Observe closely what is going on all over the planet. Open up your inner sensing system and listen to the still small voices within. Then realize you are a perfect spirit created in the image of God and are a vast multidimensional being that can do anything. You have an opportunity to just ask and receive. Consider that as you read these thoughts there are many other thoughts behind these words. Listen within to those thoughts, they may be the most important ones for you. This may be your "Wake up Call" to hang in there and with the help of your guardian angels, spiritual assistants and friends you can proceed on to stage seven. You now have the choice to get with the Light Body Awakening program and move on.

Seventh Stage of Light Body Awakening is where you open up the heart chakra and become involved in working more intently with your emotional body. Here playfulness opens up and you reach out to hug others, hug a tree, enjoy the beauties of nature, and become childlike.

The blocks lodged within your emotional body begin to come up to be cleared, because you now realize you will need those removed in order to express your divinity and your vast capabilities. Request that the mental body become synchronized with the emotional body and together these bodies will be capable of releasing all old stored emotions, much easier. As the cleansing process continues you may experience sadness, cry easily, get angry, yell, and then you want to laugh and be happy. Your activities become concentrated within the "NOW," with little concern about what happened back there in the world of illusionary space-time where past and future events were of concern. Be in the present, it really feels good being in the "Now." My past "Now" is gone and my future "Now" is where I AM "Now." The energy you save by living in the "Now" can be used for many joyous experiences, during all the coming "NOWs."

Be alert to how your emotional body is attempting to remove (drop) many of its old patterns of responding to events and people in a judgmental way. Fear related thoughts that have been stored within your bodies somewhere -- about family members, friends, co-workers, etc. need to be released. These old patterns are beginning to surface. As these patterns surface, exercise caution and hold back from becoming pulled back into previous undesirable reactive patterns or conflicts. Avoid all persistent judgmental attitudes of yourself and/or others. Your new relationships will be based on the elimination of emotional attachments and the practice of acceptance. Be patient with yourself and those who fail to realize that they damage themselves through judgmental behavior patterns.

In the seventh state of Light Body Awakening, the heart chakra opens and as a result, some individuals actually feel chest pains. These pains are different from a heart attack or an imbalance within the heart region. Once the heart chakra has opened, it can be used as a gateway that can help you travel interdimensionally. This new opportunity takes time to become functionally efficient.

On third density planet Earth, the heart chakra had a membrane that prevented you from experiencing inter-dimensionality and multi-dimensionality fully. Within the third density, you were restricted from using your heart chakra as a gateway to other dimensions by a membrane. Because of the changes initiated during the first three stages of Light Body Awakening, that membrane has been slowly removed. Removal of that membrane also gave the heart chakra predominance over your other chakras. That predominance relates to the previously discussed opening up or creation of the Unified Chakra.

Therefore, it would be quite helpful to continue the Unified Chakra meditation to assist various aspects of Light Body Awakening. Assisting the chakra merger will also help improve the efficiency of your emotional, mental, and spiritual bodies. The whole process will allow your bodies to handle increased amounts of new high frequency energies with different energetic characteristics.

During the seventh Light Body Awakening the pineal and pituitary glands begin to open up and regain their designed purpose. When the pituitary becomes fully functional, the aging process will be terminated. The death hormone production will be replaced with the production of a rejuvenation hormone. As a result, it becomes obvious that the individual gradually looks younger and more energetic. Also the pineal and pituitary glands function together to help create a rainbow of light, known as the "Arc of the Covenant." That rainbow of light energy arcs back and forth over the head from the fourth eye to the third eye. This arc of energy is part of the decoding mechanisms for higher-dimensional language that you will utilize in the future.

Another interesting change is the opening up of the fourth eye. Most people have heard of the third eye located in the center of the forehead. The fourth eye is located on the top of the head, near where the soft spot is located. For some individuals that fourth eye opens easily. For others it may take time because it has had an etheric covering that needs to be removed. That fourth eye is an important part of the sensing system that opens up your multidimensional sight.

When you are gradually working through the seventh level of Light Body Awakening, your energy system is functional within the fourth level of dimensional consciousness. Many individuals who have reached this stage of Awakening have become energy workers and Light Workers. Because of their awakened state, they are able to move subtle (spiritual) energies. Sometimes these individuals are called "Healers." To call anyone a healer can be misnomer when misused. No one can heal another individual. Every individual is responsible for healing himself or herself. Actually when an individual incarnate (spirit) is called a healer there is often a sense of ego involved. Any individual who has maintained a high Light Quotient and emphasizes Service To Others can channel energy to someone in need. Make a specific request and direct those energies, with projected intent, for your own personal repatterning or assisting others in resolving their imbalances.

Many people going though seventh-level Light Body Awakening develop what some call manic-depression. One instant they are on top of the world and feel they can do anything. The next instant they feel worthless and indicate "I can't do anything right." They bounce back and forth from the concepts that were left over from duality thinking and then jump into the concepts of multidimensional Oneness. This bounding around is one sign that the shift in consciousness is occurring. Life during this stage of Light Body Awakening has become a paradox that is being resolved through these changing manic-depressive type symptoms. Allow each modality to fully express itself and live within the center of the paradox where each modality has an opportunity for its valid expression.

One fear the mental body has during these changes is that: "If I become aware of my multidimensional nature, will I be unable to function within the physical reality?" Have no concern; you will be able to function, more efficiently when there is a need to manipulate that physical body.

Just recognize that you will be spending more time in different dimensional states of consciousness. You will also recognize that it will take practice to become familiar with a new paradigm for living. You can anticipate an expanded range of exciting experiences that open up a completely new world. New possibilities and probabilities will open up. Then additional choices during each "NOW" moment, will become available. As you progress, that deep connection with spirit becomes more real, more than ever before in remembrance.

Some may think at this point in their Light Body Awakening process. "I'm progressing so fast I'll be out of here pretty soon, therefore I might as well do what I want to." That is fine -- because you are beginning to realize you are in charge and can have all the fun you can imagine. You are striving towards finding your Divine Purpose for being on Earth.

Eighth Stage of Light Body Awakening accelerates the desirable changes in your pituitary and pineal glands. These glands become larger and change shape. When this process begins to hurt and the pain or headaches become excessive talk to your High Self and pain body and ask for the changes to be, slowed down. Talk to your pain body and let it know everything will be OK soon, just reduce the pain please. Some may prefer to have a big headache for a day or so while others would prefer to have small headaches for several weeks. One solution is talk with the brain and ask for help with the question, "Brain please release endorphins that can help reduce my pain." Talk to all of your glands and ask them to work together as a team -- as you awaken your Light Body.

Gradually as your progress through the eighth stage of Light Body Awakening, your brain begins to increase in size. As the brain increases in size, it must expand towards the soft spot at the top of the head. Also, as the brain increases in size it pushes upward, because the thick skull bones restrict its expansion in other direction. As changes proceed, the shape of the head takes on the appearance of a cone. That is your head becomes cone shaped, and justifies the use of the term "Cone Head." If you watch "Star Trek," you may recognize the physical characteristics of the "Cone Heads". Realize also that the hair follicles will gradually cease to produce hair as you proceed through the many changes and a balding, can be anticipated. Some have rebelled at the thought of these changes. One individual said, 'I had no idea this was going to happen and my head would be cone shaped." It may be in your best interest to accept the beautiful cone head and the balding and remind yourself, by stating, "I like the features and shape of my new head, they are beautiful."

As the process proceeds three small seed crystals form within the head region. Two of these crystals are located over the eyebrows. The third seed crystal is just below the hairline right above the nose. A fourth crystal, called the receiver crystal, forms on the right side of the head one and a half inches above the ear. The receiver crystal will be capable of receiving masses of information from a higher dimension recorder crystal that has stored information the Soul has experienced over many incarnation cycles, on many different planets. Once the receiver crystal becomes functional, information from the recorder crystal will be downloaded. You may suddenly have all this information flooding in and wonder where it is coming from. Now you have some idea of where all those stored thought forms you previously created have been. They are being down loaded to help you better understand how all your experiences have led you to this point in your evolutionary cycle. These thought forms flooding your consciousness have originated from your massive library of illusionary "Now" records. These records will help you make additional choices about your next exciting journey through the cosmos.

When previous experiences flood in, new pathways are being created within the brain to help with various translations of that information. In addition, the changes are designed to help hook up the various components of your multidimensional mind. By accessing the multidimensional mind you will gradually understand that you can be anywhere and do anything.

Another understanding that will be quite helpful is to tap into information about how one's communication skills relate to colors, geometrics (sacred geometry) and tones (combinations of frequencies). As these new pathways are opened up within the brain, colors, various tones, geometric forms, bands of light, and shapes of letters (which are, spirit communication symbols) become evident. When this process begins, go back and carry out the unified chakra technique, then ask that those symbols be translated into usable thought forms. These thought-forms can then be converted into a language for verbal communication. As a result, your functional activities will proceed without a logical reason. In addition, you will realize there is nothing planned for as the result of a so-called "need." Rather those activities you experience will occur within the 'NOW," occur because you want them to without any reason or perceived need. That's living in the "NOW" as described in the book "The Power of Now" by Eckhart Tolle

One sign that you are reconnecting to your multidimensional being is that people do not understand what you are doing. Since your energy fields have changed and are changing, frequently it is very difficult for them to keep up and connect with you. Those individuals who in the past connected for the purpose of coercion, manipulation, or co-dependency drop away fast. You are no longer operating within their duality state of consciousness.

The eighth level of Light Body Awakening is one of the most transformative levels. Everything is changing fast and you may find yourself talking rhyme, unable to talk, or talking backwards. As you practice using the new language, information is being stored within your new DNA encodements, your sensory system, brain, and nervous system. All of these systems are being upgraded to process information previously unavailable.

To supply energy for these changes, a new internal fifth dimensional circulatory system (called the axial system) is coming on line. As these changes that began in third stage Light Body Awakening proceed, -- a "kick-over point" occurs that makes the final connection (merging) of the axial system with the autonomic nervous system complete. This change triggers the new axial system (that replaced the circulatory system) that can now carry out its new functions. Along with this significant upgrade of the old circulatory system, the group mind becomes more functional. As a result, the group mind begins to magnify individual efforts more profoundly.

Ninth Stage of Light Body Awakening begins when the tonal languages become recognizable, are more coherent, and function as a language. Your Spirit is using these languages to shift the sixth-dimensional structure of your new blueprint into a new template for your fifth-dimensional Light Body. Simultaneously your seventh-dimensional structures are shifting into alignment with your Oversouls. Your new Alpha/Omega structures are opening around the physical body. As a result additional high frequency energies are flowing in. These changes relate to your fifth-sixth dimensional etheric structures that are being coordinated through the seventh-dimensional alignment with your Oversoul. As this process proceeds, your body may change shape. You may become taller, a lot thinner, larger, or you may grow wings. This occurs when you begin to realize you have other body types or forms that are not human like. As a result, you begin to integrate non-human identities into your human identity. Obviously, this stage of Light Body Awakening brings together many aspects and levels that make up your total reality. Remember these processes are not optional. If you have incarnated on Earth and have chosen to graduate and ascend to the New Earth, Light Body Awakening is a requirement.

Therefore, as you go through the ninth stage of Awakening you experience a powerful shift into your multidimensional self. You are becoming the Master that you know you are. You came to Earth to experience duality and all the associated challenges. As you proceed through the Light Body Awakening stages, you realize you have mastered the limitations and separation experienced in duality. As you reflect, give thanks for all of the many exciting challenges that have helped propel you forward to the "New Earth."

Now the game is shifting to a new way of life, called "Heaven on Earth." "Great Job Fellow Travelers," we are going to make the transition. Here in the ninth stage you begin your final surrender to Spirit. You will discover you do not control anything on a personal level. You will realize that throughout all of your incarnations you were a component part of a divine instrument. You are and have become "Spirit in Action." All along your Spirit has had control of all previous activities, making plans for your graduation. Spirit has designed everything so that you can regain your capabilities as a Divine instrument. Your Soul has recorded those happenings as it has evolved all along the way as your loving companion.

When this change is realized, the persistent ego-self is dissolved and a final awakening takes place. This series of experiences is both ecstatic and painful. All of these experiences have been what you have been working toward and waiting for during multiple lifetimes. Yet when you arrive at this gateway, the portal to the fifth dimensional state of consciousness, it can be frightening. The joy and ecstasy that exists beyond the ninth stage of Light Body Awakening, that is, all of the new realities that exist on the other side of the portal, is beyond description, in any known language.

Many who have picked up this book and have read this far, are working through the Ninth Stage of Light Body Awakening. To go beyond this point in your historical journey it will be important to surrender at every level of your being. Let go of the "I-self," as you think of and understand it. Let the illusion held by the ego-self fade away as you awaken to your magnificence and Devine capabilities. Then the survival fears will dropout, they become unimportant. You will feel more centered and calmer than ever before. As you strengthen your connection with your Oversoul you will feel more connected to SOURCE Energy (I AM Presence) all the time.

Note: The last three Stages of Light Body Awakening (Tenth, Eleventh, and Twelfth) are called the Spiritual Levels. Within these levels, all of your energy fields become completely unified. Your new chakra system is being fine-tuned and you will soon have chakras up through the fourteenth chakra. Then you will become fully connected to the Christ Oversoul at every level of your being.

Tenth Stage of Light Body Awakening becomes quite evident when you begin to manifest avatar abilities. For example, you can be exactly where you want to be, when you want. You have the capability to teleport and manifest through your thoughts. You become fully conscious of being a part of everything. You are All-That-Is. You complete the hookups and function from your vastness, from what the angels call "ALL THAT IS" (Your God/Goddess within) -- as a component relationship with your High Self." Consequently, you feel connected to everything. You sense a level of awareness that encompasses and knows planetary consciousness, understands the deepest part of human consciousness, and taps into the complex human genetic consciousness. Within the Tenth State of Light Body Awakening, you will have activated your DNA encodements to where you will have an unlimited number of choices for new experiences. It is up to you to choose the most appropriate combination of experiences for your continued journey. One important choice is to make sure your Mer-Ka-Ba Light Body is upgraded to the crystalline eight point Mer-Ka-Va, in 2010 (10-10-10), the twenty point star Mer-Ka-Na in 2011 (11-11-11), and twenty-four point star Mer-Ka-Ra in 2012 (12-12-12). These new Light Body Structures will be outlined in greater detail by Archangel Metatron in the workshops of the Metatronic Keys. Each of these Light Bodies are designed to help accommodate the new energy patterns and insure they are functionally efficient.

Within the book "You Can Avoid Physical Death", starting on page 133 the statement was made: *"If you have been on Earth or a related planet for at least thirteen thousand years, your Mer-Ka-Ka energy field has probably become dormant."* Thus all one thousand plus individuals within the Subtle Energy Research Program were advised to activate their Mer-Ka-Ba Light Body. Many did activate that energy body and a large number have maintained it. If you are <u>unaware</u> of the importance of the Mer-Ka-Ba Light body now is the time to do some diligent study on the subject.

As you progress through Tenth State of Light Body Awakening your old Mer-Ka-Ba vehicle, designed for the electromagnetic field surrounding the Earth, will become obsolete. It will be upgraded or converted through a re-creative process into a Crystalline Light Body Mer-Ka-Va, then converted into a Mer-Ka-Na Light Body and finally into a Crystalline bio plasma Mer-Ka-Ra Light Body vehicle. Each of these increasingly complex Light Bodies will be designed for a very specific purpose. For more details about these Light Body patterns log on to www.earth-keeper.com.

The new third phase Mer-Ka-Va is a subtle energy vehicle that will connect you to your multidimensional Angelic component part. That angelic part was released during "The Fall" when we shifted to the lower third density. As you learn how to work with your Mer-Ka-Va, you have the capability to visit planets in other solar systems, and the many different Universes. During these visits, you will become familiar with the creation of other Source systems. As a result, an understanding of how they have evolved will become evident. Also, upon your return from these journeys you will bring back many exciting opportunities to continue your conscious expansion. Once your Mer-Ka-Va is functional within the matter world and the Mer-Ka-Na, functional in the antimatter world, the old Mer-Ka-Ba will become obsolete.

The Mer-Ka-Na is a phase three crysto-bio-plasmic subtle energy Auric Light Body. The activation of your Mer-Ka-Na and becoming familiar with its functional features is imperative. That system will be required for your graduation and ascension to the fifth Dimensional state of consciousness. The further you work with your new Mer-Ka-Na, the greater energy you can carry. Thus, you will need to learn how to control that energy. This will require mental balance and self-discipline. With the development of your Mer-Va-Na Light Body, you gain the ability to navigate within the higher dimensionality and in so doing freely access greater consciousness levels.

This magnificent Mer-Ka-Ra vehicle will allow you to move through the illusions of space, time, and dimensions. Coherent crysto-light energy can be projected out from the body of a Master Mer-Ka-Ra "Healer" through the hands by beaming coherent light emanations into a patient's body. The phenomena called channeling also functions with the features of the Mer-Ka-Ra Light Body. A large percentage of the channeling is an enhanced connection with the High Self or Devine Self (Ascended High Self). Archangels and Ascended Masters do in fact communicate with certain channels and teachers, but the great majority of conscious mediums are channeling their own Higher Selves. The famous channel, Edgar Cayce channeled Ra-Ta his Ascended Higher Self.

A magnificent world is within your grasp and understanding as you activate your Light Body and learn to operate your Light Body vehicle. The above four paragraphs may be somewhat complicated and difficult to understand. When your consciousness is ready to understand, your High self will explain everything in terms you can understand. Just make connection and listen to the small voices within. Ask and Ye Shall Receive.

An event that is beyond comprehension of the human intellect, will take place at the time of ascension. The Angels, Archangels, Extraterrestrials, and Ascended Masters will hook together all the Mer-Ka-Ba and Mer-Ka-Va vehicles (thought forms) they are building to assist Earth. Once they are all hooked together, they will surround planet Earth. Once in place this multiple energetic Light Body structure will form a planetary Light Body. This planetary Mer-Ka-Va Light Body will help planet Earth to finalize her ascension to the higher fifth Dimension. As that process takes place the third dimension planet Earth will be cleared for cleansing and cease to support life forms. The old third dimension parallel Earth has been so damaged by human activities for several thousand years it is now scheduled to go through a cleanup and renewal phase. For additional understandings of these important changes, I recommend enrollment in the classes termed "The Metatronic Keys." These classes, held by James Tyberonn, have been designed from information channeled by Archangel Metatron, described at www.earth-keeper.com.

Following "The Shift" (ascension event) the Ascended Masters will work together and become directors and navigators to coordinate the required adjustments to place this solar system within a multiple star system with two suns. Then we will have additional opportunities to create a completely new pathway of evolution. A binary solar system, one with two sons, has many unique features. Those additional features will offer untold opportunities and pleasures in the future. These opportunities become available after Earth arrives in its new location. A majority (two thirds) of the solar systems in the Milky Way Galaxy are binary or multiple star systems. This planetary system is a pair of stars held together by their mutual gravitational attraction. These two stars revolve around their common center of mass.

Eleventh Stage of Light Body Awakening is where you will make your final decision to stay within your Lightbody and ascend with the New Earth. Some may ascend ahead of the planet in 2011 and function as an advanced crew to prepare for the mass ascension coming up. Others may leave and proceed for other destinations. Once you have your Mer-Ka-Ba (Mer-Ka-Va, Mer-Ka-Na, Mer-Ka-Ra) vehicles perfected and your axiotonal lines coordinated and hooked up your spin points and you new chakra system, etc. you will be capable of making a decision as to your future upcoming destination.

The axiotonal energy lines positioned across your bodies are a part of your new Light Body. These energetic patterns are similar to the ley lines of planet Earth. The axiotonal lines also connect you with other star systems and universes. Each axiotonal line positioned along energy lines called acupuncture meridians connect to energy points called "spin points." As the new energy flow patterns become functional and new genetic codes have been activated, a completely new fifth-dimensional circulatory system will become active. As energy flows in through these spin points the internal metabolic systems takes on a juvenile pattern and as a result triggers the repair and creation of new body parts. As you proceed through the Eleventh Stage of Light Body Awakening, all of your new structures will gradually be put firmly in place and then fully activated.

Another significant change that a majority of the population is currently aware of is the illusion that time is speeding up. From a third dimensional aspect time is collapsing and at some point will appear to become simultaneous, that is, there will be no time. Your sensing system will phase in and out when this happens. Sometime you will think you are everywhere at once and then think you are on a time line. As you get used to going back and forth you will gradually understand that in reality there is no time. You will realize that the concept of past and future life is an illusionary "joke" designed to help facilitate third density flowing activities. All of your lives in reality have been and always will be lived simultaneously. Even your many parallel lives on other planets and those within the spiritual realms are being lived "NOW."

As you make the choice to Awaken Your Light Body, in any parallel reality, you have affected every life your Oversoul has helped bring into existence. In fact, that decision to awaken your Light Body is even more powerful than anyone can imagine. One person choosing to become Light in one lifetime affects the whole planet across time and across all parallel realities. There are over eight million Light Workers now on planet Earth. Can you imagine what effect they as a group are having upon every human on Earth? As a group, they can do anything, as long as they follow the direction of Spirit with Love as their motivating factor.

Within the Eleventh Awakening stage, you will operate from your God/Goddess self within. As you review the events in your Awakening, you may remember the headaches, flues, and other pains and rejoice that you survived. Now it is payoff time. Because of your dedication and persistence, you have arrived to where you can do anything you desire as you manifest your original Divine Plan. Exercise care since thoughts manifest very quickly. A continual series of thoughts could propel you in different directions excessively fast, another learning experience if you choose.

Many humans have come to planet Earth at this specific "NOW" event with specific skills and a willingness to be of Service To Others. Your talents are required right "NOW" as you read these words. Step up and be counted as one who has awakened their Light Body to be of Service to the planet and to others who ask for assistance. Through your conscious activities along with millions of others, you have the power to help create the New Earth (Heaven on Earth,)

Twelfth Stage of Light Body Awakening is where you seek out that area of service where your talents will allow you to link with other like-minded individuals to make a united difference. There will soon be a need for your talents to help design and participate in different organized patterns of government, education, service, etc. to help create an effective environment for continuous spiritual evolution on the "New Earth."

Throughout your many incarnations, you have made multitudes of choices. Those choices related to different parallel possibilities that were decided by the function of mind. Obviously some of those choices followed the guidance from Your High Self by listening to the Spirit voices within. All of those possibilities (parallel realities) still exist and are scattered in the Akashic records of your many lifetimes. All of those records will become available for your review as you ascend.

Once you reach the Twelfth Stage of Light Body Awakening, all of those parallel possibilities will be gathered (merged) into one significant file. Each of those NOW POINTS -- all of those games, challenges, events, opportunities, fun times, etc. are all part of the file records. All of those events were illusions that were a part of your Creator School activities.

As you ascend with your new Light Body there will be no need to carry all of those activities in your physical body, mental body, heart, or in your emotional body. Likewise, you will have no desire to take all of your third dimensional creations with you. All the keepsakes, money, cars, houses, churches, factories will remain upon third dimension Earth and be recycled for another reality realm. When you awaken and follow Spirit, you will be able to create your new realities. Moreover, remember that all earlier choices will have been merged and placed within the one large file. You will have a clean slate in your future "Now's" to follow Spirit.

As you have completed Light Body Awakening stage eleven and twelve you will have prepared your consciousness for graduation and ascension. The twelfth stage was the final activation of a Divine Plan for planet Earth. The old third density (dimensional state of consciousness) for Earth will be closed out as Earth ascends along with those who also choose to ascend with her.

A word of caution, once you have completed your Light Body Wakening and Activation avoid allowing a "healer" or energy worker to adjust your energy patterns. There is good evidence that they could damage your energy system inadvertently when they were unaware of your status. Once you have reached Light Body Status, there will be very little need to obtain assistance from another energy worker on Earth. There may be acceptations so check with your High Self to avoid any future problems.

Section VI. Dimensional Consciousness Features

The Twelve States of dimensional consciousness can be correlated with various patterns or vibrational frequencies to provide a better understanding of spiritual evolution. The following proposed evolutionary pattern came from an unknown source.

Evolutionary Thought Patterns and Consciousness

(1) The Primary Life – Developing the Ability to Think
1. The initial development of the intellect and the spirit.
2. Begin thinking of the intellect and the spirit.
3. Striving to think of reason the reasons for life.
4. Beginning to exercise the intellect and tap the spiritual force.
5. Working out the pattern of primary reasonable actions.
6. Exercising one's will that is causing thinking and action.
7. Beginning stages of reasoning in life.

Creatures on these levels are thought to be insane or idiots whose spirit and intellect is still not spiritually developed. These forms of primary life are in a sense new spirits who have through experience, have to go through an evolutionary process of learning how to think.

(2) Reasoned Life – Developing Skills to Utilize Knowledge
1. Primary development of reason.
2. Effective realization of reason and its use.
3. Primary acknowledgment and cognition of higher influences.
4. Belief of higher influences without owning knowledge.
5. Belief of higher forces. Superstition, fear of evil, veneration of good, etc.
6. Primary recognition of the true reality. Research and development of real knowledge. The first spiritual cognitions become apparent and how they can be used becomes evident. Spiritual curing, telepathy etc.
7. Primary development of knowledge and wisdom. The present position of the average Earth human being is within this category at around the sixth level.

(3) Intellectual Life – Technologically Developed

1. High development of the intellect. High technology, second utilization of spiritual forces. Primary creation of living forms.
2. Realization and exercise of knowledge, truth and wisdom. Slow break-up of acceptances of belief.
3. First utilization of knowledge and wisdom.
4. Acknowledgment and utilization of Natures Laws, generation of hyper- technology, secondary creation of living forms.
5. Natural exercise of wisdom and knowledge, in cognition of spiritual forces.
6. Life of knowing, wisdom, truth and logic.
7. Primary cognition of true reality as real absolute.

The present position of educated Earth human beings. Includes those who have mastered their ability to control their emotions and mental capabilities.

(4) Real Life - In Harmony With Creators Design

1. Clear knowing about the true reality as real absolute.
2. Cognition of spiritual knowledge and spiritual wisdom.
3. Utilization of spiritual knowledge and spiritual wisdom.
4. Cognition of true reality of Creation and understanding Universal Laws.
5. Living within Creational Laws. Purification of the spirit and the intellect. Cognition of the true obligation force of the spirit. Complete breakdown of   acceptance of belief.
6. Aimed and controlled utilization of spiritual forces.
7. First ability to create living creatures. Includes the more spiritually advanced and scientists who have tapped Into Universal Consciousness to help define human endeavors.

(5) Creational Life

1. Creating and controlling living forms.
2. Construction of machine-like genetically created livable creatures.

3. Spiritual development of forces for control of organic forms of life.
4. Will conditioned to master life and all of its sorts and forms.
5. Position of recognition, reminiscence of earlier lives etc.
6. Kingdom of wisdom's - ISHWISH (IHWH).
   Next to the last highest power and knowledge.
7. Cognition of spiritual peace, of Universal Love and Creational harmony.

Those who have mastered their creative skills, will be able to bring into existence new life forms and other "thought forms." Some souls residing on the Pleiades have evolved to become creators of new life forms. Evidence indicated that some Pleiadians have evolved to be active within pattern five "Creational Life" and are creating new life forms.

(6) Spiritual Life – One Centered on Service To All Creations
1. Acknowledgment and realization of spiritual peace, capable of projecting Universal love and Creational harmony.
2. Living in pure spiritual forms.
3. Spiritual creations.
4. Disembodiment of spirit.
5. First spiritual existence.
6. Final spiritual existence.
7. Qualify to pass over into the Creation Life.

(7) Eternal Life - Oneness with all of Creation
1. Twilight sleep over seven periods. (Eternity's)
2. Awaking and beginning of creating in the Creation of Creations, during the seven periods.
3. Creating of living forms throughout the Omniverse.
4. Creating of new spirit. Improvement of Creation.
5. Creating of spiritual greatness within the Creation.
6. Improvement Upgrade of Creations in Creation.
7. Reaching of highest improvement in the seventh period.

The Nature of a Changing Consciousness
Assuming that consciousness concepts are the foundation on which all creations come into existence and the criterion on which spiritual

evolution is measured, then -- each individual needs to answer the following question. What is consciousness? One definition of consciousness is existence. Another is, being awake and aware of one's surroundings. In addition, we could define consciousness as constantly being mentally aware of the component parts of creation.

In terms of our human existence and potential evolutionary capabilities, we could ask the question; how does consciousness relate to quantum mechanics? Could it be possible to utilize the concepts of quantum mechanics to determine the position, time and spin of all creation (existence) in relation to consciousness? If so, then we must consider that there are space-time points that make up all of the observed creations. Science has defined these points in terms of a set of quantum numbers. To define consciousness could require a more complete understanding of quantum mechanics in relation to frequency, magnetic fields, electric fields, subtle energy, gravity, light, and many other concepts or energetic patterns that together make up existence.

Why Raise My Frequency and Consciousness

One reason for raising your consciousness is to help yourself and everyone living on planet Earth. The collective consciousness of humans living on Earth has become extremely low for thousands of years. Many have lost their spiritual connection to source and reality. One sign of this fall in consciousness is evidenced by the current confusion and chaos. Negativity has become so intense that many humans have lost contact with reality. They seek escape through physical sensations, called pleasures, or securing possessions in an attempt to satisfy their longings for happiness and joy. Because of these self-centered activities, and fixations on "worldly activities" humanity is in the process of destroying their third dimension planet Earth's capabilities to continue supporting living systems.

For thousands of years after 'The Fall," the intensity of the duality lessons have become packed full of difficult challenges. Nearing the end of the dark portion of this twenty-five-thousand-year cycle, surface dwellers on Earth have fallen to one of the lowest levels of dimensional consciousness in the Universe. Those more spiritually advanced humans living within the Earth would prefer not to have any contact with their surface sisters and brothers. All of humanity's experiences have been kept in massive computer files. Quoting from these historical records:

During previous times, that is during the history of the Earth, humans have ascended to the heights of glory during the two thousand year Light cycle, a phase related to a twenty-five-thousand-year cycle. But, during and following the twenty five thousand year dark phase, they have consistently fallen to a very low conscious level.

Humanity has reached that low level of consciousness, where a majority of humans have lost contact with their God/Goddess within. Humanity on Earth has just experienced the end of a 25,000-year dark period that has followed "The Fall" in consciousness. Humanity is now poised to enter a light period of two thousand years. Now there is an opportunity for humans to concentrate on raising their (your) consciousness to a level compatible with those energies supplied by the Great Central Sun and Photon Belt. These complex energies are the ascension energies Mother Earth is using.

Real happiness and joy that humans could experience, comes from those consciousness connections to the God/Goddess within and their Higher Selves. Many have become so confused about reality they have begun to worship some false, fabricated God/Goddess outside themselves, some unknown, ill-defined entity or "father figure" out there. They not only tend to worship an unknown, mystical God/Goddess but also an illusory Heaven they have created with streets of gold. The real God/Goddess, the I-Am-That-I-Am, the All-That-Is, or Universal consciousness resides within every human, animal, plant, and every other aspect of creation. The rise of one's consciousness relates to our individual capability to connect with those spiritual components that make up our multi-dimensional consciousness. Once connected to Source where your "Light Quotient" is optimized you and I (all of us) can receive guidance, prepare for graduation, help those needing assistance and then ascend to the "New Earth."

Happenings When Changing Consciousness

Before examining the many benefits of raising your consciousness, it will be very helpful for you to spend time becoming aware of your feelings about life. Examine the joy of living on Earth, your freedoms, and your capabilities to sense the world around you. Ask the question, how aware am I of all events taking place in nature and around me every moment of the day? Remember, consciousness is related to awareness. Awareness is also related to your health, so examine your health, and determine who or what is in control.

Think about how mentally, emotionally, and financially secure you are. Next, spend time contemplating the true meaning of freedom and what freedom means to you personally. Can you locate some factors that limit your freedom or your health? What is the possibility that these factors can be removed or un-created through transmutation? How would you like to see your life unfold? Then decide what you want for your future life on planet Earth. The creative processes available have been provided to assist you during your experiences on Earth.

As you know, everyone creates their reality by their thoughts. In addition, your thoughts attract like thoughts to magnify that original thought. The reality is, like attracts like. You have created every disease you ever experienced with your thoughts. Others may have added energy to that disease as they visualized you with the imbalance. Obviously, you created these experiences for a purpose.

The secret is to focus on the thoughts that you want to create, those things you would like to experience in the future "Now." Negative thoughts are just as powerful as positive thoughts. Thus, avoid all negative thoughts that relate to any form of fear. I repeat -- keep in mind there is nothing to fear except fear itself. As you contemplate shifting your consciousness to a higher frequency, ask these two questions. What can I dream about for a better future? In addition, are there activities or events that I would like to experience? It would be helpful to write your answers down for future reference.

Do you realize that when you raise your consciousness above Your current, limited perceptions, you can have anything you desire? Within the higher dimensional consciousness (DMC) levels, when you ask, you receive. Thus, be careful what you ask for. Your thoughts will be manifesting much more rapidly as you shift to a higher level of consciousness. As your consciousness moves to a higher level, you have opened up your heart and made a more efficient connection with your God/Goddess within. As a result, your mind will perceive that perfection and those limitless possibilities that are available just for the asking.

Change in My Activities Related to Consciousness

The changes in your life because of raising your consciousness are unlimited. Yes, raising your consciousness will gradually influence your daily activities. Raising one's consciousness is a natural process designed by the Creators of all Universes. As your consciousness rises, you become closer to the Creators and God/Goddess. You gradually recognize your real identity as an eternal and immortal part of God/Goddess, a child of love created by the Creators of Love. You will know that you not only came from love, but that by raising your consciousness, your love will continually expand. You can become more aware that you are a child of an omnipotent and glorious God/Goddess, created with all the same attributes. You are a duplicate, if you will, of God/Goddess. As your consciousness has been raised to higher frequencies, your lost memories will be restored. Greater understanding will allow you to know where you came from and what you are doing here. It will also provide guidance for your future paths throughout eternity.

Within the higher states of dimensional consciousness, you can move out of the small box in which you have been living for thousands of years and explore what else is available outside your box. You will be able to explore the Earth, this Solar System, other galaxies, and different Universes. You will gradually realize that the little box you have been confined to was an illusion. There is no need to stay confined to your box and all of the multiple illusions. You can become free and discover you are not alone; you were never alone, you are a part of All-That-Is.

Ask yourself if you are an isolated human living on the only inhabited planet within the Universe. What is your first answer? Are you an interconnected part of everyone and everything? There are millions of other planets inhabited by creations just like you. They are having experiences just as you and they are surviving. Many of these entities with numerous physical features are evolving spiritually, just like you, all connected to the same Creators.

Some scientists now believe that all planets and their moons (just like Earth) have inhabitable interior portions. Spirit indicates that on some planets, life on the surface is very difficult to impossible, so the inhabitants must live inside the planet to survive. As you raise your consciousness, you will have an opportunity to visit many of these societies within the Earth and on many different planets throughout the Universe.

When we consider that all individual creations came about through the combined activities of several Creators, each joining their consciousnesses to finalize a proposed goal, the process of conscious evolution takes on more meaning. Then we can consciously begin to understand that throughout creation anything is possible. In addition, it is very logical to realize that many different biological creations could inhabit both the exterior and interior surfaces of billions of planets. Can you realize, or imagine that all of these inhabitants are all our brothers and our sisters?

Can you fathom the concept that you are part of a vast and infinite creation of an unimaginable degree of variation in shape and form? Failing to clear out the false beliefs that place limitations on your spiritual evolution is tragic beyond description. Opening your mind to unlimited possibilities will help you understand you are not alone; the real creation extends beyond your wildest imagination.

Why limit your God/Goddess-given capabilities by clinging onto outdated beliefs and illusions? By raising your consciousness to a level that is more closely connected to the God/Goddess within; it becomes possible to restore all your divine gifts, freedoms, and capabilities. You can receive the gift of spiritual sight and visualize the physically unseen world. You can time travel, bilocate, remote view, and thus experience the joy of exploring illusionary past and future events. Your daily life will flow with ease as you focus your thoughts on the beauty of the moment and all it has to offer. You become capable of clearing out all self-punishment, old routines, false beliefs, and illusions that have held you captive for many lifetimes. Just ask your High Self to locate those entities that can use the neutrino sweep technique vertically, horizontally, and obliquely to clear all adverse energies.

As an aid to your expanded energy system, you can request that all needed energy-flow patterns without and within your bodies be opened and fine-tuned to optimize your well-being. Grace and magic become available to help you restore your health and stop aging. Within the higher states of consciousness, you have lifted yourself above the pain and suffering of the present physical, mental, and emotional limitations of the old third-dimensional state of consciousness.

My Spiritual Evolution and Shift in Consciousness

Assuming you plan to follow the outline of evolution designed by the Creators, God/Goddess, then the process of raising one's dimensional consciousness will continue from a glory to greater and greater glories on into eternity. The Lemurians, currently living within Mount Shasta in Telos have sensed that the majority of humans residing on Earth are dreaming of going to a New Earth when they leave through physical death. Could it be that the "New Earth" they are dreaming of is right here? "Now" at the end of the twenty-five-thousand-year cycle and the beginning of a new cycle unfolding on this planet, you will no longer have to physically die to go to an illusory heaven with streets of gold.

The real Heaven on Earth will manifest right here as a parallel "New Earth" for all of those who choose to ride the wave of graduation and Ascension. For those who reject this opportunity, there are other options available. Therefore, you have a choice of whether or not to answer the following yes-or-no questions about your reason for coming to Earth. Many have already answered these four questions.

1. Did you incarnate on Earth to remain in the little box of duality consciousness and continue living on some third-dimensional planet like Earth?

2. Do you still require lessons and challenges to complete a part of your contract within the little box of duality before you graduate?

3. Did you come to Earth to complete your third- and fourth-dimensional lessons in this incarnation before moving out of the little box and into Unity/Christ Consciousness?

4. Did you come to Earth to shift your consciousness to the fifth-dimensional frequencies and thereby graduate and take your renewed physical body to the "New Earth?"

Do you understand the significance of your answers to these questions? You may have already decided or are close to making your decision about graduation and Ascension. Everyone has a choice to make. There is no judgment as to what your answers are. Your choices and decisions about these four questions will significantly influence your current "Now" status. These choices will affect the status of your cosmic evolution for thousands of future experiences.

Keep in mind that within the spiritual realms there is no time or space. Thus, you have an eternity to chart your path. However, there may be an advantage of speeding up your evolution by answering *no* to the first two questions and *yes* to the second two. By choosing to answer *yes* to the second two questions, you will be moving out of duality, away from the lessons and challenges that pain and suffering have provided you. The decision to shift into a higher, fifth-dimension frequency is a choice to embrace Unity/Christ consciousness by passing through the Star Gates to the "New Earth." With this decision, a completely new reality realm opens up to a cosmic path for your spiritual evolution. Opportunities within the higher levels of consciousness have unlimited potentials.

My Sensing System In Relation to Consciousness

To be conscious involves your capability to detect and/or sense various events going on mentally and emotionally through your thoughts. Not only here on Earth and beyond the veil within the spiritual realm. That means to be continually aware mentally and emotionally of all your thoughts on Earth and beyond within the Spiritual realm. This awareness should involve using all of your sensing systems (conscious, subconscious, and superconscious) to become more conscious of all aspects of life. Notice how conscious events unfold around you during every "Now" moment. Being conscious also means listening to the God/Goddess within to answer any question that would be of assistance for helping you follow your time line. With a higher level of consciousness, it becomes possible to be aware of every event that your outer and inner sensing systems perceive and record in your conscious and subconscious minds.

Raising one's consciousness is an inside responsibility (job) and will require a dramatic change in your behavior patterns. No more living on automatic pilot, stuck mentally and emotionally in a repetitive pattern of activities that block out the world around you. It means clearing out activities that have limited spiritual value. It means stopping the madness around you from entering your thoughts and bodies. Summed up the whole process means cleaning your house, that body and physical residence, where you spend so much time. Clear out those items that hold your consciousness (thoughts) to a third density world and third state of dimensional consciousness.

Avoid mentally and emotionally tuning in to and concentrating on the many negative distractions around you. These distractions have been purposely created to divert your attention and cause confusion in your life. Once humans become confused, they are much easier to manipulate and control. When the slaves are confused, the controllers have an easier time of restricting spiritual evolution. These many confusing distractions within third density have been designed to limit your ability to raise your consciousness, advance spiritually, and graduate.

Gain control of your chattering mind and focus its activities on worthwhile thoughts. Spend time exploring activities other than those that have entrapped you in a repetitive routine. Seek the real self, the God/Goddess within. Go within and focus your being in your heart. Transfer your focus from the mind to the heart and its potential guidance for your life. Study how to live from the heart as opposed to living from the mind. Listen to the still, small voices within (God/Goddess and High Self) as your main guidance system. This is an internal knowing, free from the clutter of the ego and false beliefs. With discernment, you will also be free of the many limiting illusions humans have created.

Then use your sensing system to explore everything around you in nature, all the guests Mother Earth has been open to receive. By communicating with and honoring the presence of trees, birds, insects, and animals, you can open up and expand your consciousness. Realize you

149

have become arrogant to think you are superior to others who inhabit the planet with you. No one has a spiritual right to manipulate other creations. Visually, sense everything around you: the rocks, plants, flowers, and grass and other features of the landscape. Feel and smell the soil as your source of energy for maintaining the physical body. Work the soil with your hands to help a plant in need.

Examine the characteristics of the air, wind, clouds, sun, moon, and stars, and contemplate how they influence your life on Earth. Give thanks for how they support your life. Realize the love and patience shown by the being you call Mother Earth. She provides life-giving oxygen, water, minerals, and food for your survival as a Spirit and Soul traveling in a physical body. As you thank and honor Earth Mother and all of her guests, she will be ready and willing to assist you in raising your consciousness and vibrational frequency. Just ask members of the Spiritual Hierarchy (High Self Spiritual Council and God/Goddess within) to raise your consciousness to the most appropriate frequency.

As an unlimited, divine being having a temporary human experience, you can maximize the joy of experiencing the many challenges here on Earth. Concentrate on the wondrous opportunities you have here. Be thankful about your many choices to incarnate back to Earth and complete your third-dimension lessons. Share your insights with others of like mind and find ways to be of Service To Others and to all of creation. Because of your self-discovery and understanding of your interconnectedness with creation, you will be assisted in raising your consciousness.

Graduation, Ascension and Consciousness

One method for raising your consciousness is to focus your conscious intent on sensing the characteristics of all aspects of God/Goddess creations. Seek to know the names of and understand the many different people, animals, and plants in your world. Then seek to understand their behavior patterns. Try to understand the purpose of each one. They each have a specific purpose and a support role to play in your life on Earth. Study how the names of the many different animals and plants came about and call them by name. Thank the angels, divas, and fairies for their service to each human and plant. Thank all of the spiritual entities for all their loving care. These higher-dimensional spirit entities have a consciousness and a sensing ability in order to understand your thoughts.

There is value in working with the soil and growing plants. Placing your hands in the soil and watching plants grow have been scientifically proven to bring in healing energies to the body and Soul. Open your heart to all of that which is above and below in the visible and invisible world. Strive to communicate with the invisible world that exists within the higher frequencies. Start to open your spiritual sensing system to become aware of those realities beyond your five physical senses. Develop your sixth sense to communicate with those higher-frequency creations -- the angels, divas, and fairies. Believe that anything is possible. Remember, your beliefs create the foundation for the thoughts that create your reality. Open yourself to sense the unconditional love present within all of the wonders of creation. You will be raising your consciousness to all of the new energies that are flooding into the Solar System and planet Earth.

By shifting your consciousness to the higher frequencies at this time in history, you will be closing out the thousands of lifetimes you spent on the low-frequency planets. Your labors and many challenges throughout the centuries will be crowned during graduation and Ascension. Never in the history of the Earth has the Ascension process been made as easy as it is currently. The Creators have given permission for Mother Earth to Ascend, and she has chosen to do so. Mother Earth welcomes all who would like to join her during her Ascension.

The goal of "mass graduation" has eluded humanity for thousands of years, primarily because that opportunity only occurs every twenty-five thousand years. You can now realize that your goal in continuing to incarnate on Earth was to raise your consciousness so you could eventually ascend with your physical body to the "New Earth." The Creators and God/Goddess have chosen to offer this opportunity to you. There is still time to "Wake Up" and decide to graduate. However, if you prefer to wait for the end of another twenty-five thousand years to graduate, that is, at the end of the next cycle, that is an acceptable option. For those who were

151

unaware that graduation time is near, this is your "Wake Up" call. For those of you making preparations to graduate, continue your efforts.

Some have asked, if humanity "Now" has an opportunity to graduate from third dimension Earth, Why haven't we heard of this opportunity in the communication media? Because, the Illuminati and specific Extraterrestrial groups control the major communication media—radio, television, and the newspapers. They would rather keep you on an Earth-like planet as slaves in the third dimension for another twenty-five thousand years than let you know of this opportunity.

The subject of Ascension has been discussed in hundreds of books throughout history. In addition, here are currently over one thousand Internet Web sites that discuss and outline helpful suggestions for your graduation and Ascension. Obviously, there are many false beliefs about how you achieve Ascension. Go within during meditation, use discernment, and you will know the most appropriate path. It is up to each individual to be willing to work at finding and following his or her own spiritual path. No one else is responsible for you. Over two thousand years ago, Yeshua (Sananda or Jesus Christ) came to Earth to show humanity the way to live in order to graduate and ascend. His **basic** instructions were simple: love God/Goddess, love yourself, and then love your neighbor as yourself.

In summary, the best advice for you in the days to come is to start each day with a total commitment to embrace and align your spirit and Soul with the God/Goddess within. Then request that your heart and God/Goddess within take charge of your activities during the coming days so that everything unfolds efficiently and gracefully. In Addition, confer with your High Self and High Self Spiritual Council for guidance and assistance.

Section VII. Dimensional Consciousness States

Introduction to Dimensional States of Consciousness

The following descriptions of multidimensional consciousness are the results of our research over the past 10 years while listening to High Self, various spiritual entities, attending workshops, lectures, scanning the internet, reading magazines and by reviewing many books. We are a long way from fully remembering or even partially understanding our potential as multidimensional conscious creations. I believe we as a society are putting together the greatest of all puzzles, "Spiritual Evolution." Pieces of the puzzle are coming together thick and fast.

We each need to assist in the process. Then the more we share what we have learned and remembered about our multidimensional consciousness, the more we can enrich the collective consciousness of the Earth and all of it's inhabitants. We then assist in the "AWAKENING" throughout the galaxy. The Hathors, incarnated on Venus, are watching the solar system very closely. Their information indicates that Earth is a crossing point for many different galactic and intergalactic travelers. As a result, many intergalactic Extraterrestrials are also watching changing events on Earth and on many other planets within our galaxy.

Several Extraterrestrial spacecraft have the capability of monitoring Earthlings concerning their evolutionary status. One procedure is to monitor each human's DNA composition and frequency remotely, as humans shift from two strands to twelve strands of DNA. They are also measuring each human's degrees of spiritual awakening. Those measurements are designed to place each human on Earth into one of three categories or levels of consciousness. These three levels of monitoring are:

1. Individual humans currently living on Earth that would rather kill and die rather than awaken from their mentally induced sleep state. They remain asleep and are dangerous, since they sleepwalk and look like everyone else. Intuitively you may detect them, when you do, be careful about communicating and/or developing a relationship with them.

2. Individual humans that do not wish to be bothered and do not wish to change how they live life. They are not particularly violent, just numb and appear too involved in their repetitive behavior patterns to be

bothered with their spiritual lives. Many just appear to be a daze and remain in a sleep state -- day and night and appear to be unaware of events around them.

3. Individual humans that have awakened some time ago and those that are currently awakening. These individuals have some degree of understanding about activities occurring on Earth. Many of these individuals are willing to help as they begin to understand. Gradually they are beginning to accept their responsibilities. They have an ability to live with joy in the face of conflict.

Mentally think about these three categories. Note which consciousness group your records are most likely stored, within the Extraterrestrial computers. They have complex computers on board their "Mother Ships" that can store information about every human living on planet Earth.

To those of you who think that your historical records are off-limits, think again, there are no secrets. Now go back and study the three classifications again. Those classified within the first and second groups may read these words but most will have difficulty comprehending what they read. The third group, who do understand, must carry the load in assisting the graduation and ascension processes. For all of those classified in-group 3, the Extraterrestrials and many Earthlings are all counting on your assistance. It is obvious that you will need Spiritual courage to walk the talk and stand up to be counted, especially during the next few years. Because of rapidly changing conditions, leading up to 2012, many of these unfamiliar events could be stressful. We all need to ask for mental and emotional strength to survive the changing energies and the potentially stress related events.

As you make a detailed study of the concepts of Dimensional Consciousness (DMC), keep in mind there is another important concept known as "Dimensional Parallel Universes (DPU)," which helps define the design of reality in this "One Universe." These two concepts (DMC and DPU) are partially correlated with each other. There are twelve states of DMC (discussed below); each of which has at least twelve evolutionary levels of spiritual development.

In contrast, there are an infinite number of DPUs. Earthlings have gained access to over 100 DPUs by taking and utilizing specific energy patterns stored within these data banks. Within these DPUs, there are many different energy forms designed for specific purposes. Some DPU have stored energy forms used for creative purposes. Others have human like life forms, however different than the forms we would normally recognize.

For example, Robert Detzler of "Spiritual Response Therapy (located in Lacy, Washington) has discovered that some DPUs contain unique energy forms. Some energy forms (entities) that he has detected are, "The Loch Ness "monster", unicorns, Divas, dinosaurs, gargoyles, Pans, and Centaurs, each within a specific DPU. The Loch Ness "monster" resides in the 28th DPU and the Divas in the 20th DPU.

Preliminary evidence also indicates that the 23rd DPU contains various energy challenges that creations within the second, third and fourth DMCs take on for challenges. For example, the vibrational frequencies of each physical (e.g. viruses), mental (e.g. brain fog), and emotional (e.g. tension) challenge needed for lessons within the lower DMCs, originate from the 23rd DPU.

The second DPU appears to be a conduit for adverse energies. As a means of protection, use your accurate pendulum dowsing to determine if you have any adverse energies coming from the 23rd DPU, through the second DPU. If you detect any of these adverse energies, request that your High Self contact the appropriate spiritual team to check on the energetic features of those energies. When adverse energies are discovered have them disconnected from the 23rd DPU. Disconnect those energies that are flowing in through the second DPU conduit. You can also use accurate pendulum dowsing to ask if it would be wise to disconnect all appropriate bodies from the second DPU. Exercise caution with this request because of possible side effects. One option is to make a request for the most appropriate change – that is generally the safest procedure.

Within the Subtle Energy Research (SER) activities, we have worked with the energies from the 44th DPU for many years. Within the 44th DPU, there are millions of numbered "Power Codes." These power codes consist of a sequence of numbers separated by dashes. By repeating a "Power Code", nine times or more you can tap into the energy behind a thought form and then project that energy pattern to a designated target. For example, the power code for the Available Energy Complex is (10-3-5-5 - 4-8-4-2 - 1-9-6-7). This "Power Code" represents over thirty-two different beneficial thought forms (creative energies) that can be directed to an area of the body, or to the area of someone else's body that needs healing energy. I repeat, to pull in these energies within your consciousness visualize and repeat these numbers in sequence at least nine times during each setting. That code can pull in a host of different energies for helping energizing your many bodies such as your: physical, etheric, causal, mental, emotional, spirit, soul, astral, spiritual, love, pain, Soul body, Christ body and Holy Spirit bodies.

Another important power code is (9-9-9 - 5-5-5,) where 9 depicts completion and 5 depicts love. The complete love power code can be used for many different purposes. For example, this power code can detoxify and thus remove, from foods and liquids all adverse energies. This power code will also energize foods and harmonize them to your body before those foods are consumed. Again, remember each power code has originated from the 44th DPU library. Power code (9-9-9 - 5-5-5,) can also be used to detoxify the human body by repeating this number sequence nine times or more, depending on the severity of the toxins present.

Every "thought form" has a power code. There are millions of power codes within the library, just waiting for you to ask to use them. There are also power codes for harmonizing the antimatter components of our energy bodies. All creations have some degree of antimatter in this domain. You can access any of these power codes by going to the 44th DPU library. Your High Self can guide you through the maze to reach the library and help in the selection of any power code.

There is at least one power code and sometimes several for every thought form in every language. These numerical numbered codes are available for the asking. Use accurate pendulum dowsing to determine how many numbers make up the code, their individual sequence, and then carry out an experiment to make sure the numbers and their sequence is correct. Then when you discover the power code fails to work make needed corrections with accurate pendulum dowsing.

As you take your power back, you can make the choice to develop your imagination, remember your capabilities, and practice creating. You can augment these capabilities by tapping into specific Dimensional Parallel Universes (DPUs) for an energy format. These other DPUs contain patterns (thought forms) useful during your creations and throughout your spiritual journey.

To complete our lessons here in "Creator School" and to graduate, requires removal of all interference patterns (adverse energies of all types) and making several shifts in consciousness. Once all of the adverse energies have been cleared to an appropriate level, the most significant task is to awaken and activate your Light Body.

Then take advantage of your multidimensional consciousness by utilizing the desirable features of each dimension that will aid your evolution. That is, learn how to shift your consciousnesses to the most appropriate higher dimensional state of consciousness (DMC), when that shift is appropriate. Ask your High Self to help you shift some of energy systems from the third and fourth DMC levels to the most appropriate higher DMC's. This means making "partial shifts upward" while residing within your third to fourth low frequency dense physical body.

To make that shift involves working with your High Self and High Self Spiritual Council to help you remember and understand your signed contract. Once you remember your current contract, you will know what tasks lay ahead during this current incarnation. As a result, you can become more responsible to yourself and those other companion Souls who incarnated within you during this incarnation. Then through a series of incarnations, you will have designed a sequence of contracts that will assist your graduation from these lower third dimensional challenges.

As with any school, success requires hard work, patience, persistence, and a large measure of dedication. I repeat, to accomplish this task, you will be required to clear all of your dysfunctional features. Once you recognize what those many dysfunctions are, then you can ask your High Self to seek out spiritual help to locate the spiritual teams that can help remove these roadblocks. To facilitate any activity make sure your "Light Quotient" is maintained at an acceptable level to avoid depleting your stored energy. The "Light Quotient" is a measure of your connection to "Source Light" (ALL THAT IS). That measurement also reveals the degree to which these energies are capable of flowing through various channels, into your bodies -- while incarnated on Earth.

It is unlikely you will be able to perceive all of your dysfunctions unless you glimpse inside your consciousness and begin to know yourself. Who are you? What do you base your identity on? For example, is your identity based on what you believe about yourself? Is your identity based on, or do you describe yourself, by your current occupation? How accurate is that belief?

The more you allow currently established belief systems to create your identity, the more you damage your physical, mental, and emotional health. I heard an individual state, "I am an electrician." Is that who he truly was, or was that his occupation. Many humans have become lazy in terms of their communication skills. Exercise extreme care in your choice of words; think before you speak, when communicating. It is very easy to cut off your energy flow by making false statements. That kind of behavior will not be acceptable within the fifth DMC.

In order to develop your true multidimensional nature "be" truthful at all times. You are a spiritually advanced Soul, in the process of being perfected, "NOW." You are a magnificent creation with unlimited capabilities. Therefore, act that way without becoming egoistical. Just remember who you are, how great you are, and what tremendous potential you have.

Why develop spiritually? How does one develop spiritually? The main reason most individual Souls came to Earth school was for Soul development, a spiritual process. One non-standard question that is important to understand is, "Does having a set of religious, economic, political, or social beliefs help develop my spirituality?" The answer to that question should be yes!

The lessons learned from attachment to these illusionary false beliefs should give you a clue of some alternative beliefs. The lessons learned within these social structures are why we incarnated upon Earth within a low frequency duality environment. Within this Earth environment of false illusionary beliefs, we should have learned several important lessons.

One lesson is that these false beliefs have created so much confusion and strife that there must be a preferred way of life on Earth. You can now understand that for you and me to have a joy filled life and an exalted state of well being we need to change our beliefs. There is a very important lesson learned, from going through dealing with all of the confusion and false beliefs on Earth. From these experiences, you can now understand that there are more accurate beliefs that could help you and me accelerate our spiritual evolution. Thus, you and I need to clear those "False Beliefs" and install new beliefs that are more accurate.

We came to Earth as advanced spiritual beings, Spirits created perfect by God/Goddess. If that's true, that we were created perfect, then, where did all of the "so called" imperfections come from? It becomes obvious that we individually and/or collectively created all of these imperfections and illusions for a purpose. Since we have created them and have "hopefully" learned from them, it is now time to un-create them. To accomplish that task we are required to reverse the creative process. The procedure my High Self recommends is to change their form. You can use either phase shifting or transmutation to take the old energy and create a new energy, one that is "more perfect." You can request that the created imbalance be phase shifted ninety degrees and fed back on its self or have the created imbalance transmuted, changed energetically to a beneficial form. Remember neither you nor any entity can destroy energy; an entity can only change its form.

True spirituality based on eternal principles and Universal Laws is superior to basing one's spiritual development on duality based fear manipulated belief systems. To make an attempt to live better lives through the use of negative thought forms is totally unfounded from any known perspective. Positive thought forms like Love heal. Negative thought forms like hate destroy. Have you gained control of the thought forms you project out into the world?

As third density humans, we have missed the mark (sinned via error choices) through our attachment to false belief systems and negative thinking. Many false systems were forced upon us because of our limited understanding of reality. Many similar false belief systems have been in place on Earth for thousands of years. As a result, we now have a worldwide crisis. Are you aware of this "crisis? By slowing down and paying attention to what is happening throughout the world, you all can sense the many social and environmental features of the growing crisis.

The survival of the planet and all life is threatened by this crisis. That crisis was largely created by humanity's false belief systems used as learning tools. Those we trusted as teacher and leaders programmed these false beliefs into our different levels of consciousnesses. These old, outdated behavior patterns are destroying our children, our health, all life forms, and the planet, thus it is time to change and take on new updated behavior patterns.

Those patterns are available within the fifth density and fifth state of dimensional consciousness. The choice is, Evolve Spiritually NOW, or Die Physically and Keep on Trying to Wake Up Later on another dimension in spirit or on another third dimension planet.

Everyone needs to take care of himself or herself; no one else can live your life for you. Control the ego (egoric) mind and learn to live from the heart. Open your "Ascension Channel" by going within for "self discovery" to find all the dysfunctional behavior patterns that create and instill self-punishment. Within the Subtle Energy Research Program, we constantly observe people who punish themselves day after day, for so many different reasons. If someone knows why so many humans consider their worst enemy to be their own self, please let me know. Maybe we punish ourselves because as incarnated Spirits and Souls, riding around in a body, we fail to realize how wonderful and powerful we truly are. A few individuals feel rejected by God/Goddess. They believe they have been sent to Earth as a form of punishment. In the first place, they were not sent; they volunteered to come to Earth. Secondly, Earth is not a place of punishment. Earth is a school where you chose to learn how to become a Creator.

Ascension involves a shift in dimensional consciousness from within. I restate an urgent point about the first step in this shifting process – that is "Clear Out All Old Interfering Energies." Were those energies to remain they could function as a resistance to the new incoming high frequency energies. As those energies pass through the resistance, heat could build up. That process can result in spontaneous combustion of the physical body. Yes, that has happened many times when the human body goes up in flames. There is no need to fear – just ask your spirit team to monitor changes in your energy system. Thus, clear out the mental and emotional junk stored within your conscious, subconscious, and superconscious memory banks. Also, clear all physical junk, items that no longer serve a useful purpose out of your life, home, car, or place of work.

When the clearings are completed, you can add new high frequency adamantine particles. These are brought down from higher densities, to recreate imbalances and thus accelerate your evolutionary progress. The answers to regaining your health, saving the planet Earth, and helping make the shift to the higher dimensions are located "within" your consciousness and that of each individual Soul on Earth. Then the overall collective consciousness of every graduating Soul will help create the New Earth.

May I repeat an earlier discussion about "The Shift" or "Shift of The Ages." The decision of Earth to shift in consciousness correlates with a specific stage (phase) within the Grand Galactic Cycle of 26,000 years. We have reached the end of the dark phase of this historical cycle and have entered the light phase. Simultaneously this sector of the "Milky Way Galaxy" and our Solar system have entered the photon belt (a region containing high energy light particles, called photons), recently verified by Russian scientists. Again, remember, the arrival of the Photon Belt signals the end of the dark phase and the beginning of the light phase. The light phase has been called the millennium, a period during Earth's evolution cycle when humanity has an opportunity to "Wake Up." It will be another 26,000 years before this light phase of the cycle returns.

The resulting shift in the consciousness of the Earth and its's inhabitants is taking place right NOW, as you read these words. As a part of "The Shift," Earth is in the process of cleansing herself. <u>We will continue to see tremendous cleansing activities in the form of increases in geothermal events such as earthquakes, tsunamis, and volcanoes. Also, an increase in hurricanes, cyclones, tornadoes, and variable weather patterns will continue to occur.</u>

The turbulent storms reported throughout the world are an out-picturing of the human violence currently taking place in society. Those violent energy patterns, created by humans, must be dissipated in order for life to continue on the planet. For thousands of years Mother Earth stored these negative energies, but those loving activities are over. The Earth cannot hold any more of those energies without self-destructing.

These misdirected powerful negative "thought forms" of energy are dissipated (cleansed) and released in these storms. These cleansing events and a shift in consciousness have been prophesied for centuries. Cleansing of the Earth and of humans began several years ago and is in full swing. Predictions also indicated that these cleansing events should subside around the year 2012. Many energy shifts are occurring throughout the Universe, on our Sun, on other planets of our Solar System, and on Earth. Because of these changes, many new energies are arriving on Earth. We have an option to start remembering how to use these newly arriving energies to assist in our ascension.

On March 17, 2006, the Hathors (of Venus) delivered the following message in Spain about current events. The message read:

"This movement into your future, that some call a new Golden Age is not, in fact, guaranteed or a done deal, as the saying goes. Your future (both individually and collectively) depends upon what you choose to do or don't do NOW----- in each moment of your present reality."

The future, in other words, does not just happen, but rather it is forged in the foundry of personal choice. Spirit indicates that it is vital that you understand what you are up against as you move to create a more benevolent and life-friendly future. We say this because there are those who would shape the emerging new world and this new age of humanity according to their own selfish ends. Many of them have held the reins of the old world into the present moment through the power of money and politics. Other groups such as the religions and educational institutions have also keep control. These controlling forces will not let go of their power easily.

The Hathor transmission further states:

"Each individual on Earth needs to be prepared for erratic weather patterns, volcanic activity, earthquakes, food shortages, limited water supply, electrical supply disruptions, economic changes, limited gasoline supply, and a host of other life threatening events."

For those interested in keeping up with a rapidly changing Universe. I recommend you can read various internet web sites, many channeled with information that is over 90% accurate. The message from Matthew, received in our home by Betty Pettit on 4-7-06, was 97% accurate. Read these messages at www.matthewbooks.com. You can sign up to receive updates at Matthew-subscribe@yahoogroups.com. Then keep up by reading the "Sedona Journal of Emergence" each month for timely updates on the rapidly changing events.

There should be no fear involved in making your preparations. Look beyond the fourth DMC confusion, the lies (false beliefs) and fear propagated by the politicians, religious leaders, and news media (frequently 40% accurate). Eliminate all fear and become informed about the choices available. All of the sociological events of the third and fourth DMCs are illusions we created. Each human must choose for themselves to either buy into these illusions or find some constructive alternatives. Upon the Earth plane that's the fairness of the free will test. One choice is to continue the inner search, shift your consciousnesses, and ascend in a newly created physical body to the fifth DMC of the New Earth (some call Tara or Planet II).

In the past, everyone on Earth was required to face death at the end of a Galactic cycle. That is no longer the case. You now have a choice. To choose to live will require the creation of a new body to take with you to the fifth DMC. That body you plan to take with you should be free of sickness, pain, and all the other adverse features of a human body residing on a third-fourth DMC planet. If you were planning to graduate and arrive at the portal (doorway to the fifth DMC) in a wheel chair -- because of a sick body, you will have difficulty passing through the portal or gate. There will be guards at the gate working under the guidance of Peter, referred to as Peter in some writings that is waiting at the Golden Gate. There will also be internal portal workers checking your credentials. One check they will make is the physical condition of your body. That check is made because there would be a danger to your body -- if it were sick. A sick body cannot withstand the high frequency energies beyond the gate, in the fifth dimension.

A lack of preparation brings into play some new challenges and confusion. Everyone who has been slow to prepare needs to take action to graduate. We are besieged by disincarnates who died and left their physical body unprepared. Many spirits went up the tunnel of light and successfully joined their family. Others had no idea of what to do. They had they left their physical body with little thought about their future activities. They had never through about what happens after physical death. Many of those Souls who failed to prepare have become Earth bound (ghosts tied to a familiar location), some co-habitat with the living, and others are lost - looking for help and guidance. Many disincarnate wondering Souls need someone to help them.

Every choice you currently make will have a dramatic influence on your future – preparation time for your future is now. You are responsible for preparing to pass through the gate, no one else. After the gate (dimensional doorway) is closed, you will then be faced with another quiet different choice.

First State - Original Thought

Original thought is first cause with nothing before or after it. Original thought is also the beginning of the return to Oneness. It is where the formless first considers form and becomes aware of a specific point or very specific physical location. The first dimension is the Will of The Creator and as a practicing creator your will is your first cause and original thought. This is the consciousness of the mineral and molecular kingdom, for example the awareness of a quartz crystal or awareness of our deoxyribonucleic acid (DNA) molecules in the body. Note these creations generally lack individual self-consciousness. However, the first DMC component parts are aware that they will be the foundations on which our physical forms are constructed. Our first DMC is born of freedom and presented with many choices. The choices made have brought us individually to this point in our evolution and will help us to continue on the Soul's chosen spiritual "time track"within the lower DMCs.

Some examples of these first DMCs components are minerals, water, amino acids, proteins, and genetic codes. Tuning into first DMC is described as being centered upon a single target, a pinpoint of the basic structural features of matter, such as an adamantine particle, neutrino and/or an atom. As with all dimensions, the first DMC is always expanding as new thought forms become available to assist in one's infinite ability to create. As an extension of these infinite abilities, we (those in "Creator School") know that creations initiated by thoughts are a part of the first DMC. In order to manifest those thought forms (a first DMC activity) we utilize first density building blocks and add various forms of energies, density materials, and specific states of dimensional consciousness to complete the manifestation.

By nature, the first DMC centers at a specific point and there is a lack of complete awareness of the other points. In addition, there is a lack of awareness of associated structural features. That is, first DMC lacks awareness of all component parts that comprise a new creation. The whole process involves a series of choices when added together result in a series of creating or un-creating events. To facilitate these creative events (etheric or physical structures), from the first dimensional energies and first density energies requires some of the features of the second and third DMCs. These energies are required for efficiency. For many creative purposes, energies obtained from the first DMC, that is energies required for your creations, can be accessed from any one of the other eleven DMCs. All higher states of consciousness have access to all of the lower states of dimensional consciousness.

Second State - Awareness of Being

Second DMC adds to a first dimensional point, a sequence or a second point of awareness, sometimes defined as a time-line of individual awareness, on the lower astral plane. The second DMC is the beginning of separation and individualization. It is also another beginning stage for the return to Oneness.   Here is where consciousness perceives itself as all that exists. Second DMC entities lack a distinct "Universal" spirit, are devoid of Souls, and essentially are self-absorbed.   It is where the formless first considers form and where creativity ponders manifestation. In the simplest of terms, the second DMC is where conscious thoughts consider an idea for it's relative merit. In very rare circumstances, human spirits have become trapped in second DMC. To understand self and extend one's dimensional capabilities one must seek direction and movement.   These capabilities are required to implement the individualization of specific tasks. Self must recognize its creative awareness, potential, and have purpose as it's guide. Then to accelerate the creation; we add belief, intent, and a degree of enthusiasm to bring "IT " into reality.

The second DMC is the realm of the elementals, where there is a form of limited awareness.   Since the elementals have almost no consciousness, they must receive direction from some outside controlling force. Within second DMC, awareness through mind is not linear since there is "no time." Also in this situation higher is not always better or worse here; it just is. In Buddhism, the second DMC is called "bardos," in some religions second DMC is known as lower Hell, because of the limited awareness.

Within the second DMC is where the birth of space and time, movement, and desire originated and then gradually manifest within the third DMC. It is the starting point from which one seeks knowledge. It then establishes a base for taking that knowledge so it can be assembled into a blueprint. That assembly process requires the beginning stage of how to use knowledge through wisdom. The prevailing belief is that the second DMC is the realm of pure consciousness. Here we find the architectural plan for all creative thought and all creative movement.

The processes of birth and death take place here in the second DMC; not within the third DMC as many believe. Why do you think this is true? Because, all movement and experience begins and ends with thought and thought begins within the second DMC. Thus with thought even within the fourth DMC of the astral plane, we are using second DMC to determine the point and time of physical birth. Likewise within the third DMC of the physical plane we are using second DMC to determine when to experience death and return to the (fourth DMC) astral plane. Read this paragraph again, "carefully", since it is the basis for several multidimensional concepts.

Within the second DMC, those entities called microscopic organisms, plant species, and the lower animal kingdom reside. Yes, these creations have some degree or level of awareness. Thus, the limited development of consciousness occurring within second DMC has been referred to as that animal component of our being. The difficulty of defining second DMC is due to the fact that each individual experience determines the features within it's own unique state of consciousness.

Here in second DMC basic instincts dominate, which may be slightly different under different environmental conditions. For example, the driving force for survival in the arctic compared to survival in the African desert is an individual experience that varies with each entity. These survival instincts involve the varying needs for feeding, covering, sheltering, and fighting for survival.

In addition, the drive for procreation predominates here in second DMC. This involves the need to continue creating new physical vehicles (bodies) to maintain the species. Also, these entities are developing an instinctual need to have a respect for all of life and an ability to maintain balance throughout their challenging experiences. Those higher states of DMC all have some of these individual features of the second DMC. That is, the second DMC is a part of your multidimensional consciousness.

In order to understand the importance of the second DMC we need to become aware of all natural systems. Thus, the importance of becoming familiar with the elementals and the many second density creations discussed earlier. Understanding of various natural systems' functions is a stepping-stone to developing the third state of DMC. As part of the third DMC lessons on Earth is that we are learning to become creators. Remember Earth is a "Creator School." As part of those lessons in "Creator School", we will need to become aware of a requirement to respect and honor all the components of creation, including all manifested "thought forms" within the second DMC. Failure to continue your honoring and respecting of all previous created illusions, will significantly limit your spiritual evolution.

Those individuals and a society that destroys anything for selfish motives have a price to pay in terms of their spiritual future. Through the destruction of any part of creation, a lesson is learned. To repeat these destructive patterns repeatedly, may be quite painful and require repeated incarnations within the lower states of dimensional consciousness. Humanity upon Earth is currently faced with the consequences of raping the planet of its physical and natural resources. Removing oil, coal, minerals, rock, water, plant species, and trees from Mother Earth has caused many energetic imbalances within the Earth's structure. As a result, the negative ledger against humanity continually increases. What have humans given in return for the sacrifices made by Mother Earth?

As we begin to realize that all components of creation began as "thought forms" created by some Creator Soul working with spirit, we may need to be cautious of what we think. As we carefully examine all the component parts of a second density and second DMC, we can begin to understand that all component parts are present in their specific location for a purpose. Then we should develop a greater awareness of how each second DMC component of all natural systems fit together to comprise the whole. We develop these understandings of natural systems in order to maintain balance. Without balance, we destroy nature, mother Earth, and destroy our bodies to bring on physical death. Our physical bodies were designed to live thousands of years. What happened? What has created the massive degree of imbalance? How do we get back on "Track?" These are questions of utmost importance. The answers can help each one understand why Earth at the end of this age in 2012. Because of all the destruction humanity has inflicted on Mother Earth she has chosen to cleans herself of the excessive number of parasitic humans. Yes I am one of those parasites. In fact, most everyone reading these words has been a parasite on Mother Earth. She has been very patient these thousands of years during the dark cycle.

Before proceeding in our discussion let's tie in the concepts of conscious, subconscious and super-conscious " mind levels" as related to the lower five levels of DMC. The conscious mind is the portal to the third DMC. Here as we expand on the concept of "clock time," a linear measure that began in second DMC we need to understand more about time. To some extent, the concept of clock time has been perfected within third DMC. Clock time is used to facilitate an understanding of how a series of events can be arranged on a changing "time line." The "time line" series of past, present, and future events can then be placed in a "time frame" or loosely arranged in a series of related thought forms. These patterns are part of the Earth School curriculum. As a part of that curriculum there is a need to categorize and store these thought forms within our various computers and Akashic records. All of those records can be accessed in the future for a multitude of purposes.

The subconscious mind is the portal to the first, second and fourth dimensions. Within the first, second, and fourth DMCs the concept of time are not linear rather they are arranged in the form of a continuum, or steady state flow pattern. The super-conscious mind (spiritual connection) is the portal to the fifth DMC and beyond, where there is "no time". Within the fifth DMC, we become aware of the importance of realizing that all events within past lives, present lives, and future lives are all occurring "NOW" in "no time." Thus, past lives and future lives are illusions. However, they are real illusions and serve a purpose. In all situations and all states of DMCs "ALL EVENTS HUMANS EXPERIENCE DURING ANY INCARNATION ARE FOR EVOLUTIONARY PURPOSES AND ARE IN DEVINE ORDER."

Third State - Cause and Effect – Duality

Third Dimension adds to the second dimensional features of a point and line and all other features of the lower complex organisms, the concepts of length, height, breath, and volume. All the awareness and experience gained in the second DMC serves as a foundation for making choices in the third DMC.   This is the consciousness of the animal kingdom and higher humans. Anything within the third DMC vibrates at a maximum of 9,000 cycles per second. Here we observe the direct experience of cause and effect because of free will and choice. Our choices create the quality of life within third DMC. Each choice is processed through mind in thought in order to create a template or etheric mold for physical manifestation into the third DMC. Once that template (hologram) is created, it than can be carried through to a series of procedures, for physical manifestation. Elsewhere in this book, there is a description of that process. Consciously remember, that for a physical creation to be maintained within the physical realm, it will require a continued source of conscious energy patterns. Conscious energy patterns similar to those that brought the item into physicality will be needed for it to remain on Earth. As long as there is that conscious energy pattern available in the minds of human consciousness that structure should survive. Withdraw the human consciousness supporting energy and that physical structure will disappear. You can anticipate that many of the physical creations dotting the surface of planet Earth will disappear as consciousness is withdrawn as to hold its physical shape. This process may be quite frightening to many.

Remember the creation of a holographic template is one of the first steps in creating new body parts. Do you know how to imagine what various (body parts) templates looks like? Perfecting one's imagination is a key first step one should be learning in "Creator School." Some may say "Oh, You Are Just Imagining That"; remind them everything on Earth originated from an imagination. Everything present within the third dimension is a figment of someone's imagination or the imagination of the collective consciousness. Everything on Earth began with someone having an imaginative thought. Remove the consciousness that created the imagination (that was manifest in the physical) and all of the physical objects you observe within the world, will disappear. Some will ask -- when will this disappearing act begin?

Assuming that all galactic events are on schedule and that the three days of darkness occur at the end of 2012 that event could occur at any time. The possibility exists that during the three days of darkness when everyone goes into a deep sleep then consciousness that held the illusion in place would have been removed. However, spirit indicates that the disappearing could start and proceed over the following years.

When you are aware of this probability or possibility, you have a sense of what to expect. Thus, when your car disappears you will know that everything is proceeding on schedule. There will be no reason to fear because there is nothing you can do about the disappearances anyway. Your objective will be to accept whatever happens with joy and thanksgiving that you are coming closed to your arrival on the "New Earth." Therefore, your task is not to think adverse thoughts but to prepare consciously.

Preparation time for graduation and ascension is short, since as of December 2010 there are only two more years until December 2012, a closing-point during "The Shift." Somewhere around 2011 to 2013, the null zone (intense band of photons) of the photon belt is scheduled to arrive. The null zones light density will absorb all electromagnetic energies including light and electrical energies, to create total darkness.

States of dimensional consciousness are the blueprint and the third DMC is the architecture. Here consciousness brings into play the building process of structure and form, brought forth through belief via thought. It is the consciousness of creatorship, a realm of dominion and responsibility. Evolution is progressive here, not linear as some believe. As advancement in consciousness occurs, we have the following sequence; consciousness becomes awareness, self-awareness develops, and then source-awareness realizes from whence we came and where all creative energies originate. Some may, because of their previous programming state that everything is from "God." Alternatively, others state that, everything is from "God Source." In my opinion, the belief in the concept of a male dominated Father God is very limiting and discriminatory. What happened to a belief in Mother God? A possible alternative that may be more accurate is, "Everything is from "God/Goddess Source."

A greater understanding, based on my scientific background could be more inclusive. Thus one could state that in terms of all of creations, that which brought it into existence can be called "ALL THAT EVER WAS, EVER WILL BE AND IS or ALL THAT HAS ORIGINATED FROM THE GREAT CENTRAL SUN - THE SOURCE OF ALL THAT IS." Even this definition is restrictive because it appears to overlook or bring into consciousness the creation of an infinite number of dimensional parallel Universes (DPUs).

170

Much of my typing and printed information originated through my "High Self," as guide to information required or from direct thought forms. Thus, the above concept of creation more accurately describes what my "High Self" considers an all-encompassing "Energy Source" for creating with our limited consciousness. With this understanding then I am required to seek out some more solid knowledge on which to build some insights about "Dimensional Parallel Universes," (DPUs).

Remember your reality may be different from mine; each one is just as valid. So ignore those who question whether your reality is valid. Your reality may have a minor relationship to their reality. No two realities of individuals residing anywhere within the Universe have identical realities. To continue a debate on what is real and unreal can be immediately resoled when everyone realizes that all thought forms and physical creations are illusions. None of them are real, so what's the big deal. That is not a real car in your driveway -- it is an illusion. It is a "thought form" that can disappear when the collective consciousness that helped created it and now helps hold it on Earth, is withdrawn.

In our third DMC linear experiences, more is often considered better. Linear experiences of necessity are subject to the laws of polarity (duality). More or less debt, more or less pollution, higher or lower taxes, and high or low insurance rates are examples of the philosophy of less and more. The more is better rule does not extend to conscious dimensions above the fourth DMC. Thus, be prepared to drop the concept that more is better. Clear that false belief from your belief system. Hanging on to any false belief will slow your spiritual evolution.

Souls experiencing third DMC inhabit a gross matter physical (carbon-based) low frequency body as their vehicle for housing the Soul and movement. The time involved in using this body on Earth is relatively brief, between 70 to 100 years, compared to our total Soul existence of several million years. Generally, a Spirit with a Soul, a feature that distinguishes them from some other creations, inhabits our humanoid appearing bodies. Your new fifth DMC less dense physical body will be a silicon crystalline Light Body that has the potential to live for thousands of years. That illusionary time span (there is no time in fifth DMC) will have limited meaning after you graduate.

However, realize that scientists have created human clones and robotic humanoids. These creations are just as real illusions are just as real as you and I, but lack a Soul. In addition, we have found humans who had their Soul snatched or they gave their Heart and Soul to another entity voluntarily or sometimes forcibly. Once a large part of their Soul is gone they become robotic, have considerable difficulty relating to those with a complete Soul.

How many parts of your Soul are missing? Also, how many Soul fragments do you have attached to your body that belongs to another Soul? Some bodies actually have more than one complete soul present, primarily because of previous contracts. A majority of humans have damaged Souls with many missing Soul parts. Make sure to keep your Soul together and functionally efficient. As previously discussed, many humans have Soul fragments, taken from others without their permission. In some of these situations, an individual may have been trying to provide help without permission, a form of misguided compassion.

The physical third DMC (body) vehicle is restricted or locked into a space-time matrix held by gravity to the Earth plane (surface). However, we also come in with various spiritual bodies like the Astral body that can leave the body and travel outside the Earth plane. This type of travel is called astral travel or an "out of body experience." These experiences are very common in fact, most everyone experiences an out of body experience during their sleep. Many dreams are in actuality "out of body experiences". Learning to control your astral travels and learning to time travel, outlined in many books, are good practices for future use in other states of dimensional consciousness.

Within the lower stages of third DMC, our second DMC state of our multidimensionality also functions to provide the consciousness for survival. We also utilize other second DMC features by spending time on having enough food, sufficient cover for the body, shelter, a mate, and working to create and raise children (new physical bodies) to house souls interested in incarnating on Earth. When these thoughts are our primary conscious efforts, we need to ask; "am I missing something by concentrating on these second DMC instinctive (survival) techniques"? Yes, beyond a doubt there are many more valuable and important experiences for those souls trapped in the third DMC, other than just surviving. Those more valuable experiences, are within our feelings or memories (outlined in our contracts) of why and what we came here to accomplish, in the first place.

Every Soul incarnating on Earth outlined a contract before birth. It would be advisable to become familiar with your contract. After all, you set it up for a purpose and as your guidelines for this life. That contract was designed to help you carry out experiences that your advance your spiritual self and you Soul evolution.

As advanced spiritual beings, we came to the "Earth Plane School Room " for advanced studies in how to create or un-create various manifestations. However many have forgotten how to effectively use their creative abilities. What happened to slow our creative abilities? In part outside forces (controllers) withdrew our ability to remember, a process called "cloaking." We turned our power over to others. In addition, these creative potentials were purposely slowed down so we could track (monitor) the consequences of each creation. However, there is hope in recovering these capabilities. As we evolve in consciousness and take our power back, we can begin to "remember" who we are and continue our creative activities. That is "remembering" that we all are free to make our own decisions and learn from them. The inability to use these potentials is related to many of our false and limiting beliefs. Our creative capabilities increase as we move up through third DMC.

As you shift your consciousness through the twelve levels of third DMC evolution, you can open up to align your capabilities so that physically unseen realities beyond the veil (into the spirit realm) become just as real as the physical world. You can develop an ability to communicate with the realm of spirit and seek out help from your guides, angels and other spirits helpers. As you progress spiritually, you can consciously align yourself with your Super-consciousness (High Self). By accessing that component part of your mind, you have opened up a channel that connects you to "SOURCE" (All That Is, God). Then you have access to unlimited information from your High Self Spiritual Council and other spiritual sources for creating, maintaining your health, and becoming an unlimited multidimensional being. Then there is no limit to your capabilities.

From my experiences, one very effective method of communicating with my High Self and the unseen spiritual world is to first practice during daily meditations and listen to the "still small voices" within. During this quite time, you can also connect with members if you're High Self Spiritual Council, Angels, Spirit Guides, Central Sun

Light Beings, Spiritual Technicians, Archangels, Creators, Sananda, and an endless list of other spiritual helpers. You are listening to thoughts not audible words. Always use discernment when listening to those thoughts. There are many "fakers" in the spirit realm, whose purpose is to manipulate and cause confusion. Ask if the entity communicating is from the Light and serves the Creators and God/Goddess within.

A valuable tool to assist in these communications is accurate pendulum dowsing. Pendulum dowsing helps validate the accuracy of the one's intuition, visions and other forms of information provided by these still small voices within. Inaccurate pendulum dowsing can be very destructive. Accurate dowsing relates to belief and confidence in your capabilities, followed by spiritual protection to insure accuracy.

As previously mentioned, one helpful suggestion for speeding up your evolution is to remember why you came to Earth. A lack of interest in using the guiding concepts (within our contract) causes a tendency to drift through life. When someone is unaware of their planned contract, they have difficulty staying focused during their current incarnation. As a result, these Souls have chose the option is to keep returning to Earth lifetime after lifetime until you learned how to stay focused. Eventually you can learn to focus your attention, then proceed to complete the agreed upon lessons. You designed your contract; with the help of your High Self, thus why not follow the guidelines your group helped you set up and you agreed to be arriving here on Earth. After all, you have spent many lifetimes, each of which has a contract that was based on your proposed spirit-Soul evolutionary path. I find it disheartening that so few humans follow the guidelines of their contract.

We all know of individual Souls who are stuck in a rut, making the same mistakes repeatedly, like a broken record. Apparently, many Souls become so involved in their physical activities they become sidetracked while living on Earth. This is evident when talking with many different people. I have asked many individuals about their contract. Through the years, I have asked others about their understanding of contracts designed to assist a Soul just arriving on Earth. The majority of the time I received the following answers. -- "I did not know I had a contract." Or -- "Is It Really Important to Know about My Contract?"

Yes! It is very important to know as much as you can about why you came to Earth and what you proposed to do. Anyone can ask to see his or her contract. Time travel into the astral plane (fourth DMC) with the guidance of your High Self and ask to look in your "life contract file." Then once you have had a chance to look over the contract, request to meet with your committee and have them go over each item with you. After reviewing your contract, you may discover you would like to remove some sections or parts and add new sections or parts. Then make a proposal to your committee. With sufficient committee votes and your desire to pay attention to the new contract, approval of a new revised contract may be forthcoming.

Young and old Souls entering the third DMC often have difficulty staying aware and fully conscious of the physical, mental, and emotional reality they have chosen on Earth. For a majority of Souls currently on Earth now, those who lived on either Atlantis or Lemuria, a percentage of that difficulty is the result of a loss in their memory. Much of that memory loss goes back to "The Fall" in consciousness that occurred when Atlantis and Lemuria sank under the oceans. Consequently, those Souls and other new Souls we all have taken on a significant challenge in trying to remembering our contracts, because of the memory loss. Without a memory of our contracts and an inability to remember past lives, future live and present events, we struggle, continually looking for "THE ORIGINAL PLAN" for our lives.

As we work to develop our multidimensional consciousness capabilities, our memories will return and we will know about our contract. As you shift your consciousness to take advantage of your multidimensional capabilities, you can shift to the higher dimensional states and remember. Even though you're primary state of DMC is third and fourth you still have an important option. During meditation you can tap into your fifth, sixth, and seventh DMC.

Once there you have some access of your old memories. The challenge is to shift your overall consciousness to a higher level so that you can utilize that information in helpful way. Without an enlarged brain, characteristic of the fifth DMC you will have challenges until you have completed your Light Body awakening and activation. Thus, it is very important to strive towards Light Body awakening and take on your fifth DMC.

Many humans on Earth are unaware that a majority of the planets in our solar system have thriving societies, albeit in dimensions outside a third DMC duality pattern. A majority of these societies have evolved to fifth density (and fifth DMC) or higher. Many third DMC minded scientists appear to be unaware of other dimensional realities beyond the five senses of the third-fourth DMC. Since their reality is limited, they have reached many false conclusions.

For example, many state that "there is no life on Venus". The Hathor's, are a thriving society on Venus, based on channeled information from Tom Kenyon in Australia, by entities who have traveled through Venus on their way to Earth and others who have carried out remote viewing of Venus. The Hathors have frequently made an effort to inform Earth's scientists about other realities in different messages. Most scientists have yet to understand their messages, even believe the messages are real, apparently because these events fail to meet the tests of an artificially designed "scientific method." Some have defined these limiting "scientific" states of consciousness as "tunnel vision." Tunnel vision comes about by constantly looking down (straight ahead linearly) a narrow limiting third DMC tunnel, essentially ignoring the spiritually designed intuitive sensing systems they own to look on each side of the tunnel.

Some limiting beliefs originate from "scientific proof. "To state that something has been scientifically proven has limited value and is generally used to mislead individuals and/or groups in order to take advantage of them. Since all reality is based on beliefs, most scientific experiments (even double blinded) are controlled by the mind of the scientist who designed the experiment. Scientific proof when held up as an all-knowing "God of reality", where scientists become the "Priests of What's Real" is neither proof nor a basis for reality.

Following along with the statement "you must have scientific proof" can slow your conscious evolution and that of the planet. The so-called "scientific proof" may have been obtained by the conscious manipulation of experimental data, by using devious statistical jargon. The egoistical -- "know it all" mind set of science is just one more painful lesson humanity is faced with. Those with closed minds cherish many of these scientifically based third DMC limiting beliefs. They build their "ego" with these limited beliefs. Someone who has it all figured out, who is so close minded, and has no interest in listening to your views, should be avoided. These comments are not true of all scientists. Many scientists are waking up to understanding quantum mechanics, the unseen spiritual world and many related paradigms.

Several scientists I have known in the past have stagnated in their beliefs and as a result, they appear trapped in their illusions of reality. My experiences at Texas A&M University, following the scientific "dogma" for 26 years, revealed to me that many "scientists" become very close-minded. They become stuck in false belief systems. Be careful when considering their opinions no matter what their affiliated institution. Also watch out for those web sites or individuals who state, "Let me separate truth from fiction for you," they also have an agenda.

Those individuals, who limit their reality to their five physical senses, appear to be hiding within a tunnel of fear. Fear of the unknown, a fear that is similar to those who are fearful of physical death, unable to visit the fourth DMC where they could visit with their deceased relatives. All fears are to be eliminated and replaced with LOVE, for a myriad of reasons. Realize that a majority of all reality, over 77% resides outside the realm of third DMC. In one sense, the third state of DMC is a form of tunnel vision. The majority of our reality comes from our intuition, the inner sensing system that can communicate with other aspects of our multidimensionality. All significant scientific discoveries originate from the higher dimensional states of consciousness.

Multidimensional consciousness occurs within our conscious, subconscious, and our superconscious mental bodies. The mental processing is not an external event. That is, it does not occur "out there" somewhere. Our internal sensing system allows the human mind to process data received from our sensing systems picked up from sight, taste, smell, hearing, and feeling. These senses function in the subconscious during dream states, awake or asleep. Intergalactic travel, time travel, and remote viewing are all based on our sensing system as related to different states of DMC. These activities take place within one's consciousness. Individuals, who have taken advantage of these sensing systems (talents), have evolved to overcome the limits of the physical third DMC. As one develops their multidimensional reality they discover a vast reality of Dimensional Parallel Universes (DPUs) within, similar to the vast number of DPUs without, "So Within-So Without."

We came to Earth (Creator School) to learn how to perfect our creative skills. These skills include our ability to experience and control the emotions of happiness, stress, love, fear, and joy. Each emotion and mental challenge we have created was based on what we believe and think at that "Now Time." Those mental thoughts, energized with emotion become the building blocks on which multidimensional consciousness is awakened.

Thus, you need to become open minded, review your contracts, and get busy implementing your chosen paths (goals). Then, take control of your emotions, and perfect your creative talents to assist all of creation, yourself and others. To the extent you have accomplished this responsibility is a measure of your Soul's spiritual development. The philosophy called Service To Others (STO) is very helpful technique for accelerating spiritual development.

Another factor that limits spiritual progress is your inability to remember that your Soul originated from your Oversoul, a seventh, eight, or ninth DMC consciousness. You are one of many Soul parts that came from that Oversoul. Each of these Souls is a called parallel life and they are also a part of your Oversoul. Every human Soul residing on Earth has at least 12 parallel lives, some over 1,000 parallel lives. Also all lives currently lived in third DMC realities of past and future are a part of our "NOW" multidimensional reality. Parallel lives can be lived throughout the Universe, galaxies, and on a multitude of different planets.

Some lives may be in "spirit form" while others have incarnated on planets in physical bodies. Some lives reside in a matter world while others reside in the antimatter world. We created, (separated out) these Soul companions for expanding the consciousness of our Oversoul. Each parallel life was created so it could have it's own unique experiences and challenges that assists (expands) the conscious development of the group consciousness (Oversoul).

All parallel lives have some degree of connection. Many can sense the activities of their parallel lives. For example, a parallel life on another planet with a specific disease ailment can transfer those symptoms to the Soul residing on planet Earth through a process called "Bleed Through." This process is very common and provides the "medical establishment" with a challenge because of their difficulty in diagnosing the causes of some symptoms their patient's experience.

As each parallel life goes through its challenging experiences, the outcome of those events adds to the spiritual development of the Oversoul.

Once you have developed your fifth DMC, your capability to observe and interact with these other parallel lives (realities) on other planets will increase. Regardless, of whether they were living in the past, present and future, or possibly living (residing) in various other states of DMC.

There is another factor to consider when sensing these parallel lives from a third DMC perspective. That vision of sensing another parallel life is influenced by the emotions or thought forms (bleed through) of other humans living on the Earth currently. That bleed through can originate from a Soul that has no connection with your Oversoul family. The point is that all Souls throughout creation are connected. The challenge comes in separating out these different types of bleed through energies. Here again discernment is important as well as contact with your High Self Spiritual Council to secure their opinion to events taking place. You could with additional shifts in consciousness visit with your parallel realities on any planet in the Universe. That potential will gradually become a reality within the fifth DMC.

The most appropriate time to make connections with your spiritual assistants, High Self Spiritual Council and parallel realities is when a majority of other humans near-by are semi-resting, between 2 - 4 AM. Many have left their bodies where their conscious activities reside within their astral bodies. Whenever bleed through from other lives interferes with our life here NOW, we can clear out those energies, assist our parallel life, and block those energies from manifesting in our physical bodies. This process is accomplished, by requesting help from your High Self Spiritual Council and many other Spiritual assistants.

As we progress consciously, we learn how to work with our parallel realities. Through the spiritual evolutionary process of understanding our multidimensional realities within the third, fourth and fifth DMC we gradually become aware of where we came from (where "Home" is) and why we have taken so many side trips. Then the Soul component (entity) residing on Earth "NOW" begins to understand how the choices and insights accumulated from each multiple reality (entity) contribute to the Oversoul's evolution. Through this somewhat complicated design, the Oversoul expands it's total multidimensional realities and spiritual evolution. Progressive shifts in consciousness involve a remembering and tuning into the lessons experienced within each schoolroom experience.

As we remember and build on experiences, we can change our beliefs and/or increase their accuracy. Then, we have opened our consciousness to create beliefs that are more efficient. These new beliefs will aid in our shift in consciousness. Yes, all physical-mental-emotional activities (games people play) within third and fourth DMC, are real illusions. We are the actors involved in putting on a play. As we sit back and observe the games people play, with "Non Attachment", we can just enjoy the play. To become attached to any illusion is very unwise. All parts of the play are in Devine order, thus there is no need to judge the other actors and actresses in the play.

All acts within the play at Earth School occur for a purpose. One of our major goals, as we watch the play is to practice "Total Acceptance" of what is taking place since each actor is doing what they are supposed to do. Together we helped pick the actresses and actors, helped write and designed the play, and now we are involved in putting the play on so others can enjoy it. So let's accept each person in the play, learn from the other cast members, then thank each other, and clap when the play is over.

Everyone has free will and can choose who to associate with in the play. During these associations, each of the actors can feed back many of your weaknesses for possible strengthening. Remember you are much more efficient in recognizing the weakness in others when you have experienced that weakness. Also, consider the concept that you see your weaknesses in others, a feedback loop. Thus, there is never a justification for the judgment of any actor.

There is no need to blame anyone else for your "foul-ups". You chose those foul-ups for the lessons they provided. So eliminate those false beliefs, called "Blame Games" or "War Games." Yes, we all realize the number of actresses and actors within the play has become quite large. Thus, sometime we are drawn into a play we would have preferred to avoid. As a result, we may have also been drawn into the outcome of the play that was outside our preferred path. Regardless we would not have been involved unless there was some lesson we needed to experience. So again, we are faced with accepting the associate actresses and actors as they are and thank them for doing their job.

Regardless, even though we accept their contribution we still had free will to accept or reject their activities. Some may say to others "it was your fault or it would't have happened if you had't caused it." "They did it to me."

You create your own reality. Your EGO has failed to accept responsibility. Who is taking responsibility? Why does our ego fail to accept responsibility? In addition, why do we think you are so intelligent you can tell anyone else what to do, or say? We could give our opinion and, that's it. To violate anyone's free will is against Universal Law. There is a serious price to pay when violating Universal Laws. Within the "Subtle Energy Research Program," we have had to take several Souls to Universal Court to resolve these violations. I suggest each one reading this report, obtain a copy of some Universal Laws (in books and on the internet) and study them carefully. What we can do legally, is change ourselves to become more Loving and accepting of every member of the play - THEY JUST ARE - THE WAY THEY ARE SUPPOSED TO BE – THAT IS WHY THEY ARE HERE IN OUR PLAY.

We create and un-create by what we think, a mental body function. Whatever you think consciously and activate (energize) by verbalization, with added emotion your thought is transferred to the sub-conscious where it is acted upon. The sub-conscious has no reasoning capabilities; it will help create any thought form you bring into consciousness. The subconscious's response to your thoughts always is; "I can do that - just watch and see".

Harmful thoughts can manifest in others and ourselves. When someone asks for your prayers do you see their challenge cleared out or do you add energy to their challenge to make it more intense. Just thinking of a supposed imbalance (disease in another person) could actually help create that imbalance and obviously increase it's severity. Mentally observe all imbalances to be dissipating. Makes a big difference you know. Therefore, avoid attachments while watching the play. Then make sure you keep alert in workshops, social clubs, movies, television shows, etc. so you can avoid all of the confusion during these last days leading up to 2012. To become pulled into or become attached to the confusion will lower your dimensional state of consciousness.

Keep your shields up; avoid bringing into consciousness brain washing, controlling subliminal messages (thought forms) in video games, the movies, and on television. As you already know illusions, based on limiting beliefs, were designed for control purposes. The process of installing limiting beliefs has persisted for thousands of years on Earth. The objective has been to manipulate those who have been "dumbed down" through fear, poisons, drugs, and other hidden techniques. Those souls "dumbed down" are much easier to manipulate (control) and eliminate physically. The controllers especially notice those individuals who become familiar with the game and get in their way.

Controllers within third DMC have used the communication media, educational systems, churches, politics, and other means to convince the "dumbed down" to accept fear consciousness, even fear of physical death. Why would there be an interest in controlling other humans and reducing the world's third DMC population? Also to what degree do you realize that you have been "dumbed down," for control purposes? Spend some time studying what is happening on Earth.

In addition to the functions of the mental body in third DMC, several other bodies also have a significant influence on our creations. For example, the physical, emotional, spiritual, and I AM bodies influence our creative potentials. Thus, when we realize that the mental body is not the sole composer of one's picture of reality or the quality of one's creations we can call upon the heart to guide the mind. In addition, each component part of our reality exists in both the Matter and Anti-Matter Realms. Thus, any requests for adjustments of the matter body components should also include a similar request for adjustments to the anti-matter body.

Ideally, within the matter realm we are 93% matter and 7% anti-matter. Our parallel reality in the anti-matter realm has the mirror image of 93% anti-matter and 7% matter. When these measurements deviate from these percentages, ask that these ideal balances be re-created. You may need to research why the imbalances occurred. If you are unaware of what caused the imbalance it could return. A lack of balance between matter and anti-matter energy intensities can be harmful when either extreme is detected.

Third DMC involves an understanding of "clock time," a concept that involves motion and allows you to tune into a specific series of events (time frame) or state of consciousness on a time track and/or time line. Within those densities other than the third, there is no time. However, because God/Goddess and everything in the Universe is constantly changing, from the third density through the twelfth density this one aspect of time, change is occurring. Within the continually evolving spectrum of the Universe there are principles governing the change -- that do not change. The function that generates the change does not change. Thus, we must conclude that there are aspects of God/Goddess and the Creators that do not change. Since we are all aspects of a Creator, there are aspects of the Spirit and Soul that do not change. The challenge we have on Earth is there are not words to describe those unchanging aspects. The Founders indicate that what has been termed the "Un-manifested Void," sometimes called the thirteenth dimension. The "Un-manifested Void" is apparently an aspect of God/Goddess that does not yet know itself. This is a different aspect then the one that is unchanging.

Once you truly understand that time is energy, you can learn to time travel along a time track or time line to recover experiences in the past or future (third dimensional concepts). Some call these experiences "visions". Remember all mental thoughts (events) occur within the Now, thus so-called past and future events (visions) are in reality happening "Now." However, by using this process of recovery (time travel) we can move into a specific time frame and change an event. That is, we can change so called past or future events (visions) in NOW TIME. Yes, we have gone through this process many times with individual Souls who have had persistent challenges that are difficult to transmute. Those current challenges were the result of bleed through from a past or future life. The cause of the imbalance was elevated by going to the site where they re-lived the event, turned it into a positive experience.

Many suggest we use the concept of "clock time" wisely, realizing that time is a concept that is relative to our lower third dimensional states of consciousness. Although time appears to be linear, science now believes that time, as a sequence of measures, is in reality orientated in a circular-spiral type pattern that folds back on itself. This revised belief about time helps explain why time is gradually collapsing towards zero. As time moves along the spiral, it becomes compressed. As the diameter of the spiral changes eventually it will become compressed to zero. To many who are sensitive there is no question that time is passing much faster than it did a few years ago. We are approaching the "End of Time" as we move out of the third DMC into the fifth DMC where there will be "No Time".

Every day as we come closer to 2012 our physical work time (clock time) will decrease. In order to adapt to this change it may be helpful to consider the value of each physical activity before engagement. You may discover you can eliminate or clear out a majority of all old behavior (work) patterns; especially those that no longer serve a useful purpose. Throw away all that "old stuff" that ties you to the past behavior patterns and old memories. We have recently discovered that the dark forces have infiltrated the 'old stuff" as a means of influencing (controlling) your activities. <u>Moving "old stuff" into the fifth DMC will be impossible, so now is the time to clear it out.</u> Those old presents, pictures, nick-knacks, coins, records, etc, will be of no use. They only tie you to the third density and third DMC. If that is where you plan to reside on a future third density planet, you will have to leave your body and all that "old stuff" anyway.

Through a series of conscious and subconscious experiences, we use our sensing system of sight, hearing, touch, taste and smell in third and fourth dimensions and record all of these activities within cellular memory and/or within our Akashic (permanent) records. By remembering (time travel), we can call up these stored events and bring them into the present third - fourth - fifth DMC. As we correlate these stored events with the present moment, we gain understanding and healing. Parts of the healing results occur when these events are transmuted into a beneficial energy pattern.

Also by remembering, we can tune into our multidimensional consciousness so that our conscious, subconscious (unconscious), and super-conscious selves can merge. As a result, our true selves are revealed and we have a foundation on which to build our multidimensional realities. Then it will be possible to be simultaneously in the higher densities while experiencing the lower densities. This potential is facilitated by merging our perceived truths with previously established limiting beliefs and they have them cleared out. Then we can open up our consciousness to new more efficient beliefs with new insights. That process is called Soul evolution or a dimensional shift in consciousness as you strive to take advantage of your colossal multidimensional consciousness.

Soul evolution appears to be an awakening of life's consciousness, as discussed within Michael Newton's book "Journey of Souls". Many believe that we evolve more rapidly when we awaken and focus our attention on understanding progressive unfoldment. This process may involve, a specific experience, known as a "Wake Up" call. Some

184

"Wake"Ups" can be dramatic events that shake our very foundation so we are forced to make changes in order to survive. Other "Wake Up" calls may involve experiences termed "out of body travels" or "near death experiences." During a near death experience one or more of your many bodies present, leave and move into another state of DMC. While there, you make significant changes with the help of your High Self Spiritual Council.

Restated, once you have arrived in another state of consciousness during a "near death experience," you we may experience various forms of counseling. As a result, changes are initiated that create a new revised contract for your life; you take off on a new exciting time frame. The new time frame or altered paradigm (new contract) is designed to help you continue your physical third to fifth DMC activities. Some of these changes result in an expansion of your multidimensional consciousness, as you become much more sensitive to your higher DMC aspects.

Tuning in involves a recall of past third DMC experiences. The recall or remembering requires time travel, returning to the experience, bringing up the details, and then relating them to the current now "period." Again, note time is a concept relative to third DMC, past, present, and future or "past lives" and "future lives" are only valid concepts here in the third-fourth DMC. However, in order to take advantage of our multidimensional reality we need pay close attention to our third DMC real illusions. Then it will be helpful to consider what additional evolutionary tools are available in other DMCs, that is, tools for expanding our multidimensional consciousness. For example, consider the unconscious mind as a portal to first, second, and fourth DMCs. Remember these are timeless DMCs and have available various tools for Creator School. The unconscious mind can tap into these valuable tools.

As you learn to pass through the portals, you can access your multidimensional reality. Throughout the consciousness shifting processes, the Soul's evolution requires exercising your free will to make choices. A percentage of these choices are made in concert with a group Soul (Oversoul) or Soul Family that come together life after life to develop new more efficient and accurate belief systems. Everyone is collecting these experiences in order to know what is true for the Now Time. However, truth is always evolving, becoming more than what it was before. Thus, one could say these "Now" truths are illusions, since tomorrow, new

"Now" truths will emerge to create updated illusions. These new illusions can more closely approach the energy of "ALL THAT IS' (PURE LOVE), the only "Reality" that is not an illusion. From one perspective, Soul evolution is a process of "Knowing" by working to perceive the reality of your original design of PURE LOVE (The Highest of Truths). PURE LOVE will eventually lead you to Source (Goddess/God) (Amma/Abba), and your "Return Home." By following the commandment, "Thou Shall Love Thy Neighbor as Thyself," we can live our lives with No Attachments, No Judgments, and No Resistance.

The process of Soul evolution is in a sense subdivided into stages. Within each stage of third DMC, there are twelve levels. These are, 1. The early level of third DMC is dependent on others. 2. Next, we gain trust and respect for others and ourselves. 3. Then we concentrate on developing the capability to become self-dependent and/or self-sufficient. 4. At this point, we grasp (understand) how important Self Love is. 5. Then we make (implement) the use of Love so that it works for us individually. 6. Once we really Love ourselves we now develop a Love for others. 7. By practicing loving, we become stable, mentally and emotionally. 8. We seek out reliable information (knowledge) available to bring balance into our lives. 9. Then a desire and willingness comes into consciousness, to Love all of creation. 10. Now, we must commit time and effort to slow down and tune into the other DMC throughout all of creation. 11. Then when other Souls make requests for our help, or when we observe an imbalance in nature, we now have the tools composed of LOVE, in many forms, available to us - to be of assistance. 12. We accept our responsibility to work toward spiritual development, fine tune our consciousness, and prepare to shift to the fourth-fifth DMC.

A question each every one of us can ask is; "at what stage am I?" The next question is; " have I become self-dependent?" Just because others make their requests for your help, does not make you self-dependent or qualified to assist others in their life's major decisions. Unfortunately, many individuals offer their help and sometimes-even charge for it, while they are still in Stage 1, "The Dependent Stage." What is the clue (without judgment) that reveals their stage of development? One main feature of this stage is evidenced by a lack of responsibility for self, always dependent on someone else. Those Souls have just got started along their third DMC time line.

For an individual to be of "Service To Others" they must first Love themselves and Love others, at least you have reached stage 6. For someone to offer help to others they need to make <u>Love Work for Themselves</u> in Stage 5. It is impossible to move on to Stage 6, that is, Love Others until you complete stage 5. It is impossible to Love and accept someone else when you are unable to Love and accept yourself. Attempts to be of Service To Others (Without Love) can cause serious imbalances in those seeking help. This is a form of misguided compassion. The whole process involves a lack of self-responsibility, immature behavior patterns, limited understanding, and false beliefs that together creates confusion in self and those associated with you.

When these states of confusion are forced onto family members, these behavior patterns help create generation after generation of dysfunctional families, a common occurrence. Remember, when you lack self Love and others request your help (while you are in a state of confusion) your advice can severely damage another person. There is a price to pay for such behavior in your life and the life of another. When you become aware of your limitations you can admit you don't know how to respond to their request. Then the most effective and helpful way to respond is to suggest they confer with someone else who has a deep Love for Themselves and Others. That individual is generally beyond stage 6 and is on Earth to be of Service To Others with kindness, consideration, and Love. Ideally seek out those individuals, who have completed Stage 9 (COMPLETION). They will exude a joy and peace as you observe their desire and willingness to do their best to Love You and Love All of Creation.

Why are so many Souls having difficulty? Current social and environment conditions worldwide have placed tremendous Physical, Mental and Emotional stress on the human body. Part of this situation has resulted due to the overpopulation of planet Earth. A large number of Souls have requested permission to incarnate on Earth to take advantage of the opportunity to ascend this lifetime.

We frequently observe that many Souls do not realize that they are in trouble; they have dropped into patterns of fear, worry, tension, anxiety, depression, sadness, and impatience, all of which destroys their capabilities to function. Allowing these negative emotions to store within some region of the body, and build up in intensity is a sure recipe for

187

collapse. There is a need to release all those stored negative emotions. When you sense this is your condition, request spiritual help or if you prefer help from a Soul who has Love and the talents to help you request spiritual help. Do not delay; seek help as soon as possible in order to reverse a highly undesirable pattern.

One common example of some frequently detected negative emotions are, tension and stress. Individuals who store tension and stress within their spinal column frequently end up with a slipped disk. Each of these troubling emotions can store in a multitude of body locations, weakening that body part. A majority of all diseases have an associated emotion that is out of control. These emotions can become congealed or crystallized and lodge within a part of the body making them more difficult to remove. They can be removed with persistence. When you discover these congealed and crystallized emotions in your body or another's seek spiritual help just as you would any adverse energy. Adverse energies such as excess inflammation, plaque, cell debris, infections, colon sludge, worms, poisons, and all similar other factors that can damage the physical body. All clearings can be resolved by asking spirit. "Ask And Ye Shall Receive." Every evening before going to bed, ask that all adverse energies be transmuted, phase shifted, cleared, or removed; using whatever is most appropriate procedure.

Obviously, you will need faith and guidance from your High Self in order to understand when any one of your bodies is in a state of collapse. When long standing imbalances build up you may be required to drop back to dependency on others and request outside help. Light Workers with Spiritual Help Are Available. However, spirit helps those who help themselves. No one should violate your free will. Thus, first confer with your High Self and then always confer with the High Self of that individual from whom you are seeking help. When, someone requests your help -- again always confer with his or her High Self to avoid interfering with his or her lessons.

One alternative some Souls choose in third DMC, those who have several disharmonious imbalances, appearing as symptoms is, to avoid determining the causes. All they can think of is to get rid of the symptoms. You have heard the expression "I can't stand the pain so give me some pain killer." Most painkillers have many adverse side effects, so be careful. Many seek help from those experts who provide some form of cover-up

188

that reduces the symptoms. For example, the use of nicotine, prescription drugs, non-prescription drugs, caffeine in sodas and coffee, alcohol, mono-sodium glutamate (MSG), and nutria-sweet -- all are capable of deadening and destroying one's nervous (sensing) system. There are many healthy substitutes available for health conscious individuals.

Each of these very destructive chemicals have many adverse side effects, thus not recommended by spirit as a cure for anything. Evidence indicates they actually damage many body systems other than the physical body and slow spiritual development. These chemicals poisons are the tools (entrapments) of the manipulators. Once addicted it is difficult to break that addiction. Thus, avoid all of these chemical cover-ups.

However, a word of caution – if you have become addicted or have been programmed by some health care practitioner to stay on a prescription, seek help in withdrawing from that addiction. The withdrawal symptoms can be less than desirable and cause additional imbalances.

Dr. Sherry Rogers (MD) (36 years in Syracuse, NY) wrote in her book "Detoxify or Die": "No doctor can cure you. No medicine can cure you. However, you can cure you." She goes on to say, "You have been brainwashed."

Doctor visits and prescription medications can entrap a Soul for an entire lifetime. Doctors cannot heal a patient's body, only the body can heal. Of necessity, creativity includes the ability to destroy and/or to UN-create. Just as we create all our "dis-eases" by creating imbalances in the body, we can balance the body to assist in un-creating those same "dis-eases."

Everyone's survival is at stake because of the drugs and the poisoning of the worlds food production and distribution system. A large percentage of all "so called foods" in the stores and restaurants are poisoned with MSG, NutraSweet, propylene glycol, dyes, hormones, preservatives, flavoring agents, and thousands of other poisons. These chemical poisons destroy. The objectives for using these poisons, has been to move Souls off the "new time line." The new time line was established by the spiritual hierarchy and was designed for helping bring into existence (creation) a "New Earth."

The "illuminati's alternative time line" has been designed to limit spiritual development and keep their slaves in bondage. Because of their efforts society has gradually become "dumbed down," more easily controlled, thus, the "illuminati's plan has slowed spiritual evolution. Each Soul needs to find ways of   protecting themselves from this onslaught. The "dumbing down" of our children and adults by poisoning the food and water supply (chlorine and fluorine), along with drugs (e.g. Ritlan - nerve poison), has all been designed to destroy physical, mental, and emotional health.   In addition, the genetic engineering of foods and radiating them with microwaves and radioactive particles has speeded up the destruction of what eatable foods were formerly available.

The book "The Slow Poisoning of America" by John E, Erb www.spofamaerica.com describes a small percentage of the poisons in restaurant-marketed foods. One section in the book is entitled " Mad Cow: Coming Soon to a Grill Near You." The PRION is already here in beef, deer, and dairy products. The beef and dairy industry are scared. Are you familiar with the "Mad Cow" prion and what effect it has on the brain? Check out the internet. Also for understanding, read David Icke's books: "The Biggest Secret," "Alice In Wonderland," and the "World Trade Center Disaster." Then read "Trance Formation of America" by Cathy O"Brien and Mark Phillips. The book "The Medical Mafia" by a Canadian Medical Doctor, Guylaine Lanctot, is also very informative. So many people live in a world of complete illusion and have no idea of what is really happening. I hope that since you have read this far in the book you are attempting to know what is out there.

The most effective procedures to overcome these dark force activities is to put in practice the positive emotions of Love, Patience, Tolerance, Joy, Compassion, Faith, Honesty , etc. The objective is to clear out "so called" negative emotions which in-trap and destroy. Once "The Power Of Positive Thought" is implemented, spiritual help is requested through prayer, and self-punishment is removed, then spiritual progress is more rapid. When appropriate spiritual counseling is requested, the body is cleared of all adverse energies, energy flow patterns are restored, then Repatterning, Rejuvenation, and Restructuring can be requested to repair all 20+ bodies.

Help can also be requested to clear out all false beliefs from the third to fourth dimensional states of consciousness. Many of these created traps, those that have been designed to destroy, have their foundation tied to one or more programmed false belief systems.   When these mental programs and their associated false belief become conscious, they cause doubts about your individual capabilities. When you begin to remember that you are a perfect spiritual being, inhabiting a physical body, then you can take your power back. Then you can regain your self-confidence.

During these mental exercises, it will be helpful to avoid a sense of separation from the whole. Keep in touch with family and friends. Avoid the belief you are a victim. Why, because when someone takes on victim consciousness they believe they must become reactors. There is never a valid reason for reacting to someone's judgmental opinion. The result of such reactive behavior is -- "War," a form of self-punishment. Have you inflicted such self-punishment upon your energy system by becoming a warrior? Stop It!

Have you noticed what happens when you react? For example through an act of defense you can absorb (take in someone else's) imbalances into your consciousness and bodies. As a result, your energy becomes drained. We frequently observe people who damage their bodies by taking on "others stuff." Believing you are a victim brings on what you believe; the subconscious mind helps you - become a victim. Often criminals know when someone has taken on victimhood consciousness they are easy targets for robbery and other attacks. They broadcast fear that the criminal can sense, thus they seek out that type of consciousness.

You can also inadvertently take on someone else's stuff when attempting to respond to their request for help. Avoid misguided compassion – a common method individuals use to give away parts of their Soul. Also, avoid coming in contact with Soul snatchers or energy "sappers" who know how to place an implant in your body, attach a cord, and drain your energy. You will know intuitively who they are by staying in touch with your High Self and God/Goddess within.

In addition, when you assist another without their permission, you can take on a part of their Soul. Remember, these Soul parts are called fragments or facets. When another's Soul fragments become attached to any of your bodies, they can damage your Soul. Those other Soul facets contain energetic patterns from their original host Soul. For the health of all concerned when you discover that parts of your Soul have attached fragments from others, request that your High Self secure help to return those Soul fragments to their rightful owners.

We have an obligation to take care of our Soul (life), move out of the victim consciousness, and gain our independence. Outline a sequence of activities that will help you remember who you are. This week we received a call from an individual living in Chicago. Her High Self immediately indicated to me that she had given her "Soul and Heart away." The body had a very low level of Soul energy, only a few fragments remained.

Yes, there really are Soul snatchers everywhere, be aware. To struggle to carry on your third DMC lessons with a damaged Soul is a real intense challenge. We have also discovered that fifty –two percent of humans living on Earth have damaged Souls. Some of that damage has been carried forward from many other parallel lifetimes. As previously mentioned, there are an unlimited number of places throughout creation where parts of your Soul can become lost. They are waiting to be returned and cleaned up so that they can carry on their assigned responsibilities.

The struggle to remember who you are is sometimes a difficult task. This is especially true when you realize that society and science seek to prove that the only reality that exists must be perceived with your five physical senses. Those who accept these limiting beliefs have egos that primarily identify with the physical third DMC, a world of duality. These limiting beliefs are generally based on what society has historically believed to true and correct. Many of these limiting beliefs have been passed down from one generation to next in families, churches, politics, and schools.

This is also true of "religious" individuals or religious institutions who know they are right. They know they are right because they "have all the answers." Be cautious, especially when they try to convince you " Follow My Religion, It's Correct, The Right One" Some will say "these beliefs provide me with my foundation for living, if I were to change my beliefs I would be lost, without a foundation."

That is generally true for those who believe that their beliefs are their spiritual foundation. What you believe relates to your truth. Could their foundations have been built on shifting or sinking sands? Build your foundations on solid rock. Obviously rock is more stable than sand. Some "Wake Up" later in life when their foundations have given away. When you discover someone who knows the answers, be wary. When they resist listening to your views, leave and go on your way. No one has all the answers to anything, just partial truths. There is so much we fail to know or even begin to understand. The experience of knowing will open up as you graduate and ascend to the New Earth.

Where is the best source of truth? Are religious beliefs a good source of truth? Are religious beliefs and spiritual beliefs the same? Could TRUTH, the "real" truth be tied to the commandment: "Love Thy Neighbor as Thyself"? Those who truly Love themselves and Love others, will also have an open mindedness, desire to learn, have patience, and be willing to be open to understanding others views. Together we can help each other find truth. No one on Earth has all the answers (the truth), nor the foundations on which to judge others. Any so-called source of truth that is judgmental should be avoided. The important command, "Judge Not Least Ye Be Judged," should be taken seriously.

These attributes of Love and being open to spiritual insights are criteria for conscious evolution. These criteria are a part of the "test requirements" for graduation and ascension. Individuals within the third DMC, who hold onto limiting beliefs, have a tendency to have an "ego" that measures value in terms of professional achievement and/or the accumulation of possessions. For some the standard criteria for success are measured by the titles attached to their name. Another criterion is their physical appearance, their possessions, such as the type of car they drive, or the size and location of their house. These so-called significant accomplishments of fame and fortune are based on limiting false beliefs. To place one's attention on these third DMC physical sensing beliefs locks one into a limiting state of reality, consequently slowing spiritual evolution. Does it matter? Yes, you learn to either control "ego" now or keep repeating these same mistakes (repeatedly) until you "get it." If unable to "get it" this lifetime, on planet Earth, then transfer to another third dimension planet and try again to "get it."

To speed up the evolutionary process involves communicating with the non-physical spiritual world. If you can calibrate your conscious mind to function within the alpha and theta brain wave frequency patterns you can open portals to the other worlds. The "Silva Method," "Remote Viewing," Transcendental Meditation, and other disciplinary approaches have value in helping control one's brain wave patterns. To be sensitive in listening to your High Self is more effective within the lower brain wave frequencies.

Once these portals have been opened you can pass through and communicate with first DMC creations such as crystals and DNA, and talk with plants and animals within the second DMC. In addition, you can communicate with anything in the "astral" plane of the fourth DMC and "heaven" plane of the fifth DMC. These portals provide access to unlimited sources of information, on the physical Earth plane, astral plane, Heaven plane, other planets, other galaxies, and yes many other Universes.

Then as you progress by opening up these communication channels, you are able to visit with entities that have access to stored information in an infinite number of Dimensional Parallel Universes (DPUs.) As we seek out these component parts of our multidimensional selves and share these understandings with others, we can help to accelerate the evolution of all Souls and assist in creating a "New Earth.". As we learn responsibility for others, and ourselves we not only create a better world for others but we simultaneously create a better world for ourselves. The positive consciousness changes we make also extend out to other planets, galaxies, and Universes. Thought forms never cease to exist.

As we contemplate our future parallel fifth DMC selves, we can prepare for our endogenous natures as a part of the reality of the fifth DMC. To smoothly make the transition from our current sexual nature (male-female) to the endogenous nature (no sexual orientation), NOW is the time to start balancing our male and female attributes. Ascertain (measure by dowsing) the intensity of each sexual polarity within and work on increasing the weaker of the two. Also, balance the right and left hemispheres of the brain to utilize both your creative potentials (female) and ability to manifest in the physical (male) realms. When accomplished, our male and female aspects join into "one endogenous creation". Then we have opened a path to learn mastery of our multidimensional consciousness.

As we become multidimensional, we gain insights on how to restructure (transmute) our physical bodies by creating new body parts. We then become empowered to take on new responsibilities, under the direction of our Soul and High Self as creators in training within the "Earth School". Through these processes, we realize our spiritual powers come through us from Source (ALL THAT IS) via our super-conscious. Then through belief and faith, we can accept the opportunity to be a "clear" channel from Source. A belief, backed by the "Power of Pure Love", and step onto the bridge of fourth DMC with assurance that we are on the path to the fifth DMC where there is "No Time".

Fourth State - Evolutionary Bridge

Fourth DMC includes the components of the first, second and third DMCs (point, length, breath, height, and volume) and adds a tool of third DMC of time, for movement and discerned dimensionally. A majority of the Earth population currently reside within a combined state of third and fourth DMC. Here they are now becoming more familiar with what the characteristics of the fourth DMC are like. As we step onto the astral bridge of the fourth DMC, it appears green with a gray polarization. We realize the fourth DMC houses a very large number of Souls in less dense bodies, compared to third DMC. Within the astral plane of fourth DMC, duality still exists, just like in third DMC. Thus, one will find the forces of Light and Darkness, very active. The lower planes of third DMC have a greater percentage of Dark tendencies (entities) and the higher planes a greater percentage of Light (light Workers) tendencies.

There is obviously an intense inter-dimensional battle between light and dark underway within the fourth DMC. This is where the battle for good and evil started. The battle is obviously a continuation of the battle for the control of and manipulation of Souls. The forces of Light have been working to liberate human consciousness for eons. The forces of Light would like to see you evolve spiritually. They have constantly made an effort to contact Souls to help them evolve to the next higher evolutionary stage. Souls evolve from a third DMC perspective, to the fourth and on to the fifth DMCs perspective. In contrast, the forces of Darkness are continually working to restrict the Souls desire to evolve through this sequence. Their objective is to hold a Soul within the third & fourth DMC. We can ask Spiritual help to protect our Souls and help us overcome these forces of darkness. Make a specific request to prevent the dark forces or any other negative entity from interfering with our spiritual evolution. Also, request the Creators of Shields to provide you with an appropriate shield for protection. Avoid any fear of these dark forces. They survive on the energy of fear and are attracted to those with any degree of fear of them.

195

This fourth DMC has been called the "Will of Life" challenge. There are twelve levels within the fourth DMC. The lower levels are somewhat undesirable, since the misfits congregate there. Within the fourth DMC, the individual self (ego) uses the physical, mental, and astral bodies to attempt to achieve its driving goals. The battle between the ego mind and heart felt love is in full swing within the fourth DMC. This is where the astral body sometimes visits during sleep time or during your astral travels.

Religious group Souls who have vacated their physical bodies, because of their false beliefs of a hell and purgatory congregate in their own conscious groups here, as do others with restricting belief patterns. They join in groups as like-minded individuals to secure support for their beliefs, just as they did before they left their physical bodies in death. When you take a tour of the fourth DMC astral plane, you will observe like-minded groups in one location where they continue to support each other in their former misguided beliefs.

In addition, the first stage of Christ Consciousness, following ascension is located here. With this wide variation in spiritual attributes, the vibrational frequency varies from 9,000 to 12,000 cycles per second. A specific frequency range characterizes each of the twelve levels of the fourth DMC.

Discernment becomes very important while traveling within the fourth DMC. Humans can be influenced by dark astral beings (dark forces) from the lower fourth DMC. These dark forces are able to match the lower-vibrational frequency of negative thoughts, vices, repressed emotions, and/or unhealed or denied shadow sides of humans. As a result, since like attracts like, the dark forces feed off the pain, fear, and other dense energies generated by humans living on the physical third DMC Earth plain. Not only can they feed off these energies (lowering an individual's physical energy) but the dark forces can also cause a confused state of conscious mind, sometimes termed "brain fog." When someone calls with excessive brain fog one of the first questions is, are their attached dark forces? If so, call upon the Archangels to request they enter a hexahedron (two four sided pyramids, positioned base to base) for safe transport to a region where they can continue their evolution.

There are many examples of where possessions by dark forces have proven their capability to take control of the physical, mental, and emotional bodies, overriding the influence of one's Soul. In addition, we recently discovered that dark forces, under certain conditions, could cause a physical body to connect into the second Dimensional Parallel Universe (DPU). This connection causes the body to become more susceptibility to undesirable energies, such as infectious agents. When you sense that your immune system is less that optimum and that you may be receiving adverse energies through this DPU it may be appropriate to request spiritual help. Ask your High Self Spiritual Council (HSSC) to locate the most appropriate spiritual team to connect your reality into the most appropriate DPU. Next, ask for help to set you free and strengthen your immune system.

The dark polarity of the fourth DMC is one of the places where nightmares and astral abuse take place. As humans eliminate these low frequency influences and develop higher-vibrational patterns of thinking, feeling and doing they become attracted to the higher frequency 4th DMC Light Beings. As a result, they can be pulled free from the parasitic dark forces of the lower fourth DMC. Always hold within your consciousness the reality that "Like Attracts Like." Thus, each individual creates his or her own reality. What is attracted to any thought amplifies that thought or intensifies a "thought form" creation.

Other creative concepts are very common within the fourth DMC. For example, magic, time travel, karma, reincarnation, luck, physic surgery, mind reading, disembodies spirits, astral travel, flying, and enchantment, all originate within this astral plane. Many guides, angels, and Ascended Masters reside within the higher fourth DMC, where they are available to assist the third DMC humans – those who are receptive. Here in fourth DMC greater opportunities for spiritual growth are available. Here a Soul exemplifies a uniquely different state of being, a state of consciousness many third DMCs have difficulty understanding. However, keep in mind the importance of discernment when visiting, traveling, or communicating with entities within the fourth DMC. Work with your High Self and High Self Spiritual Council to receive guidance. Duality is still very active within the fourth DMC, in fact very active.

Here within the fourth DMC, we also should become aware of the fluid nature of our astral form, a form that is extremely mutable. For example, Souls have the conscious capability to "shape shift" (by thought) into different physical forms. Shape shifting has been known since ancient times. For example, a person who senses danger while in the woods, can transform themselves into a tree to avoid been seen. Some Native American Indians or Shamans present within the third DMC have developed those capabilities to shape shift. They have learned to ground their astral body in third DMC so completely they can temporarily change their third DMC shape and create a different fourth DMC form through visualization. As a result, they appear different in the third DMC.

From a human form, shape shifters can also take on an animal form. In addition, using these same principles it is possible for you to bilocate, appear in two locations simultaneously. Capabilities that will be carried out with ease (when perfected) as you become more aware of your multidimensional connections. One advantage of bi-locating is that you can be at work and at home simultaneously. You say, "that's impossible!" If that's your belief - so be it. We personally know of several individuals who frequently use these talents. Program deep within your conscious and subconscious minds you know that: "Whatever you believe you create." and "What You Ask For Ye Shall Receive." In addition, these are no secrets and these truths have always existed.

Humanity is currently primarily evolving to the fourth DMC, a bridge between third DMC & fifth DMC. If you visualize a bridge that expands between two great mountains, you will begin to conceive why the current period in history is unstable and challenging. A bridge is only as stable as the degree to which the designers were capable of anticipating all those factors that helped the bridge survive under all adverse conditions. Many factors are involved in creating a stable bridge.

How stable is your fourth DMC Bridge? Have you and your engineers provided all of the features that helped create a stable bridge? Will it stand the pressures and have the strength to allow you passage to the fifth DMC safely? For many the fourth DMC Bridge is unstable, swaying from side to side. Watch closely as some walk down the street and notice how they sway from side to side. You will then have a vision of what it's like when walking across a swaying bridge. If you are on such a bridge with several struggling individuals with a high degree of confusion and frustration the bridge feels unsafe. Therefore, it may take a great deal of stamina, will, and desire to steady the bridge. You may need help form others individuals on the bridge. How important is this process? As important as you believe it is.

Your consciousness, my consciousness, and the consciousness of humanity need to be raised rapidly in order to stabilize the bridge. Some may stand on the bridge a long time waiting for stabilization. Others may fall prey to the test of time and fall off the bridge. Many are standing on the same bridge trying to figure out what to do next. Very few are over half way across the bridge. Some ask what they can do to help stabilize the bridge. Each Soul on the bridge needs to take some responsibility. The successful passage depends upon the skills of each individual on the bridge. Each "High Self" of the Souls on the bridge knows the unique techniques for safe passage. We have no way to judge others standing with us. We can though, help each other by taking a positive approach and by encouraging each other. As each Soul works together and seeks help, the bridge is strengthened and stabilized. Pray and seek help in stabilizing the bridge for safe passage.

Those who thought they knew what was best for the whole, or were determined to maintain control over humanity, at all costs, have caged our minds for the last few thousand years. Finally, Souls are "Waking Up" to take their power back. The cage doors are opening and humanity has begun to explore the worlds and Universes "out there" and within themselves and others. There are now many internet web sites, books, movies, and some television programs reporting what is really happening "out there." That is, on and within the third to fourth density and dimensional states of consciousness of Earth. A different message compared to the manipulated communication media humans have programmed and brain washed individual humans for thousands of years. An alternative is now available for a seeker.

Use the power of mind along with spiritual help to understand the choices. Study about what is taking place around you each day and live your spiritual heritage. As you go within you will discover that the fourth DMC is one octave above the third DMC. The fourth DMC is where our astral bodies travel during sleep and after physical death, at least for a period. Within the fourth DMC, the concepts of time and space take on new meaning as compared to the third DMC. Perception of the past present and future become more fluid. Realize the fourth DMC vibrational rate does provide for physical vehicles to contain each individual incarnation, although with a continuation of limited consciousness. The fourth DMC physical vehicle is less dense and more astral in nature.

The effects of these shifts in consciousness can cause feelings considered less than normal, some very painful. Be patient during periods when these symptoms of clearing and readjustments take place. They will gradually ease as an awareness of the new becomes fine-tuned. However, pain and suffering will continue here in the third and fourth DMC, gradually lessening as we progress towards graduation and ascension in 2012.

Various aspects of our third DMC simultaneously occur within the fourth DMC, however at a higher frequency (vibratory rate). Since time and space within the fourth DMC are out of synchronization with the third DMC we have an awareness challenge. Unless we have developed the ability to function within our multidimensional consciousness (experience conscious of several dimensions simultaneously), our perception can become distorted. Currently this type of distortion is causing considerable confusion. Calm down, relax, and request help from your High Self when you sense a degree of confusion. Move with intention to make sure your next step is on solid ground.

Even without multidimensional consciousness, our astral body can travel into the fourth DMC while we are asleep (in an out of body experience) and review what would appear to have been several hours of activities in the third and fourth DMCs. Upon return to your physical body "clock time" resumes, with a feeling of missing time. We awaken and realize only five minutes of physical time has expired in the third DMC compared to several hours of experiences in the fourth DMC. Generally, "clock time" is forgotten in the third DMC while visiting in the fourth DMC. The perception of time was distorted, since time has collapsed in the fourth DMC.

Our fourth DMC astral bodies are where our imagination, intuition, creativity, psychic ability, lucid dreaming, magic, ability to fly and experience of out of body travels occur. As we expand our mind and become more conscious of our Soul and astral bodies, we can experience more of these qualities while present within the physical body. Many children are born with this awakened state of consciousness, that is, they have expanded capabilities characteristic of the fourth DMC. However, because of parents and misguided educational programming these capabilities (talents) are either damaged and/or destroyed. Many times, they are destroyed because of ignorance about the value to those capabilities. The controllers know of their potential so they indicate these activities are of the devil. To this author this is one the most sinister of the false beliefs propagated by the illuminati.

Those individuals who have been de-programmed (have given their power away) feel more at home within the third DMC paradigm compared to the fourth DMC. Some even believe their higher frequency fourth DMC self, does not or cannot exist. While in that third dimensional state of consciousness, these individuals are much easier to manipulate and control. Thus the constant attempts to create fear, maintain false beliefs, and call spiritual development weird, unscientific, or a "new age" philosophy of the devil, in order to slow spiritual development. Those Souls who buy into these controlling thought forms restrict their ability to awaken their Light Body, graduate, and ascend. The controllers (reptilians) know this and realize they will have lost the battle for control, if they allow you go "WAKE UP" in either the third or the fourth DMC.

Thus, their frantic efforts within both the third and fourth DMC to keep humanity "dumbed down". Within the fifth DMC, there is Unity consciousness and no controllers. The "new time line" created by a multitude of spiritual forces leads to the fifth DMC. The "old time line" is tied to the third DMC. Those in the know, (the controllers) have created their own "alternate time line" to prevent movement towards the fifth DMC time line. Which "time line" are you on? Do you know how to tell the difference? You can know by using pendulum dowsing. The choices are "Old time line, New time line, and the Controllers conservative time line, each with distinct differences.

The fourth DMC exists as a preliminary guide (manual) for the fifth DMC. It outlines the possibilities and probabilities, it is a resource which can help play out many scenarios, without the need to experience them in the physical sense. The fourth DMC allows you to practice and pretend so that your plan will be worthy of the creative beingness, that you are. The fourth DMC allows one to experience non-linear and non-physical dimensional thought forms from a third DMC perspective. This is why the fourth DMC is likened to a bridge between two worlds or two major levels of consciousness.

Within the higher levels of the fourth DMC, there are veils that seem to separate or prevent you from carrying incomplete experiences (unfinished lessons) into the fifth DMC. It is like a proving ground for thoughts and ideas and only those with expansive and creative frequencies are truly able to transit the final steps across the fourth DMC Bridge with ease. Once the challenges of the fourth DMC Bridge are brought into perspective -- through creative thought and assistance from spirit, one can become freed (cleared) from some concepts of duality. These clearings actually help propel (speed) one across the bridge into the fifth DMC realities.

From the vantage points of the fourth and fifth DMCs, you have "NOW" prepared your Soul to have the capabilities to seek out the benefits of becoming aware of your multidimensional capabilities. Opportunities you were aware of before incarnating on third DMC Earth. The challenge is that you have forgotten about your capabilities before "The Fall" in consciousness. We all experienced that dramatic shift called ''The Fall" previously, while residing upon the continents of Atlantis and Lemuria thousands of years ago Yes a majority of you reading these words were there on those continents.

That memory will return as you transition to a higher state of consciousness where the brain is upgraded (enlarged) in order to be capable of processing many of your stored records and new responsibilities. The passageway to the fifth DMC is through joy, appreciation, and ecstasy, the way to higher spiritual vibrations, to Heaven on Earth. You can pass over the fourth DMC Bridge with ease and safety. Just join with those of like mind, support each other and then ask for help when your High Self indicates there is a need for additional spiritual help.

Fifth State – Light Body - Unity of Thought

Fifth DMC encompasses an awareness of point, length, breadth, height, time, and spirit. All life forms within the fifth DMC still have an experience of "I" as an individual member of society, however inhabiting their Lightbody. The fifth DMC is similar in some ways to the third DMC, but is clearer. The haze and the veils that clutter consciousness in the lower dimensions are being lifted (diminished.) This fifth DMC also has minor features of dark and light polarities, however less pronounced, since there is neither physical suffering nor fear present.

All actions within the fifth DMC are based on Love. Love is the primary energy that helps you shift to the fifth DMC and helps develop your multidimensional capabilities. Immortality is an experimental given, a miraculous world dimensionally created where the walls of space and time, have been cleared away. Those walls that have so long limited our capabilities will have remained within the third DMC. We need not die a physical death in third DMC to experience the fifth DMC. However, physical death is one pathway to the fifth DMC. Another approved option this lifetime is to ask for, create a new physical body, and take it with you to the fifth DMC. An old worn out diseased imbalanced body will not qualify to pass through the portals into the fifth DMC. Therefore, if you would like to take your physical body with you to the New Earth it is time to clean hours and make repairs. Awaken Your Fifth DMC Light Body and plan to transition to "Heaven On Earth."

When present within the fifth DMC you love everyone and know that each individual is a part of the Divine Whole. The criteria everyone uses to perceive reality is based on your ability to accept by believing that everything -- "Will Just Be That Way. -- It's The Way Everything is Supposed to Be." There is no concern about what happened before or what will happen in the future.

There is no longer the debate as to whether anything is "possible" or "impossible" within the fifth DMC; "Everything Is." Many Lightworkers have recently come to Earth from the fifth DMC to be of assistance, to those Souls residing within the third and fourth DMC. They are waiting for your telephone or internet message if you need assistance. Many conduct workshops or give lectures on various approaches. Use discernment in selecting the most appropriate help. There are shysters' out there taking advantage of the less informed. Before committing to any training program, check out the motives of the presenters to determine if everything is presented through Love and respect.

Progression into the fifth DMC is not a miracle but the result of a dedication to shift consciousness inwardly towards thinking multi-dimensionally. The process is a natural extension of spiritual evolution and thus is a part of that which you are. The primary consciousness within the fifth DMC is androgynous (non-polar - non-sexual) stellar beings, functioning within Light Bodies. However, beings here retained their etheric foundation (template) from the third and fourth DMC combined, with the refinements and freedom to alter these forms at will. Here you can create what you think. When you desire to change your appearance, just visualize what you would like and ask. However, excessive caution because the excessive use of these capabilities, can become confusing.

Many call this fifth dimension Heaven or Nirvana, the highest realms a Soul can reach, according to some Earthly designed religions. Some go as far as stating that the Soul has evolved to a "God Like" consciousness within the fifth DMC. In actuality, the Soul has always had "God Like" properties since the individual Spirit was created in the image of God and the Soul was created to record that Spirits spiritual development.

To believe that the highest state of DMC attainable is the fifth DMC is a "False Belief." As outlined within Section VI there are twelve states of dimensional consciousness know on Earth. These states of DMCs are available for Souls who are interested in returning to Source "ALL THAT IS." We plan to discuss the sixth through the twelfth states of DMC, in the next few pages. As you will begin to understand those more advanced Souls who have shifted their consciousnesses above the ninth DMC are highly developed in terms of their spiritual evolutionary status and capabilities, they have ascended to a level of Godliness.

Flying dreams, as well as dreams of healing and attending classes occur within the fifth DMC. Many times in a near death experience, a Soul will travel up a long tunnel of light to enter the fifth DMC. The tunnel traverses the darkness (through the fourth DMC) and ends in a bright opening of golden light of the fifth DMC to meet relatives, friends and various spirit forms. Here spiritual counseling may be offered during a near death experience to assist the Soul in making a decision to stay or return to their physical body. Sometimes just a brief visit within the fifth DMC will result in a dramatic shift in an individual's consciousness. The Soul realizes that death is not the end, but is like an opening, a doorway and passing into another room. Because of this type experience, the phrase "doorway to heaven" has been used to describe stepping through an opening into a new glorious realm.

The fifth DMC is where humans (residing within the third and fourth DMCs) dream their lives into a time and space realty, and then wake up in third and fourth DMCs and live out their dreams. These dreams have been are called "lucid dreaming." The fourth DMC is also the place where white magic happens. White magic deals with using various energy tools to heal and strengthen the human bodies. Many of these tools are within but also there are tools like crystals that can be used externally. The field of white magic is a massive energy field in which the highest good of all concerned is used to assist you, humanity, and the Earth.

In contrast, the lower levels of the fifth DMC are where the dark polarity persists. Within the lower levels of the fifth DMC, there are powerful dark lords who utilize black magic and control. These are skilled dark angels, masters, sorcerers, and rulers of the lower astral planes and underworlds. If a person develops psychic powers, and mind control capabilities without developing the heart and spiritual integrity, this is where they are ruled from and go during sleep. In addition, when they become attached to these energies some may join these states of consciousness (dark lords of black magic) after physical death.

Many now are gradually shifting their consciousness where they are having experiences in the third, fourth, and fifth dimensions and above, periodically shifting from one DMC to the other. As a result, sometimes life seems so accelerated that you wonder how you will complete what used to be one weeks's task in one day, and at other times, you wonder why life seems to have come to a screeching halt.

Within the fifth DMC you have moved into a period (sequential event time frame) that many refer to as collapse of time, the "end of time" where there is "no time". In the fifth DMC, time does not pass, but you can pass into time. Time in the fifth DMC is perceived as the Eternal NOW or The Present. That means that what you feel and experience in the present moment is the only essentially important experience. The past and the future have no relevance as such. What you create and experience in this moment is what you are and what you will be, unless you shift your intention. Exercise caution, the time lag between thought and manifestation is very short. As you focus on the present moment, experience it fully in its immediacy, then you will find that time will stretch for you into an eternity. This process sounds magical, and to lower DMCs the fifth DMC is a magical place, a powerful place! So, what you focus your attention on NOW will rapidly manifest in your life. Through this process, you become aware of your creative powers, within the fifth DMC your potential has expanded beyond anything you could have dreamed of in third DMC.

The fifth DMC is different because it takes place in conscious awareness of the Now where linear sequential time becomes a tool, rather than a guiding force. Gradually it will become easier to make attunements of all bodies, mental, and spiritual to open up your awareness. Space also takes on new realities within the fifth DMC. You will remember that space and distance are only illusions of the material third DMC plane.

One example that may be of help to grasp one aspect of fifth DMC involves the choice to experience physical movements. Following the choice to experience movement, you will feel like you are experiencing a combination of flying and treading water. Part of the reason for these sensations is due to the lower density of our fifth DMC light bodies compared to the third DMC dense physical bodies. In third DMC, gravity of Earth held these dense bodies close to the surface. Our Light Bodies, like our astral bodies, are mutable and can easily change form. Just as you can change your location or experience with desire in the fifth DMC, you can also change the form of your physical body. That is, change the shape of your physical body that "encompasses" your Soul consciousness. This is a modified version of "shape shifting" as previously mentioned within the third and fourth DMC discussions.

You can practice your new found capability of changing locations or form just by visualizing a location or form and willing yourself to experience these activities. What form would you like? Note however that excessively rapid shifts in form or location may be an impediment to stability. Excessive rapid shifting could cause a lack of internal stability. With practice, one can control the desire to experience these new capabilities logically. Lack of control can cause some new challenges.

The shortest distance between two points is not a straight line or curved line in the fifth DMC. The shortest distance is traversed by simply duplicating one's self and by thought arriving at the desired destination. You will always be immediately connected to others who are your social and heart family, no matter where they may be on the planet. Within the fifth DMC, we all will have the ability to link telepathically with anyone we desire. Thus, every human is connected to every other human on an energetic level. We can also connect to all animals and plant life. Once these principles are understood consciously the "Paradise" of the fifth DMC will have been created, a "New Earth."

Within Fifth DMC Paradise there will be no polarities (such as poor/rich, smart/dumb, pretty/ugly, good/bad, hot/cold, and weak/strong. As one contemplates these features, we each realize what a dramatic shift in consciousness is taking place <u>NOW</u> and will continue. Once fifth DMC becomes established you will become more fully aware that all events will occur in "Now Time" and all reality exists simultaneously. You may develop the capability to enter into any portion of Earth's space-time matrix or continuum. However, keep in mind that once you have entered into another continuum, you are bound by the progression of that "time line". For example, when you enter the third DMC you are bound to the structural features of that state of consciousness. Returning from any space-time matrix or continuum into another space-time continuum is as simple as asking. A word of caution may be in place here. These activities like any activity require some degree of training and practice. Exercise caution until you become familiar with your new home. Just by asking, you can receive assistance.

These added capabilities within the fifth DMC open up a multitude of opportunities and/or possibilities, very rapidly. Here you have the option to choose the opportunity that best exemplifies the most promising or appropriate outcome. Exercise extreme care in making these choices since the effort required to un-create may slow spiritual development.

When faced with several choices where it is difficult to decide, one possibility is to filter each choice through Love. Love raised to the level of "Pure Unconditional Love" is capable of cleansing everything. The objective is to pass the various choices through a cleansing process. Then use discernment and listen to your High Self to discover the ranking of each choice. This process assists the mental body in making the most appropriate choice.

Fear, in any form cannot survive and function within the fifth DMC. An example was given in a workshop discussion where a Soul within the fifth DMC became so fearful the thought of having a gun for protection came into his consciousness. Instantly a gun manifests in his hand. Now what does he do with a gun? Obviously, some unfinished lesson may need review. His fear was a residue that failed to be cleared out of his third state of DMC. A continued recall of such behavior patterns is unacceptable in the fifth DMC. When excessive, these "thought forms" of fear, force one back to the fourth and event the third DMC to complete his unresolved lessons. Fear needs to be eliminated before entering the fifth DMC since it has no value there.

The Light Being aspect of fifth DMC contains most of the personal spiritual Guides to humans, such as the serving Angels, Christ Consciousness, Ascended Masters, The Great White Brotherhood, and Over-Lighting Divas. The frequency of these Beings cannot be measured because they are beyond time and space limitations. The fifth DMC brings harmony with the Divine Will of God/Goddess/All That Is.

Thus Love centered creative probabilities will take into consideration the best choice that exemplifies a desired state of well-being and stable mental and emotional health. Here there is no need for a testing period for trial and error procedures, to resolve various challenges. You are free in the fifth DMC to have a joy filled sequential experience while living within a circular or spiral frame of reference.

The fifth DMC experience does not require the mind to spend as much time processing thoughts when compared to the third to fourth DMC. As a result, the mind and heart will be freed to pursue endeavors that are more creative. You still have access to your third DMC linear thinking but with fifth DMC capabilities. For example, you are now capable of expanding --- *beyond the gaps and spaces between thoughts where we communicated with Spirit within the third* DMC. These limitations of linear mind/time awareness have dissipated in fifth DMC.

In the oneness (unity consciousness) of the fifth DMC, there is no exchange or reward for services rendered. In fifth DMC, we experience the feeling of sharing. There is no separation like that experienced in third DMC Earth. Therefore, you have no need to form symbols of energy exchange, such as money. Where there is unity of heart and mind, there is no greater reward, and nothing is requested in exchange for Unconditional Love.

In the fifth DMC and beyond obviously there is "No Time," rather what previously appeared, as time is now perceived as a space-time continuum. In the fifth DMC, there is "No Time" because in these higher dimensions there is a Unity of space, time, and polarity. Not only is there "No Time" or Space, but also since there is a lack of polarity there is no good/bad. Thus, conflicts at all levels of society will no longer exist.

There will be no need for pain and sickness. Your fifth DMC self will have integrated the lessons of the lower dimensional selves and you will have no need for suffering. However, you can re-join your third and fourth DMC realities through different visualization techniques for specific purposes. In many cases where you have perfected your multidimensional capabilities, you will automatically have an awareness of the fourth and third DMC event. There will be no sense of separation you will be able to experience your third and fourth DMCs realities within the same moment as you are experiencing your fifth DMC realities.

Future generations will discover alterations in the genetic make-up of their fifth DMC bodies. Genetic mutations will occur that are now characteristics of the more advanced races commonly called the indigo, crystal, and violet races. These genetically more advanced Souls (individuals, many children worldwide) have come to assist in the burdensome evolutionary changes now taking place in and on the Earth. Thus for these indigo, crystal and violet Souls the shift in consciousness will be much easier, a very natural experience. However, keep in mind the controllers are fearful of these more advanced Souls and are attempting to destroy their capabilities with drugs. Whenever possible seek to protect these advanced Souls since they came to help Earth move humanity onto the new "time line" to the fifth DMC. You can reduce the adverse affects of these happenings by asking spirit to neutralize the drugs in someone's body. Any drug can be inactivated, transmuted into a beneficial energy, phase shifted 180 degrees, or the drug toxicity can be cleared from substances (pills or liquid) within any container such as a bottle.

In addition, you can help yourself by constantly attuning your bodies to the new incoming frequencies. Every few days ask that all your bodies, the old and new to be attuned to the newly arriving energies. In addition, it is very important to ask for automatic upgrades in your holographic template (blueprint). Then request that all energy patterns be balanced, harmonized, integrated, and aligned for optimum performance.

As we move into fifth DMC, many changes will be noted in science, religion, art, and politics. These areas of social change are long overdue. Third DMC humans have been manipulated for so long they have become out of tune with spiritual principles and Universal Laws. Thus, many struggle just to stay alive. Some have lost their touch with the spiritual forces that brought them to Earth in the first place. The distortions have become so acute many have "tuned out" in their attempts to clean up or escape from the situation. Those behavior patterns will be phased out quickly after the year 2012.

Many in positions of "power" who are programmed for Service To Self will be removed from office and some removed from the planet. All social institutions will be reshaped to reflect the spiritual value of each individual. The revised social format will be designed so that everyone can contribute to the good of the whole. Disagreement and discord will just loom over the distant horizon within the lower dimensional states of consciousness. The changes in consciousness that allowed you to enter the fifth DMC will terminate the long-standing battle between the mind and the heart. Finally, that battle will be resolved (be put to rest) and the heart will win.

The first levels of the fifth DMC are the beginning of Ascension, a state of consciousness where there is multidimensionality. As you become more familiar with your fifth density self you realize that you have access to many steps leading to other higher levels of the fifth DMC.

As you stand on the lower steps (lower levels of fifth DMC), you can think about the many possibilities as you progress up the steps within the fifth DMC. Here you can live in unity with your male and female expression of "My" being. Here all individual realities are androgynous, lack male and female features.

Now you realize how important it was in the third and fourth DMCs to balance your male and female attributes. Here in the fifth DMC you realize you are implementing perfection and living unconditional love, unconditional acceptance, unconditional forgiveness, and as a result have created an "I Am That I Am." You will then have a personal identity that is within the unity of All That Is. Now you know that all your thoughts can manifest instantly within the Light Body that "I Am." The new me lives forever in the NOW. Then as you step up on the ladder, you become aware of not only the other levels of consciousness in the fifth DMC but may other possibilities within the sixth through the twelfth DMCs. Many new possibilities can open up quickly as you consider the unlimited opportunities within this range of your multidimensionality.

Through these many levels of challenges, you now realize how multidimensional you truly are. Everyone in fifth DMC is having evolutionary experiences of the Spirit (Soul), involved in the process of returning towards Source.

Sixth State - Unconditional Love

Sixth dimension contains all the attributes of the previous dimensions. However, this dimension is often bypassed by Souls in an evolutionary sense. It is the realm of the Higher Council where the archangels interface with Earth. Here is where the Council of the Elders is headquartering. The sixth dimension is the beginning of collective consciousness. Melchizedek consciousness exists within this dimension. To become a part of sixth DMC requires that each entering Soul must have high moral standards and have a strong foundation of unconditional Love. Only mature Souls who have been teachers capable of nurturing Love in others, take on this type of consciousness. This Love leads and guides through all experiences. Thus, the individuals who spend time in the sixth DMC need to have a high intellect and have a capability to understand humanity and society. In addition, one must have a capability to resolve opportunities (problems) and challenges of others. Those Souls currently on Earth, who have these capabilities, have experienced the sixth DMC.

Most humans have difficulty meeting the entrance standards of sixth DMC, thus favor moving on to other states of DMCs. This is especially true once a Soul becomes aware of the challenges within the sixth DMC. This is where many Souls frequently work during sleep. The most significant preparation is to develop a complete understanding of "Unconditional (Fundamental) Love" before moving to the sixth level of DMC. Within the sixth DMC, one will be learning to develop "Spiritual Love". Preparation for sixth DMC began within the lessons gained within third to fourth to fifth DMCs. Because of the potential value of spending time in the sixth DMC, many consider the effort worthwhile. Anyone interested can expand her or his multidimensional consciousness here.

This is the dimension where the High Self communicates with you and connects you on a Soul and spirit level. When your Oversoul decided to sub-divide into several Soul units, that decision was based on the concept that as each Soul moved out into the cosmos it would have distinct experiences. Each Soul is expressing different parallel realities to expand the overall capabilities of the Oversoul. The sixth DMC is where all of these individual Soul fragments rejoin in one energy body called the High Oversoul. Restated this is where all individual Souls share the same Oversoul Higher Self and become the High Oversoul. Beings on this level can choose to project human-like forms if it serves a purpose. Their projections actually exist as pure geometric forms, which are characteristic of the sixth DMC.

The sixth DMC is the realm of sacred geometry. Since sacred geometry is so important in creating, we as practicing creators can tap into sacred geometric formulation and related information in the sixth DMC. In Creation, this is one of several realities where not only sacred geometry but also other creative tools such as color, and sound take on geometric forms and numerological significance. When entities residing within sixth DMC wish to communicate with one another, they simply blend their energy fields and consciousnesses together as one.

Through the process of blending communicators, there is formed a unique hologram that exemplifies and correlates with their collective communicative desires and states of consciousnesses. Both entities then experience the essential nature of the other, mainly through a process of comparing what each has to offer the other for their understandings. The blending hologram provides a sense of knowing, that is, without actually feeling or using other communicative skills you have become the other entity.

The sixth DMC can be thought of as a country back road rather than a well-traveled highway. Here the etheric terrain is different; it is rough and bumpy, energetically speaking. To enter the sixth DMC requires courage and fortitude. It is a honeycomb of dimensions within dimensions, the destination of the true seeker. One could spend many "so called" lifetimes here and never become bored. It welcomes those who are willing to see beyond the obvious, and willing to take on challenges. The sixth DMC will assist each individual's Light Body in an examination of their depth of understanding. Within the sixth DMC is where all of the languages, symbols, and computer codes used for communication started.

The sixth DMC holds the templates for DNA patterns of all types of species', including humankind. Here the Light languages are stored along with the Akashic records of every creation and everything that has taken the form of a thought. Thus, complete files on every Soul that exists are stored here in a Library. Your every thought, feeling, action, sensed items, emotion, etc. during all of your thousands of incarnations are stored in the sixth DMC library.

Here you are required to be your own teacher. There is no one entity (teacher) to follow nor is there anyone to help lead you through. Rather the sixth DMC invites the seeker to go within and understand "All That Is." One objective within sixth DMC is to experience and understand the value of solitude. It is the realm where the emphasis is placed on individual experiences, those that desire to become a "master/teacher." As you experience solitude, the seeker will discover what lies beyond the horizon, discover what occurs underneath the purpose, and discover what movements will be provided for the future destiny of Souls and Oversouls.

The experiences gained through these disciplinary experiences can prepare a Soul for specific services. Those interested in visiting other worlds as ambassadors and/or representatives, are frequently advised to spend time within the sixth DMC. The features of the sixth DMC is like a cosmic bridge to the Higher Realms." Within the sixth DMC, there is a weaving of understanding and wisdom from a variety of other dimensions and perspectives. These understandings come from the knowledge and wisdom from within the Soul and Oversoul. Here the Soul has an infusion of Light through the Oversoul from the One Source (ALL THAT IS).

The result is a significant shift in consciousness. The rigors and self-discipline a seeker encounters within the sixth DMC involves having to work through a difficult, rough, and bumpy etheric terrain. Through a myriad of individual experiences within this terrain and by internally seeking out new perspectives, the results are a tempering and fine-tuning of one's consciousness. As one moves on from the sixth DMC, the experiences here pay off with a ten-fold return on all previously committed self-discipline and other personal investments.

The gains in terms of previous commitments, in comparison to the accomplishments, are far more than what one would normally anticipate. That gain is approximately a 1 to 10 ratio. That gain calculation is based on the assumption that you complete all assigned agreements (commitments).

One need not experience the sixth DMC; it is not a spiritual requirement. As mentioned, the sixth DMC is primarily designed for those Souls who have an interest in becoming a "master/teacher." Thus, the rewards go beyond the goal of "becoming," the efforts prepare you to become a channel for future service within many other spiritual realms.

Thus, those who make the choice to submit themselves for these disciplinary and solitary experiences will truly learn to rely on Spirit to watch over and provide for them. The vibrational lessons and significant instinctive capabilities gained are available for those who choose to pass through the sixth DMC.

Seventh State - Creative Expression

Seventh DMC in contrast to the sixth DMC is considered to be less demanding, thus a very delightful experience for the majority. It is considered the DMC of good fortune, the creative dimension, and the realm of pure expressions in pure sound, pure tone, pure geometry, and various harmonics. All Souls (beings) within this conscious state exist as expressions of an essence. That essence is expressed these listed harmonics. Hear each individuality, and collective group have their own recognizable frequency in one or more of these expressions.

The seventh DMC has been characterized by a multitude of indescribable features. Here you have available all the creative tools to design the most magnificent creations imaginable, with a high degree of refinement as etheric like forms. Physical forms can no longer be projected by consciousness in the seventh DMC, without the creator stepping down dimensionally. That means that there are no physical creations in the seventh DMC

Soul patterns are formed by sound frequencies. Visually they appear as nebulous flows of color and movement. These varying spiral patterns are the primary describable forms to be detected. When various entities wish to communicate, they simply combine their sound, blend colors, and create new nebulous ethereal like patterns. From these experiential procedures, each consciousnesses involved is energized and each fully comprehends the consciousness of the other one.

There is also a greater understanding of reality here, which comes about because of the principle of "the whole is greater than the sum of its parts." Because of the uniting of Souls, the seventh DMC is the level of collective consciousness. Remember here is where all your parallel life Soul parts and parts or groups of other Souls have united as ONE. They are all members of the same Soul Family experience themselves as the same being within the seventh DMC. However, what is unique is that each Soul is capable of maintaining a sense of individuality.

Within the seventh DMC, an entity truly learns the art of creative manifestation, a magical art of creating and seeing the perfection in that created. The seventh DMC invites what a third DMC could call perfection, or in other words, the artist working with master teachers for bringing into manifestation that which approaches an exalted level of perfection. Here one's skills are perfected and fine-tuned to put the final touches on one's ability to create a unique and all inspiring manifestation. It has been called the dimension of the alchemist, where one gains an ability to transform energy and matter back and forth into new forms.

Here all elements are equal, in the sense that all elements have their own unique and special properties. One obtains the skills to recognize the unique properties of each element. From that understanding, you can discover how they can be assembled together in different patterns. As a result, there is the potential to create a multitude of different highly creative combinations and patterns. Thus, one can create or bring into being new previously unrecognized creations.

While engaged within the seventh DMC the individual spirit becomes a possibility thinker. In many ways, the seventh DMC is like the fifth DMC. However, the seventh DMC is much less physical and less dense with a finer texture and a delicate beauty.

The seventh DMC is where students and teachers meet with masters to perfect their arts. Those with an interest in music, art, cosmic science, intergalactic commerce, mathematics, and healing specialties perform within an atmosphere that erases barriers of separation and brings worlds of knowledge together into a unique multidimensional setting. The phrase, "When the student is ready the teacher will appear" could have well been coined here, because quite literally that is what happens here. The seventh DMC is considered the favorite of many and it is easy to see why. Forty-four Research Associates within the Subtle Energy Research Corporation program have already visited and worked with the seventh DMC to check out all the opportunities available.

Souls within the seventh DMC have a goal of service. The seventh DMC is the realm of pure Melchizedek consciousness, as was the fifth DMC for Christ Consciousness. Here hearts are filled with Love and everything they do is for the benefit of others. Those with experience within the seventh DMC devote considerable effort in guiding Souls in the lower dimensions. Particularly those Souls (disincarnates) within the fourth DMC who are disorientated after having just left their physical bodies behind in the third DMC. Many of these wondering Souls need all the help they can to continue with their spiritual journey.

On occasion, those Souls who primarily reside within the seventh DMC allow themselves to be born again in physical bodies of the third DMC, in order to be of Loving Service To Others. These Souls have reached what may be called an exalted plane of accomplishments. The type Love practiced and taught here is termed "Forgiving Love," a Love that transcends beyond the concepts of good and evil. Souls of the seventh DMC realize that Souls within the materialistic third DMC are blind in a spiritual sense, and need help. However, because of their Love and realization that the Souls in the third DMC have free will they will only help when asked. They realize the third DMC incarnate purposely signed up for the blindness, as a means of understanding duality concepts.

The second DMC and seventh DMC have a very special relationship, just as the second chakra and seventh chakra of the human body have a special relationship. Five units separate both. However, in sacred geometry five unites the two. Thus, we observe that the unique energy of the five both separates and unites. It is like the cosmic in breath and out breath of "All That Is." Each in breath and out breath has their own unique place in the evolution of consciousness. The second DMC provides the architecture of physical life and expression. The seventh DMC is where the design for that architecture originated.

The seventh DMC emphasizes the building of spiritual and divine presence in all endeavors. Those souls who have reached this understanding of creation have a state of consciousness where virtue surpasses intelligence. For those Souls who have experienced the seventh DMC there is a state of forgiving love that comes from their heart.

Here in the seventh DMC you can become familiar with completely new concepts about the corridors of space and time and discover the most appropriate way to experience them. These concepts of space and time are unique and could be viewed as platforms or pavilions where energies are exchanged and reinterpreted. For those interested in some very interesting concepts about space and time and their importance in the design of the Universes, they will find the seventh DMC a very intriguing experience. From the skills gained here, you may have the opportunity to put those skills to use in the future, as you help create new Universes.

The seventh DMC is the first portal to other dimensions within various Dimensional Parallel Universes (DPUs) of infinite expression. There are an infinite number of DPUs, each with it's own unique properties. Some Oversouls may consider the challenges of visiting these DPUs to gain additional skills for creating. It appears that the opportunities available within the seventh DMC are unlimited as one seeks out various tools in different DPUs.

Eighth State - Universal Travelers

The eighth DMC is known as the state of consciousness where one develops the skill to become a traveler of many Universes. Here you have an opportunity to choose from many possibilities, make exchanges, and become involved in some very important decisions. One important combination of experiences is to bring together compassion and empathy. In fact, this combination has been the hallmark of Souls who have experienced the eight state of DMC. Giving without discrimination - a true form of compassion is one prime example of the capabilities gained here. It is a bestowing on others the attributes of pure Love, which the Soul has accumulated. These attributes of Love have been gained through many varied experiences. It is a Love like the Great Central Sun, inexhaustible. Souls who have passed through the eighth DMC are truly qualified to become skilled leaders. When you meet a Soul, who has worked here in the eighth DMC you will note that each one exudes the "Essence of Love."

When you have had that Soul touch your life the enabling consciousness will help you resolve your doubts, and can instill within you a spiritual awakening that changes your Soul's path, a path for service to all of creation. Those Souls who have had these life changing experiences shine out within the third through fifth DMCs crowd, They have a Light to share with others and in so doing change the world around them. You just like to be close to them, they inspire those in their presence.

Souls currently who have or are currently experiencing the states of eighth DMC can be called upon to provide spiritual insights. Most of those called upon are highly integrated group Minds or group Souls. Here there is a loss of the sense of "me" or any semblance of separateness. Souls communicate within the eighth DMC by sharing real-life holograms. When you travel multi-dimensionally into the eighth DMC you will experience considerable difficulty keeping your consciousness together because just with a brief encounter you are becoming pure "we." You almost immediately become a part of a group Soul. As a result, your sensing system may indicate to you that you have gone to sleep or just blanked out. By intention as you pull back from the eighth DMC into the lower DMCs you regain your sense of "I." With practice this experience of moving in and out of eight DMC becomes less dramatic and actually exciting.

The trademarks of the eighth DMC are pure color and very precise energy flow patterns. When attempts are made to discern Entities within this dimension they appear to exist as complex states of consciousness emanating color, light, and movement. When communicating with one another, it is more of a synergistic experience during which either entity (being) can sense varying differences between its 'self and others entities, and understand what those mean.

Another unique feature of the eight DMC is the absence of tones and sound. Because of the absence of sound, Group Soul expression in the eight DMC, take on a concept or "realm" of what is generally called the "VOID." Within the void and entity can experience one's wholeness and uniqueness as pure essence and consciousness in oneness of expression. Because of these features and many more, the eighth DMC is known as a place (location in consciousness) for solace and deep rest.

Souls who have mastered those conscious states of the eighth DMC have a unique capability to be of service. Each Soul is a component part of a highly integrated group. When you become part of a Group of Souls residing within the eighth DMC you will be able to call upon all of your previous experiences within the all other states of DMCs. In addition, you can go elsewhere throughout the Universe to be of assistance in expanding your multidimensional consciousness.

For example, lets theorize that your Soul as a fourth DMC had an interest in withdrawing from it's physical body. Then you could call upon an eight DMC (Soul Group) to assist you with that decision. The capabilities of the eight DMC could help outline various possibilities for consideration by your Soul. The eighth DMC group Soul has access to your Akashic records and multidimensional status. Then through a complete review of these records, the Soul Group, within the eight DMC, could prepare an outline of all your accomplishments in terms of your spiritual evolution. Once reviewed, these records could provide the basis for outlining various probabilities or possibilities that would be helpful for making your Now decisions.

Then you could review the entire presentation and have a sound basis on which to make your decision. Obviously, your decision would take into consideration the potential impact that a change would have on your (inquiring Soul's) future evolutionary path. The eighth DMC could then continue to help you analyze these potentials. Keep in mind that all these options would be available before there is a need to make a decision to withdraw or remain in fourth DMC. Then your inquiring Soul, residing within fourth DMC physical body, must decide. That decision is tempered by your free will and will be spelled out in accordance with various guidelines spelled out in Universal Laws. The decisions and the consequences of that decision now lie in your fourth DMC. However, now you will have a basis for retaining the current "time track" or choose one of the options presented for your consideration by the eighth DMC Group Soul. The choice is yours to make. Obviously a choice based on the mass of accumulated data gathered and presented to you by an evolved eighth DMC Group Soul.

The eighth DMC state of being is well traveled by a majority of all entities. One hundred percent of the Research Associates within the Subtle Energy Research program have visited, traveled through, or in some manner experienced the eighth state of DMC. It is a state of consciousness where one form of energy can be exchanged for another for the purpose of neutralizing or removing it harmlessly. Many Extraterrestrial travelers from throughout the Universe and beyond are very familiar with the eighth DMC portal, an opening to a source of insight and council. It is here that the Extraterrestrial entities can take on a physical body or receive an infusion of compatible energy that will sustain their own bodies while within an Earth like matrix (environment) for a given purpose.

The eighth DMC is considered a realm where the sciences of physics, chemistry energy, and creation are understood. Many future discoveries in science, for future use on the lower DMCs planets, like the

Earth are held here for a retrieval in NOW time. These future discoveries can be made available (released) when the consciousness reaches an acceptable level of understanding upon a planet seeking new technologies. Then the release of these creative patterns will be based upon the capabilities of those making the request. Those making the request must have evolved sufficiently so that their consciousness has the capability of using those new discoveries for improving planetary conditions.

The eighth DMC can be used to process materials (essences or elements) from throughout other parts of the Universe. When entities are interested in transferring materials from one domain (e.g. galaxy) to another, a need exists to insure the safety of all concerned. Let's say you would like to import some material from another planet in another galaxy to Earth. Those items would have to pass through the eighth DMC in order to insure their safety to the inhabitants of Earth. The point is, these items may have been perfectly safe and beneficial elsewhere but because of their frequency emissions, they could be highly poisonous or damaging to Earth inhabitants.

Thus, Universal Law requires that these items be processed before being introduced into a new environment. The processing involves more than an inspection. The item in question may need to be chemically and structurally (energetically) examined, then possibly altered within the eighth DMC to render it compatible and safe to all of Earth's inhabitants. We participating residents of the Universe all need to insist and insure that these Universal Laws of safety are followed during all of these transfer requests.

In some circumstances, the technologies available within eighth DMC may be unable to adjust the detrimental energies of the item under consideration. That is, not all energies can be adjusted so that they are stable and safe. Some with very high frequencies are unadapted to the lower frequencies of the consciousness of Earth inhabitants. Some of these energies may eventually become safely adjusted after the Earth and its inhabitants shift to a higher state of consciousness. We have discovered in our research that if we have specific challenges we can ask for help. When we request that our Spiritual Assistants help shift our consciousness to a higher state, some imbalances just fall away.

This process is most dramatic when a third and fourth state of DMC is flooded with the power code for Complete Love (9-9-9-9-9-9-9-9) for (completion) and (5-5-5-5-5-5-5) for (Love). Complete Pure Love heals, as has been scientifically proven in laboratories and hospitals here on Earth. Thus, you have permission to project this power code sequence to anyone as long as his or her High Self has given permission. For the understanding and safety of all concerned use accurate pendulum dowsing by asking the most appropriate question about the target individuals' statues. Take readings only when permission is granted. When permission is granted then take readings before and after the use of any power code. Again, this will help insure the safety of all involved individuals.

Frequently there are requests from off planet entities form throughout the Universe to visit or incarnate on planet Earth. Once approval is granted and it is found to be relatively safe for all concerned, then permission is granted. Those off planet entities that are found compatible and beneficial for Earth's inhabitants are introduced at specific intervals. Many different animals and plants have arrived on Earth, from other locations throughout this Universe and from other Universes via the eighth DMC. They were inspected thoroughly before transfer to Earth.

However, in all cases Universal Law requires that these entities (ET's, plants, and animals) pass through the screening and conscious energy adjustments within the eighth DMC before they are allowed on planet Earth. The same screening and adjustment procedures are used for transferring non-physical (etheric) properties to the Earth.

Various species of plants or animals that choose to depart the Earth plane energetically can also often choose to use the eighth DMC for assistance. This is because; energetically speaking the eighth DMC is relatively soft. This eighth DMC is less abrupt and more subtle than other DMCs. It is a soothing and inviting environment. The inviting feelings, characteristic of the eighth DMC make it a preferred choice for beings that have just emerged from a harsher dimensional climate. Likewise, it is very helpful and frequently required for those who are on their way to a harsher dimensional climate on another planet to pass through the eighth DMC before a transfer.

Ninth State - Spiritual Complex

A majority of all Souls that have incarnated on Earth are being directly influenced by various energies of the Earth. That includes all energies from the first density and first DMC up to the eighth density and eighth DMC. Once you take into consideration the features of the ninth DMC you will need to expand your mental capabilities to think in terms of spiritual worlds of other planets beyond this solar system and even beyond the Milky Way galaxy. The ninth DMC is the collective consciousness of planets, star systems, galaxies, and Dimensional Parallel Universes (DPUs). Once again, it is very difficult to grasp a sense of "I" because states of consciousness states within the ninth DMC are so vast that everything is Oneness, a Unity Consciousness of indescribable Unitarian concepts without any separations.

Thus, if you visit the ninth DMC it is essentially impossible to remain conscious of being a separate entity. To experience the ninth DMC briefly shift your mental abilities to where you have all the imagination you can possibly assemble. Can you just imagine yourself as every star, every planet, every life form, and every installer etheric creation? Obviously if you have a state of consciousness similar to mine, that task is impossible in my state of "Now." However, with a shift in consciousness and belief that anything is possible that task will be obtainable. Group Souls within the ninth DMC have had sufficient experience to offer guidance to the inhabitants of any evolving Universe or terrestrial spirit groups on various planets anywhere, any creation that seeks guidance.

These Souls Groups residing within ninth DMC have helped provide the basic tenets for a majority of the many religious philosophies found on many different worlds. In their original form, these religious philosophies were provided and organized to provide spiritual guidelines for various evolutionary stages of spiritual growth. Originally, these philosophies provided the highest form of Love available to humankind. This love may be described as God Incarnate Love, Pure Love, or Unconditional Love. This type of Love is restricted to Soul Groups chosen by ALL THAT IS (God) as Divine instruments. Once chosen, each Collective Soul Group functions as supreme representatives of ALL THAT IS (God).

222

However, keep in mind that once these religious philosophies arrive on a planet those who desired to control the masses frequently manipulated these highly spiritual guidelines.   Why do you think these philosophies are so frequently manipulated? They were manipulated to create religions with a degree of truth to make them sound spiritual but not sufficiently filled with spiritual truths that would allow the population to evolve rapidly from a spiritual perspective.   The objective is to slow spiritual evolution to allow more challenges and movement in learning how to create efficiently.   The experiences required becoming skilled in making the appropriate movements and illusionary creations requires patience, persistence, and forbearance all attributed related to spiritual evolution. The point is that the manipulation of religious philosophy is a paradox. There are beneficial aspects and detrimental aspects.

All of the religions on Earth have been manipulated to slow Soul and spiritual development. By slowing spiritual growth through promotion of half-truths and by withholding true reality it is possible to create fear, doubt and judgmental attitudes within the population, about one's capabilities. By slowing spiritual development through "dumbing down" of the population, individuals have a tendency to give their power to the religious leaders or controllers.   Such manipulation has been in existence throughout the history of the Earth and on many other lower DMC planets. Evidence indicates this is purposely allowed to exist as another form of learning. As the Soul evolves these discrepancies between spirituality and religiously become quite evident. However, keep in mind that the manipulations have also created a challenge to overcome. By overcoming the challenge, one grows spiritually.   The secret is to "Wake Up" to what has been created, face the challenge and resolve to make a decision to follow a spiritual path.   The religious path was a foundation for that change. Without those religious experiences, you would not have a solid basis for making an informed decision or choice.

Such manipulation of the masses is evident in all the major religions on Earth. A true Loving religion would never sanction war and all the discriminatory characteristics that major religions currently endorse, including Christianity. Remember Jesus words about LOVE. Why would most religious groups play down the importance of Love in practice? "By their fruits ye shall know them" is the foundation for Spiritual Love. With Spiritual Love comes acceptance of All That Is, ALL of God's Creations.

There is never a spiritual basis for judging another Soul. Yes, there are legal justifications within the laws of the land for making judgments. Close study of these laws in relation to Universal Laws and the Law of Love will need revising in the fifth DMC state of being.

Those contemplating working with the consciousness of the ninth DMC will discover it is the dimension of the final exam, but any perceived barriers or boundaries concerning the exam are self-imposed. The ninth DMC invites checking and double checking of all that "One Is - Or Believes about one's Reality." Here one is able to ascertain the real from the false. Here false beliefs can be immediately checked for their accuracy. Move your consciousness into the ninth DMC and ask for an analysis of your beliefs. Wait for the answer in meditation as an aid in knowing what needs changing in your life.

The consciousness of the ninth DMC carries the perfection of All That Is, Ever Has Been, and Or Ever Will Be. The ninth DMC invites completions, attainments, and transformations and is accessible to those who present themselves as sincerely interested in receiving assistance. Very few humans are aware of these opportunities within the ninth DMC. Possibly one reason for its minimal use is because of the false beliefs, about the entrance requirements. My guide and research indicates that the ninth DMC lacks entrance requirements. The ninth DMC is readily accessible for those who are prepared spiritually to understand and comprehend that which is available.

To visit and participate in the consciousnesses of the ninth DMC is a choice you need to make, based on the intended purpose, for that visit (experience). When one chooses to take advantage of the services provided (in the ninth DMC) all aspects of self that are perceived to be less than whole, are measured or held up and compared to One Standard, "All That Is". Those energies measured and perceived to be less than whole or imbalanced are recorded and one can request that these deficiencies be addressed. The ninth DMC Soul Groups (Oneness Light Beings), when asked, can restore and bring into balance all energy patterns needing attention.

To take advantage of these services is beyond human third, fourth and fifth DMC reasoning capabilities and counter to the majority of the belief systems present on Earth. However, just knowing about the ninth DMC services available should spark your interest in meeting the qualifications to inquire. Then you can pass through and check them out, and/or experience the many desirable features of the ninth DMC.

Energies characteristic of the ninth DMC are the true source of all healing. You may visit the ninth DMC wing of the Spiritual Hospital, adjacent to the Rejuvenation Temple any time. Both the Temple and Hospital, for use in the United States, are located in the Astral plane (fourth DMC) 100 miles east of Dallas Texas, two miles East of Tyler, Texas. The hospital is on the east side of the temple with it's own entrance. There are no financial charges for assistance. When you approach sleep at night or any time in meditation you can request that your High Self Spiritual Council assist your visit to the Spiritual Hospital near Tyler or in similar Spiritual Hospitals at other locations on Earth. An alternative is to visit the healing facilities on the Extraterrestrial Arcturian Mother Ship, the fifth dimension facilities in Telos inside Mt Shasta, or many other spiritual healing centers on Earth.

Remember, during these visits, your physical body stays in place awaiting the return of your consciousnesses. When visiting the Spiritual Hospital near Tyler, Texas, use the east entrance and check in at the registration desk by filling out the appropriate forms. Within the Spiritual Hospital, there is a large number of professional staff (over 1200) available to consider your needs. In addition, there are guides for visitors who would like to take a tour. One our Research Associate and his friend took a tour of the beautiful facilities and upon returning to their bodies in Los Angeles they recalled their experiences and recorded them.

One very important service available within the Spiritual Hospital is located within the ninth DMC ward. Several staff at the hospital have been trained to align and re-align your axiatonal lines, following your request. Every human body has it's own specifically designed axiatonal lines across its surface. These axiatonal energy lines are similar to Earth's ley lines in that they carry energy and cannot be permanently damaged, only altered and thrown out of alignment. They are like a cosmic link to All That Is. When the axiatonal lines are adjusted, a response similar to the activation of the kundalini energy awakening occurs. The axiatonal lines carry the perfection of the Soul. Adjusting the axiatonal lines and their associated spin points has the capability to restore all aspects of self, when perceived or proven to be out of balance or less than whole.

225

We are now attempting to determine why these axiatonal lines become misaligned and how to keep them aligned. Keep in mind that each alignment is temporary. Several factors appear to shift the axiatonal lines out of alignment. One factor is the accumulation of adverse emotional energies such as stress and tension. In addition, some preliminary evidence indicates that energy pulses from another Dimensional Parallel Universe can damage your axiatonal lines. That is, a trigger pulse similar to a trigger pulse used to synchronize radars functional features. You can use accurate pendulum dowsing to measure the degree of axiatonal line alignments. When damage is detected, determine what caused the damage. Then request the ninth DMC Soul Groups align and realign your axiatonal lines for optimum energy transfer though the spin points located across the surface of your body.

True healing flows along these axiatonal lines and in through the spin points. Any time you have been ill or come close to death and have chosen to recover, it is because your High Self has requested that you visit the ninth DMC healing centers and have your axiatonal lines aligned and realigned. Once realigned the perfection implanted in the axiatonal lines of your Soul path are re-patterned for synchronization with your time line. When you choose to go to the ninth DMC for assistance go with intent and integrity. The request is in your hands, no other Soul (being) can do this for you.

The best any energy worker or healer can do is to remind you of the opportunity to go to the ninth DMC hospital ward, located within the Spiritual Hospital. Work with your High Self and other spiritual assistants to locate the hospital, the ward, and for other directions. To prepare yourself, first have your personality and emotional body aligned with your Soul body. Then align your physical body with your Soul body. Also, it is always helpful to align and synchronize all your energy bodies with the Holy Spirit Body. These preliminary alignments will begin to activate the axiatonal lines. Then you must specifically ask that your axiatonal lines be aligned and realigned to provide energy to all of the appropriate spin points.

To insure your peace of mind during these procedures, ask your High Self or those who directed you to the ninth DMC, to protect your body and personality. The ninth DMC provides many types of services to help your spiritual development. Your visit poses no threat and presents

226

no surprises. How mild or harsh the ninth DMC environment and treatments are, is strictly up to your belief, acceptance and faith in yourself.

When you move your consciousness to the ninth DMC for assistance, you are guaranteed to have revealed to you a multitude of challenges such as any perceived fears, illusions, false beliefs, paradoxes, or discomforts that exist at the Soul level. Once revealed you now have a basis for action in removing their adverse affects on all of your energy bodies. Some call the ninth DMC "a consciousness of initiation," because here you have become an initiate for spiritual insight.

The ninth DMC offers you the opportunity to discard the need for physical embodiment; it is the door to many non-physical realities. Here the physical body is viewed as a limiting vehicle for Soul's awareness. That awareness can be conscious or unconscious. Every time you encounter a milestone of opportunity in your life, your High Self interacts with the ninth DMC to provide council. Sometimes the ninth DMC entities will invite lessons from the past or the future (experienced in physical third DMC or astral fourth DMC) to join you in the Now to expand on those lessons. Integrating these past and future experiences with current lessons can improve multidimensional awareness, to move towards Unity (Christ) Consciousness of the fifth DMC.

The ninth DMC is very helpful because it can continually prepare you for your life's on-going purposes. Here, you are encouraged to accept with patience each challenge and the strength to learn thereby. The ninth DMC can direct you to your greatest obstacles in order to help you see them without having to face them directly. You can ask to experience these obstacles holographically, rather than having to carry them out physically.

For example, at night you can ask to go to the ninth DMC to see what challenge is coming up in your life, that is, one that is currently aligned to manifest in the near future. While there, you can ask for and receive various ways to evaluate different options, related to upcoming challenging events. Upon your return to your physical body, you can write these experiences down, just like you record your dreams and astral travels each morning. With these insights and various options available, you then can proceed in a more organized and purposeful "time frame" to move through the challenges. When you prefer to experience the upcoming (new Now experiences) challenges, but believe the process would cause excessive imbalances in the physical body, you can then ask to experience them holographically. Ask that a holographic duplicate of you and the experience be created. Then request that the duplicate hologram go through the experience, in your place. You will have had the experience holographically (upon a hologram of yourself) avoiding an accumulation of anticipated physical imbalances. Now you have a basis for dealing with the upcoming challenge.

Also, when any problem or opportunity for growth, is anticipated in the future, you can secure assistance in the ninth DMC. Advice will be provided to facilitate that opportunity. Also with the help of ninth DMC Light Bodies, you can choose to walk away from an experience or turn the other cheek when a supposed challenge looms on the horizon. That is, choose the option considered the most efficient in assisting you with your contract lessons. If you have walked away from a challenge (opportunity) in the past and failed to complete it, and then through a series of circumstances, you discovered how important that challenge was, you can take action. You can now ask for that challenge (opportunity) to be called back into consciousness and completed.

The ninth DMC is a proving ground and you always have the option to move at your own pace there. There are no timed tests, pass or fail evaluations, or ultimatums. It is the consciousness realm of growth via personal choices and awareness.

The ninth DMC is also a source of assistance for those who have come to earth from non-physical worlds. The assistance is available in the form of cosmic attunements. The attunements allow the spiritual entity (Soul) to remain (or return) with their bodies for extended periods without adverse affects to their natural state of being. For many extraterrestrials, this ninth DMC is the closest to their cosmic home and the furthest from the third DMC of Earth. This is also true for non-physical humanoids (e.g. Spiritual entities) present within this sector of the Universe. The assistance provided can significantly help those who do not wish to surrender their bodies in order to receive the rest and restoration they require. Assistance is available within the ninth DMC regardless of what form these physical or non-physical humanoids arrive for assistance,

Tenth State - Upper Creation Realm

The tenth DMC is quite different from all other DMC's discussed. The levels of dimensional consciousness that lie within and between the tenth DMC through the twelfth DMC have been called the "Upper Creation Realm." These three dimensions of consciousness are not linear in any way, so it is impossible to move from one to the other. Inhabitants of the tenth DMC no longer have individual personal attributes. Thus, it is a realm where no complex Light Beings (Etheric Appearing Entities) can benefit from taking on a humanoid form and incarnating on or within those states of DMC within the "Lower Creation Realm." It quickly becomes evident that the logical human mind lacks the capability to understand the complexities of the tenth DMC. We have been told that the energy patterns and structural matrixes are purposeful realms only accessible in unique ways. Currently we are unable to understand because of a lack of terminology to describe the matrixes. A detailed search within the physical and spiritual realms has revealed that we humanoids residing on the Earth plane currently have limited information about the tenth DMC. Likewise, we have no details or any guidance about how to enter the tenth DMC.

It has been established that humans on Earth <u>cannot</u> consciously access the tenth DMC from any other state of DMC. The reason for this situation appears to be related to the complex nature of the assistance available. Souls (entities and group Souls) evolving through the first DMC through the ninth DMC lack sufficient conscious awareness to know when and/or how to request assistance. The tenth DMC is the source of the Rays and the home of what are called the Elohim, (the name of God used in the Hebrew Bible).

The tenth DMC is where Light is differentiated into component units that make up all of creation. Many sources indicate that every physical creation is in reality a form of light differentiated from the tenth DMC and downloaded into lower frequency templates and holograms. From these forms, lower frequency manifestations can occur. We were also told that the tenth DMC is the source of all plans for creations within the lower levels of DMC.

Light Beings can have a sense of a unity called "I" at this level of consciousness, but it will be quite different from that which those residing within the lower states of DMC. Again, spirit indicates we currently lack the terminology to describe the activities of these Light Beings.

Those who need assistance within the tenth DMC, simply find themselves there. Let me emphasize; there is no currently known way to ask to be admitted to tenth DMC realm to receive assistance. The energies available there, just are. If anyone reading this review has experienced the tenth DMC and have the ability to remember (recall) their experiences, please help the rest of us hear of your experiences and learn from them.

For those who have experienced the tenth DMC by just finding themselves there, they report that the number of classrooms, teachers, and forms of assistance are very few in number. Universal Consciousness has informed us that there are different types of consciousnesses in the tenth DMC realm. These three types are, "Grand Sun Consciousness", "Moon Consciousness" and "Earth Consciousness." How these consciousnesses relate is currently unavailable on the Earth plain.

The tenth DMC, in part appears be designed for energetic BEGINNINGS and to assist those needing help in finding their way through the cosmos. Inhabiting Light Beings present within the tenth DMC have roles that bear some type of relationship to creation and evolution. The tenth DMC contains the Light of the Worlds that is the Light in everything. For example, that Light, "The Christ Consciousness" (a consciousness earlier known as Immanuel, presently " Sananda") came from the tenth DMC. High Self indicates He was "propelled" to Earth from the tenth DMC into human form with the help of the Archangels for a very specific purpose.

Additional evidence indicates that the evolutionary purpose for Immanuel's appearance was spiritual in nature, to help speed up Soul growth on Earth. In no way was Immanuel's purpose designed to take away the lessons that each Soul had agreed to experience within the lower DMC's. Immanuel said when HE came to Earth, (on several occasions in different forms) that, He came to illustrate, by example that, "I Am the Truth, The Light, and the Way". Many have interpreted that phrase to mean HE came from "Creator Source" to "Show the Way" spiritually. I can find no valid reference that he came to provide the foundation for or to create any religious organization. Immanuel came for Spiritual purposes, to assist all Souls in their evolutionary journey throughout the Universes.

This tenth DMC appears to be one station along the pathway back to Creator Source. Assuming this statement is accurate, then all Souls on their return path must experience some form of presence or activity within the tenth DMC. Theoretically, existing evidence indicates that the tenth DMC state of being contains many complicated spiritual understandings. These theories are based on reports from Souls who have passed through the tenth DMC. They have reported the capability of entities residing within tenth DMC is such that their "awareness" can project itself into any conceivable form. In addition, Souls within the tenth DMC can project their conceived awareness throughout the millions of Universes and beyond into a "Source System" of creation.

For example, an entity capable of implementing tenth DMC concepts could project their awareness into any seventh DMC form, anywhere. By so doing, they could convey some creative or spiritual concepts from the tenth DMC to speed up, or assist seventh DMC Souls in their evolutionary status. Such assistance could become available upon any planet within any galaxy in any Universe.

To gain one more perspective about the tenth DMC let's note the following. Remember that some of the activities within the ninth DMC involved asking and solving questions that have never been asked. Some evidence indicates that similar circumstances may be related to how some Souls just all at once appear within the tenth DMC realm. These circumstances involve paradoxes that have never been resolved through existing experiential challenges (opportunities). Thus, the tenth DMC can help resolve the irresolvable, through some resolution procedure we cannot understand.

One simple example has been channeled in to illustrate this possibility. Let's assume that your Soul has a very urgent challenge (a paradox) and needs to receive assistance within the tenth DMC. Imagine you had already completed all the experiences that you had set out to experience in your lifetime contracts and as a result, they all have been completed successfully. However intuitively your Soul (High Self) may indicate to you that your incarnations within the lower DMC's may be lacking in some way, thus you need some additional experiences. You consciously and sub-consciously believe you need another opportunity for service. That is, the Soul (High Self) indicates that some additional training is required - you are incomplete in some way, "you are lacking an unknown".

You call out to Elohim (God), as your highest spiritual understanding, for help. Your request is for an answer in some form that will assist you in finding direction and resolution. Without directly making a request to go to the tenth DMC, other than praying to God, you discover you have arrived in the tenth DMC. Obviously, those in service within the tenth DMC would have been aware of your situation and you would have automatically arrived without making a specific request. Apparently, you arrived because of the serious nature of the paradox. As a result you awaken later on Earth, having passed through the tenth DMC, and now have become aware of a whole new purpose for continuing your Earthly incarnation. Thus, assistance was available following prayer, and when you did qualify for assistance, it was because of the individual circumstances. In this example note that a remembrance of events taking place within the tenth DMC did not return to the Earth plane as a conscious memory of resolution procedures and how the proposed revised plan was formatted.

Remember there is a challenge for those who need this kind of assistance. There is no channel for making a direct request. If you find your purpose has become too difficult or so distasteful that you would like to receive assistance from tenth DMC then choose another path. When you desire to exchange your original purpose for a different purpose, request that your High Self find an approach that is open for assistance from a more familiar "Source."

Working through the tenth DMC is generally almost impossible. Here is where you need spiritual help from more advanced spiritual entities. Again, we restate, the decisions and consideration required to make a direct request within the tenth DMC are outside the normal channels of human reasoning. These decisions are made on more advanced (developed) planes of consciousness. Such decisions apparently take place in response to an urgent spiritual need, a need that can be accessed through prayer. The urgency of the need from entities inhabiting the lower dimensions appears to be an indirect means of accessing the services available within the tenth DMC.

As mentioned earlier, a few individual Souls have found themselves within the tenth DMC, without making requests. Apparently, they satisfied the criteria needed to receive assistance. As emphasized before they just find themselves in the tenth DMC. These are the facts (that's how it is); no judgment is involved.

Another possible reason access is restricted is because of the unstable physical, mental, and emotional conditions (self-created or group-created) of many Souls currently residing on Earth and related planets. Many Souls have great concern about their purpose and exist in a state of extreme confusion on Earth. In fact, many entities from other planets, galaxies and universes are here studying these states of confusion and sickness, with the goal of providing assistance. However, until that assistance becomes available to the masses we must seek other help. If all the Souls currently wishing to exchange, trade, or return their purpose for being on Earth, spirit indicates, that line would be longer than a comet's trail. There would no way to handle the masses of direct requests for assistance within the states of tenth DMC.

However, the question persists as to how some Souls just find themselves in the tenth DMC receiving assistance. Evidently, under very different and difficult circumstances a Soul in desperate need can be given a second chance. The above example was an illustration of how one Soul found themselves in the tenth DMC. Thus, a Soul may have reached a point in their evolution where it is extremely difficult or impossible to continue along the originally (previously) established "time frame", "time track", and "time line." Their condition is hopelessness beyond understanding.

Very tragic circumstances may be one way of meeting the qualifications. What type of tragic circumstance could qualify a Soul for assistance within the tenth DMC? Spirit has provided another example to help provide "food for thought," a consideration.

Let's say that the karmic purpose for an individual Soul was that he be placed in prison for 50 years. During the period of imprisonment, many things will have changed within society on the outside. Many social and environmental factors could have been altered relative to the Soul's original contract. Now assume that by the end of his incarnation in prison, all of the other Souls the prisoner had pledged devotion to in this life have passed into the spirit realm or changed consciously. These companions may have already discovered the means within themselves to move forward without his assistance. The imprisoned Soul and other associated companion Souls may have also found forgiveness within themselves that allowed others to be forgiven as well. Under these circumstances, there would be no purpose for the imprisoned Soul to fulfill his contract upon release from prison. However, the released prisoner yearns to live a purposeful life and return to or find an extended evolutionary path on Earth. That yearning (possibly through prayer) under these circumstances could automatically connect the imprisoned soul's consciousness to the tenth DMC for help.

Other extreme examples believed to have previously qualified a Soul for assistance within tenth DMC are as follows. 1. Tragic circumstances that separate the Soul from it's divine plan. 2. The experiences of an individual Soul has lead up to a point where the original Soul would like to leave their physical body. This would allow a walk-in (another Soul through contract) to take over its body, that is still in good physical condition. Why waste a good body when another Soul could use that body as it's vehicle. This is a common occurrence. We have individuals in the Subtle Energy Research Program who are "Walk in's. One "Walk In" many know, since she is quite famous on television, is making a difference spiritually, in the lives of many. 3. A condition called crib death may qualify for additional guidance. In many of these crib deaths, the Soul withdraws from the physical body because of extreme fear, unable to continue it's proposed incarnation, 4. A type of aborted path, where the "time track" has become distorted and the Soul has lost direction, and 5. Under extreme conditions a Soul, lifetime after lifetime, ends up committing suicide and/or continually commits homicides lifetime after lifetime.

Keep in mind, a Soul that has chosen to come to Earth for the associated lessons the Earth environment provides, does not receive a new life or a new purpose simply because they have terminated their own physical life. Also, if one person (Soul) terminates their physical life or terminates the life of another Soul, neither soul qualifies for direct assistance within the tenth DMC. These activities (experiences) are frequently a part of each Soul's contract before arriving on the physical Earth plane. In many cases, each Soul who commits homicide and the victim both have agreed to go through these experiences for the lessons they provide. As a result, each Soul better understands the value of physical life on planet Earth and the opportunities such a life provides.

In the coming Now, in the fifth density and fifth DMC or above we will have more insight about the tenth DMC. So, stay tuned and report any discoveries you make.

Eleventh State – Servants of Creation

The eleventh DMC is the access point or place for the intercession invoked by those beings of angelic origin. It holds the frequency of the miraculous, the point before creation and a state of exquisite expectancy just like the moment before a sneeze or an orgasm. The terrestrial system extends only as far as the tenth DMC. However, the Solar System does have an eleventh DMC. The eleventh DMC is the field of all possibilities infused with purpose and presence. It is the realm of the being known as Archangel Metatron, and the realm of a host of other Archangels. Many have been told that within the eleventh DMC is where prayers are processed for future answers.

However, it would be an error to direct your prayers to the eleventh DMC. It is improper to direct your prayers to the eleventh DMC because there is no mechanism to receive them there. Thus, do not direct your prayers to the eleventh DMC. Your Soul cannot access or participate within the eleventh DMC at will. However, you can access it's energy indirectly by assuming a position of faith, trust, and hope in all of your desires and aspirations. You can invite an angelic entity (e.g. Archangel) within the eleventh DMC to come dine with and council you.

The eleventh DMC supports angelic energies that support physical and non-physical realities including those on the third DMC, of the Earth plane or other third DMC planets. These angelic energies (spirit frequencies) receive their guidance and instructions from the Universal consciousness (ALL CONSCIOUSNESS) of ALL THAT IS, called GOD by many, in simple terms. The angelic frequencies are attracted to that which is perfect and to that which is imperfect. This is why angels are most often experienced by what humanity would call saints and sinners. This does not mean you must fit into one of these categories to receive assistance from the angelic frequencies. It does mean that you must first place yourself into a state of receptivity before you are open to receive assistance from the supporting angelic realm of the eleventh DMC.

For example, if you have made a prayer for assistance to ALL THAT IS (GOD) for the healing of a disease, you must be willing to participate in your own healing or help create your own miracle, as the case may be. In most situations, you have created the disease for the associated learning experiences. Every experience within all states of DMC is a lesson, each Soul has previously agreed to in their contracts before coming to Earth or any planet. Many realize there are no accidents. All "so-called" accidents are planned by the Souls involved in the experiences.

Each Soul has the capabilities of creating a disease (imbalance) but that same Soul also has an equal capability to un-create any disease. In other words, any imbalance can be brought back into balance, with proper understanding. All current understanding indicates that ALL THAT IS (GOD) will instruct the angelic spirits to assist you in proportion to your willingness to participate in working through your lessons. That is why sometimes it seems that some prayers are answered while others are not (unanswered). All prayers are received vibrationally and are answered the same way. In all cases, the will of ALL THAT IS (GOD) and the will of that individual Soul must be taken into consideration, before the answer to a prayer is released. This is one reason that the eleventh DMC exists, to assist in the complicated process of answering prayers.

We all realize that "ALL THAT IS" (GOD/GODDES within) has assigned angels, guides, and a High Self Spiritual Council to assist all Spirits with their Souls appearing as human beings incarnated on Earth. These spiritual assistants are there for individual help. The response to a prayer requests will be determined by many different factors. The answer depends on the individual's request. What some perceive as a no answer is just that; a "no" is the answer. Spirit cannot live a Soul's experiences and carry out their lessons for them. The Soul would then loose the value of the challenges and associated experiences that the challenges were designed to provided. Spirit indicates that the subject of challenges and answered prayers would require several books to cover the subject in complete detail.

The eleventh DMC is also an access point for angelic beings incarnating within physical bodies upon the Earth plane. Angels appearing in physical bodies are here to have a human experience and be of assistance to humanity while they are here. These angels appearing in "human garb" have a unique ability to assist humans, as no other beings can. They bring to Earth spiritual understandings gleamed from the consciousness of ALL THAT IS (GOD/GODDES). These human appearing angelic beings are present in all occupations on planet Earth. Only a small percentage of angels incarnate in physical bodies, most angels reside within a "spirit form" while active on planet Earth. As mentioned, each Soul present on Earth has been assigned one or more angels as assistants. Angels appreciate your communications and appreciate thanks for the services they provide. Have you talked to your angels today and thanked them? They are patiently waiting. A thank you feels good and makes a difference you know.

Within eleventh DMC, all the Planetary Akashic records, the Galactic Akashic Records, and the records for an entire Source System are stored in a massive "computer like" library. The Universe we currently reside within is in one, of many Source Systems. If we were to travel to another Source System, your experiences would be entirely different. To date I have received limited information on a Souls capability to access any of these records, while residing within the lower DMCs.

We all realize that it is difficult to access the Akashic records of humans on Earth, based on the experiences of Edgar Cayce. Remember the keeper of the records was only allowed to reveal that portion of the record that was related to a specific question being asked. In these cases, the answer provided would have helped the seeker to understand. In addition, the answer would not interfere with, but help Soul growth. Too much information can be damaging to a Soul incarnated within the lower DMCs because of their limited mental capabilities.

Twelfth State – Creators and Founders

The twelfth DMC blends mind, consciousness, and awareness with heart, soul, and purpose. Within the twelfth DMC, the mind no longer exists as an individual aspect of self. Rather the mind is as an expanded awareness of united purpose of Oneness, individual distinctions become completely meaningless, and all is Spirit. The human mind is a dimensional aspect of Universal mind, which exists beyond linear past, present, or future concepts used in third DMC.

The twelfth DMC allows access to all of your lifetimes present anywhere at any "Now Time" residing in many different forms, even those in non-human form. Each parallel reality of Souls within the twelfth DMC has multidimensional capabilities that can be perfected within and through the process of continued Spiritual evolution. If you ever tap into the twelfth DMC, you will never be the same again because you cannot sustain the same degree of separation if you have experienced complete Unity.

Very few souls on Earth take advantage of the opportunity to access the twelfth DMC. Why; because most souls do not consider themselves worthy of experiencing this elevated state of dimensional consciousness. Some may limit their access because they are not interested in receiving what some may call preferential treatment. In the twelfth DMC you can call up all your experiences during many parallel lifetimes, review each one as if they were a movie that involved all your interactions with other Souls.

Those who have gone through this experience indicate that once you go through the review you began to understand (why and how) what you have become relates to a series of planned experiences. The whole review process occurs so rapidly the human mind could not comprehend. As the review progresses you experience all these events without the feeling of being directly attached to the event or fact, that those were your experiences. You appear as an actor in the play. Then you begin to understand the illusions that helped construct the play. The exciting part of this massive review is that you gain a Universal concept of what is real in spiritual terms. The illusions associated with all the false beliefs fall away and you become one with ALL THAT IS (Unity or Christ Consciousness). More beliefs that are accurate will be available to help you accelerate your spiritual journey when you make a concerted effort to shift your multidimensional consciousness upward.

The twelfth DMC is accessed by a desire to be in a creative state of oneness with Source (ALL THAT IS) (GOD). There are no other prerequisites to access the twelfth DMC, only desire. This dimension offers no classes, no lessons and you need no password to gain admission. This is the last dimension of imperfection in the series form one through twelve. Following twelfth (DMC) is the first Dimension of Perfection (DMP). Research has yet to uncover the characteristics of the Dimensions of Perfection (DMPs). It appears that the Dimensions of Perfection is a region of reality currently only accessible to the more spiritually advanced Light Beings. The fact that humanity is now aware of evolutionary experiences beyond the twelve DMCs opens up a completely new phase of creation waiting to be explored. Our human understanding is very limited because of what happened during "The Fall" when everyone on Earth has a shift in consciousness to a lower density and a host of other factors that erased our memory. So little do we know, we are currently very limited is several ways on this lowly and beautiful third-fourth density Earth.

There are twelve experiences or layers of density within the twelfth DMC. Each layer has a subtle but specific aspect of creative divinity. When you enter the twelfth DMC, you will automatically find yourself in the creative density that is most appropriate for you. Within each density, there are 360 degrees or aspects of alignments. In addition, because the twelfth DMC is not linear in scope there is an infinite amount of space between the alignments of creative energies. It is an extension of the creative mind of All That Is (GOD). It is unlimited in the original richness of ideas and possibilities that are yours for the asking and taking. That is, provided you have the skills to use these riches and ideas for the evolutionary purpose outlined by (ALL THAT IS, THE CREATOR GODS). Thus, the twelfth DMC makes available an unlimited selection of creative expressions that are available to all who choose to participate in and use them wisely. It is an unlimited unconditional platform of expression. For the student in the "Creator School" of Earth it's like a gigantic storehouse of unlimited possibilities. It will be exciting to choose some of these conscious expressions and use them to help solve many of our cultural and social challenges after we ascend. That is a real possibility for those possibility thinkers reading.

In the twelfth DMC, the mind no longer exists as an individual aspect of self, but becomes a component part of an expanded awareness within a united purpose. However, the expanded awareness has a built in guarantee that all Souls are unique among all others. You are not only unique among all others but you also have your very own ideas, concerns, desires, and perfections, different from any other Soul. All advanced kingdoms and realms have access to the twelfth DMC and perfect their

God like features through experiences within these states of consciousness. The twelfth DMC is where the positions of understanding the whole of Creations are implanted.

For example, the wolf is instilled in knowing when it should fear the human, a cow gains understanding that humans may eat it someday, and a horse knows it is destined to assist the human in his work and play. It is the dimension in which the tree learns how to plant its roots and extend it's branches. It is the dimension where each bird is assigned it's very own song. It is here within the twelfth DMC that the dinosaurs learned of their transformation.

The twelfth DMC has no relationship to time, however herein lies the key to those who designed these concepts of the past and the future, via the beauty and perfection of the present. It holds the cosmic code for all that you have been as well as the creative instructions for all that you can become. It is both your becoming and your undoing. It contains all that you could want or hope to be for this "Now Time." The ultimate is available for assisting each Soul in their many multidimensional creations within the twelfth DMC.

Time and Dimensional States of Consciousness

Dimensional concepts are a convenient method of categorizing, organizing, and understanding different states of consciousness in relation to different internal vibratory rates. Higher vibratory rates like Love are more closely attuned to truth, compared to low vibratory rates of fear and false beliefs. The term consciousness relates to awareness or a state of knowing, a perceived degree of reality. Reality in terms of perceived truth is relative to experience since our individual truths are constantly changing. To gain a perception of conscious awareness we have provided a perspective or a brief description of the first through the twelfth DMCs. All of these twelve states of DMC function together to make up each individuals multidimensional reality.

Once your multidimensional reality has been perceived, it will serve as an important evolutionary capability, through which you can accelerate your spiritual development. This involves the ability to simultaneously and sequentially become aware of and participate in several dimensional consciousnesses within "Now Time." Why "Now

Time?" Because, all of our activities within any state of dimensional consciousness all occur in the current NOW time. All past events occurred in the NOW, all current events occur NOW, and all future events will occur NOW.

The "Wake Up" call is NOW. Determine your capabilities (talents) to know why you are here and decide what part of your contract you are working on. Go within to know what's the most efficient approach, ask your High Self, and then proceed with that task. Exercise care when "false prophets" offer advice. When your intuition or High Self guides your discernment and that advice is offered in Love and patience without strings, you are more likely to avoid "false prophets."

The "controllers and false prophets" have hidden agendas designed to restrict your spiritual development. They are purposely trying to hold you on the "old time lines". Be watchful and use discernment. Some reveal themselves and their motives when they say, "Let's do it my way." "My way is the correct way." Others individuals may have a hidden agenda and attempt to revive the "Good Old Days" or come with the old tired statement of; "That's Not the Way We Used to Do It".

Controllers (sometimes called conservatives) resist change. Living consciously in the past or future are very destructive behavior patterns that slow spiritual growth. The most productive life style for success and joy is to live in the "NOW," find out the "new time line" mother Earth is on, and then stick to it.

Many individuals on Earth have developed the capability to experience several levels of consciousness within a "Now Time" frame of reference. These multidimensional abilities provide anyone interested, additional knowledge and tools for helping to improve the accuracy of their belief systems. With multidimensional consciousness, you are more aware of many different states of consciousness and can become a possibility thinker and improve your imaginative capabilities. As a result, you can experience a greater sense of "Well Being" and have greater success in creating.

Currently the lower five multidimensional realities (first through fifth) emanate from our third DMC perspective of them. Understanding all five of these dimensions is an important start for the Soul's evolution. It is important to understand that each dimension has its own unique features and no one specific individual DMC is better than another is. In a true sense, a larger or higher number does not indicate a more elevated state. States of Dimensional Consciousness just are, a part of all creation, and each one contains unique features and/or qualities of it's own. The twelve levels of reality within all twelve states of dimensional consciousness are huge and vast. Those who have multidimensional consciousness have an awareness and ability to utilize the features of many levels within several dimensions simultaneously.

However, while consciously residing within one or more of these states of DMCs we by no means understand truth, the whole truth, and nothing but the truth. Truth is a matter of perception. What is your truth (reality) one day will change tomorrow and may be quite different from another's truth or reality. The same concept applies to your physical body. What is good for your body today may be harmful tomorrow. <u>This is true of everything in life, for example eating the same foods, taking the same supplements, using the same sleep patterns, or same exercise patterns because of their repetitive nature, creates serious stress on many of your bodies.</u> Being stuck in a rut or pattern of life day after day is very unhealthy and very destructive. Accurate pendulum dowsing let's you know what's best for each NOW. Always use accurate pendulum dowsing or your fine tuned intuition to make sure your proposed activities will be beneficial.

As an aid in recovering your multidimensional capabilities, new high frequency energies are arriving on planet Earth to help you. Many of these high frequency energies are difficult to adjust to, because they are incompatible with your lower frequency bodies. Many humans are adjusting rapidly. Also, predictions indicate that a large percentage of humanity is becoming aware of and rapidly shifting their reality into other dimensions. The process of shifting from the third and fourth DMC to the fifth DMC and taking our physical bodies with us is one proven form of ASCENSION.

Ascension involves shifting (expanding) your conscious realities from one state to another. To realize your multidimensional reality you must be able to expand your awareness to other dimensions beyond the physical Earth school of third and fourth DMCs. As an aid to increasing your awareness, Sprit has provided information about all twelve states of DMC, discussed above.

To take advantage and facilitate your understanding of the first through twelfth states of dimensional consciousness you can ask your High Self, High and Self Spiritual Council (HSSC) to help. One very important area is to seek out Spiritual Assistants and ask them to make appropriate clearings of all your bodies. Many old blocking energies need to be removed as soon as possible. Discordant energies create a resistance to the flow of the new energies that could be very harmful. Everyone is familiar to what happens when electrical energy flows through wires of high resistance, they heat up. That is what causes spontaneous combustion of the human body; this a rare event.

To receive you must ask the most appropriate question. You have been told "Ask and Ye Shall Receive": thus, you need to figure out what the question is, and then, just ask. For example to remove discordant energy, ask "the Central Sun Light Beings" to use shafts of Light" to sweeps out any undesirable energy present within your many bodies. We can ask "The Seven Creators of Souls" to use high-speed neutrinos (above 100,000 miles per second) to sweep other undesirable energies out. You can also ask spirit to add higher speed neutrinos to a malfunctional part of your bodies. Damaged and imbalanced areas have low speed neutrinos. You can ask your "High Self Spiritual Council" to seek out spiritual teams to use " Sacred Geometric Forms" to sweep clean your lower bodies. You can also ask that the stem cells within your organs and glands to be activated to help create your new organs and glands. All of these Spiritual Assistants and thousands more have agreed to respond to your requests. The objective is to "Wake Up" and prepare for ascension.

Once sweeps have been completed then you should request that sprits add back energies that repattern, rejuvenate, and restructure imbalances. By strengthening your connections to Source and making sure all your energy flow circuits are clear and balanced, you have paved the way for restoring your health and well-being while residing on Earth. These tasks must be completed as soon as possible. Why do you need to act as soon as possible? That depends on your choices in terms of when you would like to graduate and ascend.

Assuming you would like to take advantage of the mass ascension opportunity around 2012, and beyond, then time is fleeting away. To qualify for graduation you will need new energies to help create your new body parts, energies to maintain the new parts and energies to prepare all your bodies for ascension. You cannot take a sick weak body with you to the fifth DMC. To withstand the higher frequencies you will need a comparable fifth DMC high frequency body, similar to the New Earth.

To facilitate the alignment and realignment of your energy systems you should ask that your "axiatonal lines" be brought into balance and spin points cleared. There is a unique procedure outlined in more detail in the ninth DMC section above. Also, constantly ask for spiritual help to maximize your chakra functions, gird connections, meridians and collaterals, brain string connections, slip string balance (right-left, front-back and top-bottom), center the hara line, and maintain all other energy flow patterns.

Yes, work and time are required for you to carry out these tasks. I assume you want to keep healthy, experience a high degree of well being, and be prepared for ascension. If that is your goal then remember to carry out those daily responsibilities that favor a healthy body. For example, do not forget to make sure your thyroid has adequate iodine for its production of hormones. Then every evening before sleeping make sure all adverse energies your body has picked up during the day are cleaned out, transmuted, phase shifted, or uncreated with the help of your Spiritual assistants. Those who help themselves, spirit will help, but spirit will not live your life for you.

As you proceed along and through these paths of DMCs, it will be helpful to request that each state of DMC be synchronized, harmonized and brought into resonance with all other levels of DMC. All of your bodies need to be prepared for a systematic shift from each state of DMC to another and into each facet of your multidimensional consciousness.

To help maintain a healthy body you will need to make sure it is supplied with all required the nutrients. That means, 70 to 80 minerals in a plant derived form, vitamins in liquid suspension, enzymes from fresh fruits and vegetables, fatty acids, fulvic acid, oxygen, clustered water with a counter-clockwise spin, and over 40 different energies from Source and the Cosmos, using the "Power Code" (10-3-5-5 - 4 -8-4-2 - 1-9-6-7.) Also, as mentioned earlier, sweep clean all bodies, have energy flow patterns maximized, and request that all of your bodies be harmonized with the Holy Spirit body. To insure harmony between all body parts have all organs, glands, and tissues harmonized and synchronized with each other. Talk to you body part and thank them for their work.

Then remember, that if you have made a prayer for assistance to ALL THAT IS (GOD) for the "healing" of a disease, you must be willing to participate in your own "healing" or help create your own miracle, as the case may be. In most situations, you have created the disease for the associated learning experiences. Every experience within all states of DMC is a "chosen lesson." Each Spirit (Soul) has previously agreed to experience these lessons in their contracts, before coming to Earth. Many realize there are no accidents. All "so-called" accidents are planned by the group of Souls involved in the experience of that event.

Conclusions – About Dimensional Consciousness

In classical mechanics, a third dimension concept, the feature of each creation has been defined as a continuous range of physically observable "entities" based on some detectable form. For example, those entities could be described as the composite energies of electrons associated with atoms. However, classical mechanics is unable to consider that these creations are the result of concepts that have originated from a Creator. Therefore, they do not exist in the absence of a creator.

It has been very difficult for science to measure concepts and grasp an understanding of subtle energies. Concepts are conscious beings formed by the brain. These concepts have an identity and the mind has the ability to contain or store them for future use. Consciousness then takes these concepts to create a format or hologram as a blueprint for creating. Then a consciousness is required to bring that hologram into physical existence.

As mentioned many times, to complete your lessons here in "Creator School" and graduate, requires several shifts in consciousness. The most significant overall objective is to develop your multidimensional consciousness. That is, learn how to shift your consciousnesses to the higher dimensions, (most appropriate ones) those above the third to fourth DMC levels while residing in a low frequency physical body. To make that shift involves remembering and understanding your signed contracts. Once you remember your contracts and thus your tasks and responsibilities in each life, you have a greater potential that you will graduate from these lower dimensional challenges. As with any school, success requires hard work, patience, persistence, and a large measure of dedication. To accomplish this task you will be require to clear out your dysfunctional features. All of those you individually created or those that were programmed into your consciousness. Once you recognize what those dysfunctions are, then you can ask your High Self to seek out spiritual help to remove these roadblocks.

There are lessons to be learned and comprehended as to how these third DMC creations speed up spiritual evolution. There is evidence that once there is an understanding about how beneficial these dysfunctional patterns and misguided belief systems are one can proceed spiritually. The object has been to come up with techniques and procedures for clearing all of these experiences out and move on to other spiritual challenges of less dramatic proportions.

What you have learned from those attachments should help you realize the need to change your beliefs. You came to Earth as advanced spiritual beings, created perfectly. If that's true, where did all of your imperfections come from? You individually have created many of these imperfections. In addition, there are entities that have collectively helped create many "road blocks" to slow graduation for you and everyone else. That's part of the duality game. The objective was to provide you a challenge whereby you could learn how to clear the roadblocks and proceed on down the road towards your chosen goals.

These dysfunctional patterns can be un-created. Again, you need to keep asking the question why did I create those individual dysfunctional imbalances. You will need to answer that question for each creation. You can state, "That's impossible". If that is your belief then it is impossible. Failure to find the answer and know what that lesson was about -- is another choice and lesson. Otherwise how will you know what lesson was involved, to what extent it was completed, and what will you will need to ask for, to receive assistance.

You must also consider that all of the events associated with a new creation, must somehow involve the essence of mind. You will also find it helpful to understand that all creations of mind are composed of energy of different frequencies. Through the process of bringing together these various energy forms (frequencies) is what you came to Earth to learn. Remember that the creative process will take some form that is observable by the mind, that mind that (the individual) who originated the creation. We should also consider how we could apply these reasoning processes to describe non-physical spiritual entities. All of these activities can be monitored by using accurate pendulum dowsing. The degree of success relates to the level of your spiritual development. The level of your spiritual development determines your ability to pass the tests for graduation and ascension.

For many lifetimes, "we" have missed the mark through our attachment to many false belief systems. These false systems, many forced upon us, because of our limited understanding of reality, have been in place here on Earth for thousands of years. As a result, we now have a worldwide crisis. Are you aware of this crisis? By slowing down and paying attention to what is happening throughout the world, you can sense the many features of the growing crisis. The survival of the planet and all life is threatened by this crisis. A major part of this crisis has been caused by installing false belief systems into the human consciousness.

These old, outdated behavior patterns are destroying our children, our health, all life forms, and the planet. Consequently, Earth is having difficulty supporting the current overpopulation. The choice is: "Evolve Spiritually NOW," or Die physically and Keep on Trying to "Wake up Later" in another dimension. Everyone needs to take care of himself or herself and where possible help those who are in need of help. Control the ego (egoric) mind and learn to live from the heart. Open your "Ascension Channel" by going within for self-discovery to find all the dysfunctional behavior patterns that have helped create the self-punishment taking place within and around you in others. Then awaken and activate your fifth DMC Light Body to be ready for passage through the appropriate portals (doorways) to the higher dimensional states of consciousness.

Section VIII. Other Factors Affecting Ascension

Quantum Numbers and Creation

One frame of reference used to understand the Universe, creations and evolution is contained within a concept that time (movement or flow) is composed of quantum numbers. In quantum mechanics, a state can be defined by its quantum numbers. The question then is, how many quantum numbers are needed to describe any given system or creation? There is no Universal answer to that question. I know of no source energy that has that answer. That is, an answer that would apply to all creations. However, to describe an individual system (creation) one must find the answer to that question. Otherwise, third dimensional consciousness will continue to have difficulty defining all aspects of the creative process.

However, consider that we humans perceive events to be changing continuously and there is a continuous flow of time to allow for these changes. Within quantum physics there is the theory that the third DMC concept of flowing time is only an illusion. That theory is based on the very small difference between successive time quantum numbers.

We must also consider that the quantum numbers used to define a system should be independent of each other. Consequently, in different situations, different sets of quantum numbers may be required to describe an individual system (creation).

To accurately describe any creation, in terms of its quantum state we should be able to describe the functional features of all electrons in relation to the atoms that make up that creation. Therefore, for accuracy we will be required to measure the angular quantum numbers and orbital quantum numbers of a creation. This is important in order to describe the shape of an atomic orbital, since orbital patterns influence the chemical bonds and bond angles. These bonding features in turn influence the characteristics of all creations. Spectroscopy reveals that two electrons can occupy a single orbital. However, two electrons can never have the exact quantum state or the same set of quantum numbers.

To elaborate, the states of these quantum numbers require a greater understanding of quantum physics and a series of mathematical formulas. These formula help describe spin-orbital interactions and how consciousness influences these energy levels. Thus, a more complete description of how quantum numbers are derived will help resolve many questions in science. Once humanity understands and comprehends the value of using quantum numbers, there will come a better understanding of the creative process. In addition, these efforts can help humans comprehend the extent to which any 'thought form" is in reality a creation.

One area of concern that we have discovered, is the large number of malfunctional creations present that clutter the landscape. Their creators of these malfunctional creations have abandoned them, just left without un-creating them. Apparently, when they abandoned them they gave no thought about the effect those creations would have on the environment and other humans. Those malfunctional thought forms clutter the energy fields and have an adverse influence on all of humanity. As third density Earth goes through a cleansing process these malfunctional creations will need to be cleared.

At this point in the discussion, I emphasize the importance of being very careful what you think. Think only positive loving concepts, those that have the ability to change your life and everyone else on the planet. Also, avoid creating malfunctional creations through an understanding of the purpose of your creations. Always ask when proposing a new creation -- will my proposed new creation hinder or benefit humanity? When creating a malfunctional creation, un-create is soon a possible.

Back to the question of creation, we need to ask, is it necessary to know quantum physics in order to create? Obviously the answer is NO. However as you shift consciousness it will be very - very important to monitor your every thought. Always program you consciousness to remember that thoughts are creations. As you strive to adjust to the new realities associated with transcendence and ascension an inability to control your thoughts could short circuit (slow down) you graduation and ascension.

The Universe has a logical structure composed of many physical features that exist all at once in no time, "Now." However, the physical features of the Universe are changing and for change to take place there must be flow. Flow related to change in some sense must considerer a form of time to bring about that change. It appears that this form of time is like a spatial position and relates to an intrinsic quantum number of a space-time point. Two points can have different time quantum number without there being any point with an intermediate time quantum number. The creative process requires flow, thus it is important to understand these concepts to understand the process of creation.

In other words, from a spiritual perspective there is actually no time, just as there is no space -- from a spiritual perspective. What we perceive is the position and time quantum numbers of space-time points, and since our existence depends on their differences, we sense that time is flowing. Thus, time either flows or does not flow, depending on how you look at it. From one point of view, time is an illusion just as space is an illusion. From another reference frame, the universe expands in time with flow. Our Universe is made of time energy, so the flow of time is real to us within the lower dimensional states of consciousness. This is where the manipulation of physical matter to develop or bring into being physical illusions requires the illusion of time for the survival of humanity within third density.

Third Dimension Illusion of Space and Time

Science has difficulty in describing any given creation because of the fact that the space we live within, like time, is an illusion. Any attempt to completely describe the ordering of the Universe and all physical creations using third DMC concepts, world be almost impossible and if accomplished, would be very weak at best. All aspects of the challenge are illusive. Because in order to make a complete observation or detailed ordering of any creation we would have to specify the relative positions of all points, both in space and in time. In reality, all of these points are illusive.

Also, keep in mind that consciousness is continually changing the features of any creation. Thus, once we have made that observation, at a series of quantum numbers, then as time flows that analysis now takes on new parameters. In addition, we also will have difficulty accurately describing any given creation because of the changes brought about with a continually changing consciousness. The collective consciousness is in the process of creating all future realities and likewise future creations. The fluid nature of reality within the lower densities makes it impossible to state, with any degree of accuracy, the differences between what is real and what is illusion.

One approach is to realize that the only non-illusionary component we Souls are aware of is the "Creators consciousness." From this perspective everything else that humans visualize, such as trees, houses, oceans, planets, galaxies and Universes are all illusions.

Anything that can exist, no matter how complex, may exist because its existence is the creator of that existence. Thus, the observation of a Universe is equivalent to the creation of that Universe. In addition, it may only exist as a virtual Universe since it most frequently persists for such a short time, therefore it may never be observed. The many creations, such as a new Universe are in reality just an unrealized potential for their existence.

Likewise, many of your concepts have a very limited time span in which to manifest. Obviously, this concept of limited time has value in controlling the creation of an excessive number of useless non-functional or malfunctional creations.

Every thought that creates an energetic concept always exists and when attracted by a like thought could take on additional energy. Eventually that thought form could manifest in some undetermined or a conceivable physical form. These concepts are utilized by our controllers as they purposely divert out creative skills away from coming up with more perfect creations that would make life within the third density much more pleasant.

One good example is the withholding of free energy technology that could not only eliminate pollution of the planet but also free up the drain on destroying Earth's natural resources. Such free energy technology has been known for thousands of years. You could have a fuel cell located behind your house that could supply all the electrical energy you needed for a lifetime, free of charge. That is a proven spiritual and scientific fact.

What Is Free Will and Free Choice?

First, let us realize we live within one of the most controlled societies within the Universe, on a planet we call Earth. Humanity's free will has essentially been removed from consciousness with very few minor exceptions. Thus, before we can really deal with the value of free choice we must clear out all those thought forms that have taken our power away. To evolve spiritually, humanity will be required to take their "power back" from all of the controllers and manipulators.

The human mind also must deal with a paradox. Until that task is accomplished, there will be certain conditions where our ability to make a free choice will be very limited. Under many circumstances, there will be no free choices (none) available. The question of the extent to which free will is involved in making a choice for a specific creation is very difficult to prove scientifically.

From one point of view, all choices available are in reality one choice since existence simply creates and observes itself. The one choice chosen does not create differences. If you have been programmed to make that choice then you only have that one choice. With only one choice than what is created does not change and is the only choice observed. Therefore, any question about having a choice is meaningless.

However, there is a question of how to view choices from a random point of view. When a random choice is made without consideration of all possibilities then that choice will determine what is specifically observed. Then the question of choice becomes very important. Thus in order to be able to make a free choice it will be very important to remove all previous programs stored within your spirit bodies, consciousness, DNA and cellular structures.

Thus, quantum mechanics indicates that there is a probability for two different points of view concerning free will. Within the first instance, during the creation process, there is in reality a lack of free choice. However, if the second random point of view is predominant then during the creative process there is free choice. Your state of consciousness will influence and determine your ability to make individual choices. The subject of free will and free choice is very important. I suggest you give this topic additional consideration in your future deliberations with your High Self. To ignore this suggestion will only limit your view of the world and a more accurate understanding of reality.

Creation Particles and Physical Entities

What we are beginning to understand is: (1) existence has certain characteristics, (2) existence has a beginning in time, (3) With freedom of choice creations are brought into existence, (4) existence self-organizes, and (5) existence can occur in many places and always has specific characteristics based upon the thoughts that created that existence.

Consciousness upon third DMC Earth exists within space-time in the form of ourselves. We (ourselves) have come into existence and thereafter our self observes what we have created during a period of illusionary flowing time or within a time tract, time frame, or on a time line. All concepts that deal with time are third DMC concepts and in reality only apply within the reference frame in which time exists. Consequently, once you move outside of the third DMC new concepts will be required to comprehend existence. There will be many workshops and classes to help resolve these issues in fifth DMC settings.

Therefore we are constantly faced with the question of how particles come together to form a creation without some form of time to account for an ongoing process. Without time there would be no particles coming together in a flowing pattern, since particle formation had to precede the existence before self could observe itself — thus there must be some form of flowing time. We know that creations are made from the historical gathering of particles, atoms, and molecules present within the Universe that consciousness has brought together. A majority of those creations have existed within a very short period compared to eternity. Everything we observe within the physical world is the historical record of that third dimensional time involving creative process.

Existence sees itself and all of the concepts of all parallel Universes all at once. It sees an Infinite set of concepts, however, the Universe and its history are a single concept and our selves can be called a single concept. On this basis, there is no time as we experience it, but every concept has one or more intrinsic quantum numbers that correspond to our perceived time. These energetic particles make up our many different bodies. Therefore, these bodies are made of and created from ordered sequences of concepts. Each concept will have a different time quantum number. From this point of view, time is an illusion. With our current third fourth states of dimensional consciousness, we cannot totally grasp this aspect of concepts and their importance in relation to an illusionary reality. Graduation and ascension to the fifth DMC will open up many helpful concepts to resolve these creative principles.

God/Goddess – Creators and Creation Consciousness

The transcendent, atemporal unchanging aspect of existence has been termed Spirit, Soul, and God/Goddess within. This component part of reality is a conscious being that is constantly evolving through the concepts of flowing time, characteristics of the lower dimensions as currently viewed. Each creator God and each creative human consciousness generally view the familiar by using different ways of looking at existence. Also, each may take a different approach to take advantage of the opportunity or existing potentials to create. These concepts are in a sense the same thing; we could say that existence (looking at ourselves) is the aspect of God/Goddess within. As we look at ourselves, we are observing the creation, which brought about the looking capabilities. We are a thought created from Source energy that has the capability of looking at its self.

The creation of clones of a living entity involves taking certain physically controlled genetic features of that entity and duplicating them to form an identical creation. Upon close examination of these clones, we discover they are devoid of a Spirit or Soul. Thus, they are easy to manipulate and control, just like mechanical robots. All creations set in motion by some Creator or God appear to have a Spirit or Soul that helps prolong their life span. These clones, those that lack a Spirit or Soul, have a relatively short life span.

The question arises as to the source of that Spirit or Soul (brought about through the natural creative processes), designed by the Creators or Gods. A second question is how does the presence of the Sprit or Soul help prolong the life of that clone? Would it be possible to take a clone and make the necessary adjustments to install a Spirit and Soul? That process has been carried out in the temples of Egypt, many years ago, according to the Edgar Cayce records. However — to my understanding that process is unavailable to humanity currently. Consequently, the millions of clones of plants, animals, and humans that science has been involved in creating have limited capabilities. They apparently have value.

Just look at the celery stalks within the market place and notice how uniform in design they are. A large majority of those uniform bunches of celery are clones. They originated from a genetically designed cell that exhibited certain desirable properties as chosen by those who believe "They Knew" which clone would produce a uniform healthy marketable item.

Creative Concepts and Creation of a New Body

Following is an abbreviated (summarized) procedure for creating new body parts. To comprehend this complete sequence I recommend you seek out an instruction manual and work closely with the many spiritual assistants that are very familiar with the creative processes.

First, visualize a body part that needs repair or replacement. Based upon the features of the structural features of this imaginary body part, request that your spiritual assistants create a similar etheric "thought form." That thought form has been called the "Ideal Morphogenetic Field." The "Morphogenetic Field than can be used to create the Holographic template (blueprint) that represents the body part in question. Realizing that all creations have polarities, we then request that the two distinct polarities be established. As you proceed request that these two polarities position themselves to form a triadic three-dimensional template (mold or blueprint).

The features of the template should be likened to a proven or established morphogenetic energy field. That is, it should appear similar to a known structure of that body part as viewed within the body or on a representative picture of that part present within the physical world. Imagine that the morphogenetic energy field appears within your mind as a normal healthy functional body part represented by a three dimensional triadic template.

Then within this triadic template insert plasmic light energy into the visualized morphogenetic field. Next, insert the most appropriate natural encodement (DNA-like language codes) to guide the biochemical processes that will make up the formation of your new body part. This newly inserted DNA code should first affect the etheric template. The DNA code then needs to instruct the etheric template to download or upload the appropriate energy required to create the physical vibrational

255

pattern. At this point in the creation, the plasmic light language also follows the instructions associated with the DNA code. The detailed arrangements of the newly creating body part are filling in the energy patterns established by the visualization of the morphogenetic energy field.

By closely observing the ongoing process intuitively (via visualization), you can make any necessary adjustments to create the most desirable physical structure. By working with the etheric template to densify the energy field, there is an upload or download period called the "time lag." In order to proceed to create something a "light-plasmic" energy is required. When sufficient light-plasmic energy is available, it gradually becomes compressed for several reasons. Then the compressed plasma helps create the desired physical structure. As the etheric mold is downloaded or uploaded into the physical realm, gradual changes should occur within the body part under repair or replacement. The overall process may require a flow of time to allow for the most functionally efficient new part. The time it takes to complete your new creations will improve with experience. You may need to repeat the above sequence of steps more than once. Ask your Spiritual assistants how many times and the extent to which you will need to repeat any details.

There are many similar procedures to complete this creative process. Go within and ask for guidance as you develop your own unique procedures. Everyone reading is a divine creation made in the image of God with all the creative skills needed to carry out these creative processes. Through the process of belief, that is by removing any doubts about your capabilities, when guided by the God/Goddess within and you High Self Spiritual Council anything is possible. When possible there may be an advantage of working with others of like mind to assist in the process.

However, avoid allowing anyone with limiting beliefs that could inadvertently or purposely sabotage or in any manner damage your creative energy flow patterns. Always remember every thought form created in mind has an energy pattern that radiates out from its creator.

This overall creative process is influenced by the degree to which you are connected to source energy and your "Light Quotient." Ideally you should maintain your "Light Quotient" at optimum or above. This means being connected to the creative energy source so that these creative energies can flow through you to create your proposed holographic template.

There is also value in raising your dimensional consciousness to that which is optimum for you; this will aid in the creative process. At the higher frequencies, additional spiritual energies are available. The power of attention and intention tied in with belief can also make a significant difference. Then add a little enthusiasm to your project and watch it manifest more rapidly.

Realize that there is a "Cosmic Law" that states *"A thought form manifested as an illusion within the physical realm cannot continue to exist without conscious energy to support its existence.* Remove that consciousness energy and the imaginary "thought form" disappears. The consciousness that brought the creation into existence continues to sustain its features. All manmade illusions, created by consciousness, only maintain their physical features when that created thought form remains to give it energy to continue its existence.

There are no eternal permanent unified consciousness energy fields within the Universe. That is, one large enough to maintain all physically created illusions. This is also true for any illusionary physically appearing planet in the Universe. These structures are held in physicality by their Creators consciousness. This is also true of your Spirit a non-physical (non-illusionary) reality that is maintained as a part of the creators consciousness. To maintain a physically manifested thought form there must be conscious energy present to maintain it. There are very few procedures know upon the Earth plane for maintaining a conscious physical illusionary energy field. One good preservation procedure is quick freezing. Within Siberia, several complete Wooly Mammoths have been discovered after thousands of years locked in ice. There are obviously some exceptions in terms of the survival of physical bones of ancient animals.

Gradually without consciousness support, a majority of all physical illusionary forms will disappear. This is why archeologists studying ancient societies frequently can only find items made of naturally occurring materials and some bones. For example, the many complicated vehicles used in Atlantis for transportation have disappeared. Again, some physical creations have been discovered buried deep in coal mines. Obviously naturally occurring stone structures like the pyramids survive.

Keep in mind your physical body and all of your body parts are physical illusions created from thought forms for use by your spirit. This is why when the spirit and consciousness is removed during the physical death process the physical body goes back "To Dust." Yes, there are procedures for slowing the decomposition processes. The future rate at which many conscious creations disappear will be interesting to observe from a fifth DMC perspective.

Through the creative processes, using holographic templates based on morphogenetic fields of the thought form under consideration you can change a malfunctional body part into a functional body part. Every human was given these creative capabilities as a component part of the God/Goddess within, that was made in the image of The I-AM-THAT-I-AM. You came to "Creator School" on Earth for learning how to create. Then follow through with your creative potentials, and ignore those who have lost their connection to Source and are struggling to find their way. Ignore their negative pessimistic attitudes and comments about their current states of understanding about anything you have chosen to attempt. Seek out those with an open mind interested in helping society.

When your High Self suggests you disconnect from these individuals, then do so. There is no need trying to convert someone trapped in third DMC duality-limiting consciousness. When they are ready, they may come to you for help. Until they are ready to "take their power back" and work up to their potential, you will be wasting conscious energy in making an effort to convince anyone of anything. When an individual is ready to know and understand, they will know.

Temporal and Atemporal States of Reality

Another important concept to consider is that existence can be atemporal, eternal, and unchanging and still be compatible with the temporal, changing Universe in which we find ourselves. We reside within a Universe that exists in time, has a beginning and an end, and seems to be a one-time deal. One approach to understanding these states of reality is to consider that temporal (with time) and atemporal (without time) are both significant and legitimate states. However, they are a component part (paradox) of the creation, just as light can be a particle and a wave at the same time. However, we can only see it one way or the other during a single observation. Therefore, existence can be either viewed as both atemporal and temporal and thus are complementary ways for existence to observe itself. We in a sense have a dichotomy between the temporal and atemporal existence observed.

Within the concept model of reality we have discussed above all of creation can be classified either as atemporal or temporal. However, paradoxes are inherent in both realities because all reality is self-referential and logic is severely limited.

The atemporal is a spiritual concept and is timeless, transcendent, has multiple facets, and thinks itself into existence, or creates itself and observes itself. Existence is consciousness and relies upon mind-derived concepts. These concepts are true to themselves and have meaning in the evolutionary spiritual concept of change.

The temporal is time dependent and relates more directly with the physical vehicle we occupy while incarnated upon a physical planet within the Universe. The temporal also utilizes the mind-derived concepts that determine the quality of physical life. There is frequently a choice of free will in our temporal Universe that resides within the framework of time. From a multitude of quantum events, a single alternative is selected for our lessons and eventual evolution. Then with the utilization of the flow of time, change is brought about through the manifestation of mind-derived concepts. One of those choices was to decide which Universe and planet would provide the greatest opportunities to most efficiently carry out our lessons each incarnation.

Space-Time Points Outside of Time-Space

Time that we perceive as flowing is considered a component part of any creation. However, according to many scientific experiments, time is considered an illusion. These traditional scientific experiments indicate there is no justification for stating that time flows.

From the standpoint of quantum numbers of space-time points we observe time flowing. From nonphysical reality within the fourth dimension, our thoughts create space-time and physical reality in the form of particles and forces. We know that from these thoughts that life forms evolved, including humans. From the self-aware concepts that arise within our brains, we know that consciousness must have space-time within the third-fourth dimensions in order to manifest our creations.

Our selves represent an existence observing itself within time, that is, from the reference point in which time exists within the third-fourth dimensions. The Spiritual "Self" (via consciousness) creates itself within some dimension and exists forever, so the spirit self continues to exist outside of time even when we physically pass from the third dimension Earth. Our spirit self continues to evolve within the spiritual fourth dimension (astral plane) and beyond within some spirit form. Also, although we may be consciously unaware of our physical reality during sleep as we venture out on astral body trips we still exist as a created self wherever we are.

Science believes that we are never conscious of being asleep; however, we can become conscious of our dream states and out of out of body travels. We become fully conscious in the third dimension when we wake up during the night or when we awake in the morning. There is no time outside of time. Time is a component part of the third dimension. There is no time during the dreaming experience where we have a chance to experience what it is like to be outside the flow of time. During the dreaming experience, we have moved into another state of dimensional consciousness beyond the third dimension. During our astral trips, we are traveling outside of time. When we exist within the third dimension, we realize the flow of time has helped create our physical body. That body would not exist without the flow of time. Most "thinkers" believe that time flows because without a flowing time to allow for uploading or downloading no-thing would come into physicality. There would be no physical creations for consciousness to observe.

Time as Change During Flow

Let us consider that time is change and change requires time. Anything must be a certain way before it can change and be different. If absolutely nothing changes, there can be no perception of time. Such a non-perception is impossible for us even to imagine, because we are made of time.

Not to perceive time, for us, is not to exist. On the other hand, if there could be time without change, it would be indistinguishable from no time at all. If there is no change, eternity is indistinguishable from an instant. As always, there are different indistinguishable ways for something to happen. Within quantum mechanics, it is logical that both ways may be observed and considered accurate. Therefore, it is not meaningless to examine the consequences of having time without change.

We can theorize that there is more than one frame of reference on which to observe time. Within a temporal Universe, we have defined the creative process as involving flowing time. The way we currently experience time, it is a component part of the creative process. Therefore, within the third dimension state of consciousness we cannot experience timelessness.

However, a timeless being, one who is atemporal and exists outside the framework of time, apparently lacks the ability to create. That is, an atemporal spirit being is unable to experience the creative process. Thus, one reason for incarnating upon a low frequency planet is to experience the creative processes.

Based on the theories within Quantum mechanics there are many other possibilities. To take advantage of these possibilities one would have to consider different parameters. These different parameters could then encompass different domains. These creations have been called temporal Universes or parallel Universes. These temporal and/or parallel Universes are displaced in time-space. However, the possibility exists that these parallel Universes have their own unique features and may continue to exist when another parallel Universe ceases to exist. Theoretically, there are an infinite number of dimensional parallel Universes. Each DMP is displaced in time and residing in parallel realities just like our current Universe appears to be.

From a theoretical standpoint, consciousness observes itself in time not only as yourself, and myself but in all other conscious selves throughout these parallel Universes. Thus, there could be countless selves in Universes identical to yours and mine but all of them displaced in time. This possibility can occur because existence of consciousness could manifest in other parallel realities. Therefore, the Spirit-Soul has a choice to experience a multitude of creative activities. Always realize that each reality exists with both the matter and antimatter paradigms.

Maintenance and Repair of the Physical Body

In order to facilitate a smooth ascension from third DMC to fifth DMC my Spirit guides indicate it will be important to clear out all interfering energies and keep the body as healthy as possible.

The **Number One Challenge** is to insure that your body is receiving adequate nutrition in an assimilative (usable) form, as previously discussed. Then obtain adequate spiritual energy to maintain all body functions. Our energy bodies need 42 different spiritual energies originating from the 44th DPU to function efficiently. These 42 energies are available by repeating the Available Energy Complex power code, (10-3-5-5 - 4-8-4-2 - 1-9-6-7).

Make sure you have adequate nutrition and use the power codes daily to maintain a healthy body. These 42 energies flow through 120 different channels to each major component part of the physical and many other bodies. A series of valves regulate the energy flow patterns and must be maintained (cleared of blocks) for optimum balanced distribution. The flow rate is greatly influenced by the functional efficiency of these 120 energy flow channels. Any blockages within one or more of these channels can cause challenges that cascade (split up) into and throughout various bodies.

In 2005, the energy flow rate was approximately 12% of the potential available, because that was the level, the low frequency third density body could accept safely. That level had been increased to 23% as of 2007 since our bodies were more capable of accepting these energies. However, this flow rate is still low. Spirit indicates that the flow rate valves will slowly be increased for those planning to ascend. The current objective is have a flow rate of somewhere between 44% and 77% (depending on individual differences) by 2010. Remember, as previously mentioned, those increased flow rates may be felt within many of your bodies and could cause some discomfort.

The **Number Two Challenge** is to insure that all energy flow circuits outside and within the body are capable of delivering the energies to sites where they are required. Some of these many different energy pathways are still under study within the Subtle Energy Research Program.

262

The required 42 spiritual energies originated from the 44th DPU and Source energy. Evidence indicates they flow through the cosmic lattice (a bee comb like design) prevailing throughout the Universe, into the grid surrounding the Earth and through the various component parts of the auric field including the chakras, spin points, core star, and acupuncture points. From these entrance points to the physical body, they flow through the meridians and collaterals to reach their site of use. To maintain balance make sure the six slip strings (front, back, top, bottom, right, and left are balanced. Then make sure the axiatonal lines crisscrossing the body's surface are clear and functional.

1. Chakra alignments - The chakras are energy vortexes that move energy in and out of the body. Each chakra has a dual swirl (vortex) interlaced with each other. The outward expression (exhale) moves clockwise and allows energy to be released from the body into the environment. The inward expression (inhale) moves counter-clockwise and pulls energy into the body. The energy pulled in then is concentrated and pumped to the etheric and physical bodies. Thus, chakra imbalances have a direct influence on energy flow patterns throughout the body, especially the gland associated with each chakra.

The chakras of most humans currently living on Earth have become very stressed. Many are so stressed they are only partially functional and some even closed. The physical, mental and emotional pace that many humans go through during the day drains your energy and poor sleep patterns provide limited time to recharge the body each night. Frequently these series of events force the base and crown chakras to shift into a survival mode. In this mode you are either down and sleeping or up and running for short periods. When the chakras are closed down to any degree, you are restricting energy flow patterns throughout the body. The limited spin and sluggish spin limits the quality of energy flow. Consequently, energy stagnation and erratic energy flow may develop and restrict the availability of energy flow through the meridians and other flow channels. Energy stagnation and interrupted flow to various organs and glands can cause all kinds of imbalances and expressed symptoms.

For a healthy body it is highly important to make sure your chakra system is operating properly and aligned for maximum energy flow. Every chakra influences the associated organs and glands. When a chakra is malfunctional, there is a lack of energy flow into that part of the body. Use pendulum dowsing to check the functional efficiency of each chakra. Since the chakras are a major component of the auric field make sure you aura is intact, without holes, or tears to reduce the changes that any adverse energy could gain entrance.

One outline for working with your chakras are presented in the book "Extraordinary Living Through Chakra Wisdom" by Rick Vrenios. This is a very comprehensive guide to the Chakra Systems function and alignment. For ordering, go on line to www.reikicouncil.com.

2. Meridian adjustments - Meridians are channels through which 42 different types of energy (Available Energy Complex) flows into, across, and through the body to connect and supply all organs, glands, muscles, and tissues with these life-sustaining impulses.

Associated with the meridian are over 500 acupuncture points that have been mapped and used to determine imbalances that relate to different diseases. When the flow of energy to and through a certain point is insufficient or becomes blocked, patterns of cellular disruption can be detected. The AEC actually holds the organs and other body parts in place. When the AEC becomes weakened, a malfunction of the organs and glands can occur in which they decline in their output of hormones and other regulatory chemical compounds. .

The functional efficiency of the meridians not only is involved in the development of the body but also helps maintain the normal healthy function, of all body parts. It is highly important that you constantly monitor all major meridians to determine their functional efficiency. There are 12 major meridians. Six of these meridians are considered to be yin and six are yang. Obviously, there are many minor meridians called collaterals that extend out from the major meridians to create your total network of internal energy flow circuits. Acupuncture is used to remove blockages and redirect energy flow when a meridian circuit is damaged or destroyed inadvertently. There are professional humans and spiritual acupuncturists that you may call upon to fine-tune your meridians and collaterals.

You may ask, "What's the big deal about my meridians?" "I lack the understanding and skills to bother with knowing when a certain meridian is malfunctional." Obviously if you would like to remain healthy, it will be important to monitor the efficiency of your meridians. Again, with accurate pendulum dowsing one can ask about and obtain accurate readings concerning the functional efficiency of all meridians. Once an imbalance is detected, you may visit an acupuncturist or ask the spiritual acupuncturists to make the necessary adjustments in the external etheric meridians and internal energy meridians. The use of colored physical or etheric needles appears to be an appropriate request to facilitate optimizing energy flow patterns.

The **Number Three Challenge** is to obtain the appropriate concentration of High Energy Phosphate (adenosine-tri-phosphatase or ATP & ADP) bonds and blood sugar to maintain the requirements for photon energy flow internally. A majority of all humans are malnourished, because of a multitude of factors. As mentioned above foods produced on farms are very low in quality. Humans have essentially destroyed the soils on which plants are grown. The continuous removal of crops from field soils gradually depletes those souls of minerals. As the food is transported to market very small quantities of these trace minerals are left in the soil. Rather the trace minerals eventually end up in sewer systems, city dumps, waste disposal systems, septic systems, rivers, and lakes.

A majority of all foods (throughout the world) are grown on nutrient deficient soils. Consequently, a majority of soils worldwide are devoid of organic acids (e.g. fulvic acid) and trace minerals. As a result, a majority of all foods (throughout the world) are grown on nutrient deficient soils. When the consumer purchases foods within the market place those foods lack utilizable minerals, vitamins, and other essential nutritional factors. This is why supplements are a requirement for health.

When there is a lack of minerals within the soil then growing plants become nutritionally stressed. A stressed plant is highly susceptible to diseases and insects. Sick plants are attacked by a multitude of disease inciting agents such as fungi, viruses, yeasts, bacteria, algae, and insects. To harvest a crop, producers (farmers and gardeners) have declared war on these "SO CALLED PESTS" by treating them with poisonous pesticides. Then the food processors come along and add an unheard number of chemicals to the foods as marketing tools, further reducing product quality. Consequently, the consumer is faced with eating sick plant produce, lacking vitamins and minerals that contain various pesticide and hormone like compounds. Then as mentioned in order to reach the market the processor adds more treatments so the product looks palatable. When you place food into your mouth, are you aware of the quality of the product you are consuming? Everyone on Earth is currently challenged, in their attempts to secure adequate nutrition and to avoid those low frequency contaminants that adversely affect the body in a multitude of ways. The health care industry is booming because of this one factor.

An emergency measure is to clear your food and drink of these contaminants, and harmonize (energize) that food, to your consciousness (by intent) use the two power codes (9-9-9 - 5-5-5) and (3-3-3-3.) Hold your hands over the food; repeat the codes aloud at least nine times without verbalizing the dashes. You will be surprised what a difference this makes not only in the quality of the food but also in helping keep poisons out of you blood and body parts, especially the liver. When you discipline yourself to use the power codes, they could save you from many health challenges.

However, in terms of securing nutritious food one of the best approaches is to grow your own foods. Through careful study, you can determine what additives are appropriate for your garden soil and how to adjust each plants environment to maximize production of healthy nutritious plant products. Always request help from the plant Divas to assist the plants in optimizing quality and production volume.

Warning: Avoid purchasing and consuming foods packaged in plastic. Many plastics are partially volatile, that is they vaporize under most conditions, especially when recently constituted. The vaporized plastic enters the food and you consume plastic. The human body is not designed to digest plastic, even low-grade plastic called margarine. Consequently, that plastic ends up in your circulatory system, liver, and other body parts. Recent television programs have emphasized the danger of breathing, eating, and drinking plastic. Avoid drinking and eating out of plastic bottles and other plastic containers.

The **Number Four Challenge** relates to the ability of the body to assimilate and absorb the nutrients present within the food. From the digestive track, nutrients need to be moved into the blood of the circulatory system. Then the circulatory system must deliver these nutrients to various, tissues, glands, and organs. Assimilation starts in the mouth during the mastication (chewing slowly) of foods where ideally the salivary glands provide mucin, serous and mucus to aid digestion. The food then passes though the esophagus and enters the stomach. Within the stomach, the macerated food should become mixed with hydrochloric acid and other digestive juices secreted by the cells in the lining of the stomach. These partially digested foods then pass through the duodenum, colon and into the intestines. Bile is added in the duodenum from the gallbladder, to emulsify fats. The beneficial bacteria within the colon then aid in digestion to release various beneficial factors. Accessory glands along the walls of the digestive track also aid the digestive process.

Nutrients released from the digested food should be absorbed through the walls of the digestive tract. When the walls are covered with sludge -- absorption is limited. Lack of absorption is one component part of malnutrition. The answer, clean the colon walls with a colon "scrubbing out" procedure.

Three top liquid mineral- vitamin products marketed within the United States in 2006 are:
1. Vital-Earth Minerals, LLC Grand Junction, CO 1-866-291-4400 www.vitalearth.org
2. American Yongevity, Chula Vista, CA 1-800-892-3197 www.americanlongevity.net
3. Innovative Technologies Corporation, Dade City, FL 1-800-482-2637 www.glacialmilk.net

Thus to maintain the appropriate mineral energy levels use accurate pendulum dowsing to periodically monitor your mineral energies. When any reading drops below + 5 take a liquid colloidal fulvic acid based blend of 60+ liquid mineral elements and when possible consume liquid vitamins. Select liquid products proven to contain fulvic acid, at least fifty different minerals, and all of the vitamins. These minerals and vitamins function as cofactors (catalysts) in all chemical reactions taking place within the physical body. Avoid taking in highly processed capsules and pills, those being promoted as supplying your daily requirements. Most of these products are marketed for the benefit of those who produce and market them. With few exceptions most pills and capsules have limited value, some very harmful, and most are a waste of money.

Then to maintain the electrical system of the body make sure you have adequate electrolytes. These charged ions function to carry electrical impulses throughout the body.

There are three top electrolytes for helping maintain the electromagnetic flow patterns:

1. Emer'gen-C in Health Food Stores,   Alacer Corp, Foothill Ranch, CA www.alacercorp.com
2. Pedialyte in Grocery Stores, Abbott Laboratories, Columbus, OH
3. Gatorade Aid Drink in Grocery Stores - Quaker Foods, Disadvantage is high sugar content.

The **Number Five Challenge** is to keep your bodies clean. One option is to sweep-clean your bodies. Spirit has provided us with three types of "Sweep-Clearing" procedures. These procedures use: (1) Shafts of light" (2) High Speed Neutrinos, and (3) Sacred Geometric Forms – These procedures are described in more detail below. These sweeping procedures will only sweep out a certain percentage of the adverse energies at any one time. The objective is to avoid placing excessive stress (via rapid changes) on your bodies by making fast changes. Thus, one will need to repeat their requests of the spiritual technicians such as the Central Sun "Light Beings" and others for sweeping out adverse energies periodically. Since our daily activities will be unable to avoid all intakes of adverse energies, these sweeping procedures should be ongoing throughout your life. Some may ask how often I will need to make this request. Accurate pendulum dowsing will provide that answer.

Details of sweep procedure #1. Three light shaft orientations (vertical, horizontal, and diagonal) are used by the "Central Sun Light Beings" to sweep all undesirable energies from all 22 + bodies. They first align a vertical shaft of light down through the length of the body. This shaft of light is vibrated back and forth sideways to break loose undesirable stuck energies in both the matter and anti-matter components. A horizontal shaft of light is then passed back and forth up and down perpendicular to the vertical shaft using a sweeping motion. These "Light Beings" continue sweeping until a certain percentage of the adverse energies are removed from all bodies, including both the matter and anti-matter bodies. Similarly, a diagonal (45° angel) shaft of light is vibrated at an angle to dislodge a certain percentage of energies stuck within that matter and antimatter plane. Once the "Central Sun Light Beings" have completed responding to your requests, thank them for their assistance.

Details of sweep procedure #2. The high-speed neutrino sweep involves contacting the seven "Creators of Souls" to use neutrinos (small particles that make up all physical reality within the Universes.) These neutrinos are used to clean out those adverse energies missed during the shafts of light sweepings. Use a sweeping procedure similar to the one used with shafts of light.

In the beginning stages of the neutrino sweep it is advisable to sweep a few bodies, at one time. Initially the bodies are swept in the following sequence: (1) physical, (2) etheric, (3) emotional, (4) mental, (5) spiritual, (6) soul, (7) I AM, (8) Christ, (9) Holy Spirit, (10) Spirit, (11) three Astral bodies, and other (12) all other bodies categorized between 14 through 24. You may alter that sequence request, depending on the circumstances.

Sometimes several bodies may be swept together. Following the completion of these initial sweeping sequences all 24 bodies (matter and antimatter) can be swept simultaneously. The sweeping speed of the neutrinos used may vary over time because a lower speed is used in the initial stages. In terms of the sweeping speeds used by the "Creators of Souls," the range is between 122,000 and 444,000 miles/second. I suggest you request that the "Creators of Souls" use the most appropriate neutrino speed to carry out the individual sweepings.

Recall that the speed of light is 186,000 miles/second. Some newly arriving babies have physical bodies where the neutrino speed is close to 200,000 miles/second. During the aging of the physical body, the neutrino speed can eventually decrease to less than 80,000 miles/second. Use accurate pendulum dowsing to determine the neutrino speed of any body, system, organ, or tissue.

Generally, there are differences in neutrino speeds of body parts and individual bodies. For example, a stressed emotional body may have a very low neutrino speed. When the neutrino speed is low, this is a sign of energy pattern deterioration. The best procedure is to measure the speed of a certain body part and then ask what would be the most appropriate

269

neutrino speed for that body part. If less than desirable then request for appropriate adjustments.

Any time you sense a weakness, make a request of the "Creators of Souls" to increase the neutrino speed within the weakened area to an appropriate speed. In that request, you may need to monitor the requested changes as they relate to the overall energy levels of each body and body part. Here the objective is to maintain balance so that any one component is within an appropriate energy speed and intensity.

These procedures have, when periodically utilized helped reverse the aging and deterioration of a body, systems, organ, gland, tissue, and liquid suspensions. To insure that progress in being made use accurate pendulum dowsing to monitor all energy systems. Periodically measure the neutrino speed of a specific body organ, say the liver, as a protective measure. A low reading could indicate a potential imbalance is in progress and therefore a need for additional physical and spiritual assistance before obvious symptoms develop.

Once you pinpoint the challenge, say for example the liver, you can ask that your spiritual assistants sweep clean the liver. Once you have determined it has been cleaned, then request that the cleaned organ have the neutrino speed increased to its appropriate level. Make sure that before and after the treatment, you measure the current neutrino speed within the organ and record those reading for future reference. Then when the "Creators of Souls" have completed responding to your requests thank them for their assistance.

Details of sweep procedure #3. Sacred Geometric Forms can also be used to sweep various component parts of your energy systems. Every structural component of physical reality has a sacred geometric from that creates the template design. For example, every cell within the body exhibits a certain shape that correlates with a sacred geometric pattern. Thus as "Creators in Training" we each may want to study "Sacred Geometry" in order to best understand how to perfect our creations. If you were interested in creating a new gall bladder, it would be helpful to have some concept of the many different geometric forms that together form the etheric template for that gall bladder. The same concept applies to every component physical part of our energy systems, physical, mental, emotional, and spiritual.

Because of the significance of "Sacred Geometric Forms" as the building blocks of our creation, we have an opportunity to use them in sweeping out undesirable stuck energies that no longer serve our purposes. There are thousands of sacred geometric forms, each with an associated spiritual connection. Therefore, we have found that the most efficient approach to working with spirit is to make a request to your High Self Spiritual Council to locate those spirits best qualified to determine which sacred geometric forms would be most suitable for sweeping. Then ask that they use those forms to sweep clean specific areas of the energy system or all energy systems. When complete thank them for their services.

Stabilization of your magnetic fields is also highly important. As you know, your magnetic field is tied to the magnetic field of the Earth. For example, the rate of your heartbeat is in synchronization with the Schuman resonance of frequency of the Earth. When you leave the surface of the Earth and take an airline flight say at 30,000 feet you have lost your synchronizing magnetic pulse. This causes many different imbalances within the body. This is why many airline pilots have shorter life spans. Remember the astronauts on board the space stations have to have an artificial magnetic field in the station in order to have any semblance of normality. This subject would take several additional pages to address. Thus, do your own research on how magnetic fields influence your body and potential to graduate and ascend.

Maintenance of memory relates to your three magnetic fields, the field of the brain, the field of the body, and the magnetic field of the Earth. Remember many dramatic changes are occurring within the galaxy, solar system, and planet. As a result, the magnetic fields of the Earth have a tendency to wobble and as the intensity of the magnetic field changes, there is the possibility that brain damage may occur and that the body's magnetic fields can be altered adversely.

Since all recordings of thought and memory recall are electromagnetic events (in part), we may experience a reduction in our mental capabilities. Maintaining an optimum level all 60+ minerals in the body will help stabilize the magnetic fields of our brain and body. Also make sure your Mer-Ka-Ba and series of updated Light Body structures (Mer-Ka-Va, Mer-Ka-Vic, Mer-Ka-Na, and others) are maintained as we proceed through the Earth changes, photon belt, and a multitude of other upcoming changes as the Earth's magnetic field continues to change.

The Importance of Ecstasy, and Joy

1. Ecstasy is a state of consciousness that can radically shift the harmonics of multidimensional conscious by collapse of the "old world" third DMC reality and attunement to the "new world" of fifth DMC reality. Dark forces working through religion, politics, and education systems control many of humanity's behavior and survival patterns within the third DMC. Then in addition, various poisons and drugs are used to damage the nerves and various body parts. As a result, there is a suppression of human consciousness. That suppression of consciousness is frequently evidenced by a damaged emotional body. In association with a damaged emotional body, you will discover that many fear related emotions increase in intensity and persist longer. For example tension, stress, anxiety, worry, and depression, become stored within specific locations inside body parts. One location that stress energy is commonly stored is within the spinal column. Excessive stress stored within the spinal column weakens the bone to disk stability, increasing the possibility of having a disk slip out of place. Just an abrupt twist of the back may be sufficient to slip a disk.

Again, I keep reminding the reader that all energy patterns, anything you can think of, can be measure using accurate pendulum dowsing. When stress or any stored emotion is detected have your spirit team remove them.

These series of events, associated with the activities of the emotional body, can destroy an individual's level of ecstasy. The Hathors of Venus indicate that the ecstatic state of being is a necessary evolutionary catalyst for multi-dimensional awareness. The Hathors also recommend the following procedure to activate the ecstatic state of ecstasy and bliss. The procedure involves visualization where you adjust the vortex of cellular DNA. These states of consciousness of mind, emotion, and feeling can be amplified by use of the following practice.

"Focus on the prana tube running through the center of the body. Practice moving your awareness from the perineum (area near the anus) to the crown chakra (top of the head). Then with your awareness on the perineum think (recall) of something that brought you pleasure. Then

272

move this awareness of pleasure up the prana tube to the crown chakra. As you move that awareness, do you sense the feelings of pleasure? Have that pleasurable feeling move up to the top of the head and then visualize a beautiful flower. As the pleasure connects to the flower, see the flower opening up. Then the pleasure first turns into bliss and then into ecstasy. Bliss is maximum pleasure, and bliss can be maximized to create ecstasy. Then rest in this feeling of ecstasy for as long as you wish. With practice, you can generate ecstasy at any time. Use accurate pendulum dowsing to determine your level of bliss and ecstasy, using a scale of minus ten to plus ten, with plus ten indicating total bliss. Make sure to taka a reading before and after this exercise. Those measurements will help you know when the technique requested, and used, has been successful and to what degree progress has been made in optimizing your bliss and ecstasy. Some key examples of the ecstatic state are, Love (sharing with others) and Orgasm (sexual pleasure with the opposite sex)."

2. Joy – Joy is related to bliss and includes a feeling of being filled with happiness. Joy is related to happiness, but it is a deeper experience. In joy, one moves out of self-centeredness and seeks an orientation towards others. Joy gets us out of ourselves and connects us to others. In fact, if you are willing to give up an internal drive to be happy through any conceivable means, and willing to seek joy, you can find all he joy you desire.

Joy connects the human energy system to the creative powers of the energies available within the Dimensional Parallel Universes. These creative tools, available for the asking, are some of the tools used in Creator School. Joy and faith work together to assist us in gaining respect and finding value in others and ourselves. These feelings exist in the context and container of Love. To Love breaks us out of our limited self-interest. We NOW take our mind off ourselves and with that Love reach out to others with Joy and Faith. Then we bring meaning to our life and expand our multidimensional consciousness.

Self-forgiveness is one of the keys to Joy. Self-forgiveness is about understanding oneself and all actions with other component parts of creation. In addition, your understanding of the ego and the extent that it tries to control your daily activities, can be of considerable value. If the ego always wants to be in control and you allow the ego to maintain control then you are in trouble. The ego mind may indicate you are unworthy; therefore, you need to emphasize self-judgment. The ego mind then can argue that self-forgiveness is not necessary because self-judgment is more important. Likewise, the ego mind may say that because you are unworthy, self-forgiveness is impossible. When you follow these instructions of the ego mind, guess what. You are now in more trouble.

Remember the ego mind is not interested in your joy; it is more interested in maintaining control, even at the expense of causing your death. That may sound extreme, however there are instances where it is believed death was caused by an ego who was unable to maintain control of its' physical body housing. From this mental state take control of the ego mind and live from the heart with Love. Controlling our chattering ego mind is one of our major challenges on Earth.

Expressing Love is what we are here for, a process that brings joy. That Love and joy takes us gently into seeing what we need to do, so we can then forgive ourselves for our "so-called unworthiness and our self-judgment."

Then with the rebirth of self Love, joy is imminent. Be kind and gentle with all that you are. Your Soul was created perfect, a perfect part of God/Goddess within. You have a right to be here. Let the river of Love and Joy take you home in all of your glory.

Holons - Geometric Shapes For Energy Stabilization

Everything in the universe is constructed from sacred geometric forms. Every cell within your bodies is based on a sacred geometric form (shape). Physical life begins as a geometric shape. Your first eight cells, which led up to the creation of your physical body, appeared in a spherical form (shape). As cell reproduction proceeds the sphere changed to a tetrahedron, to a star, to a cube and then to a torus. The torus is a doughnut like structure with unique energy characteristics. A tube torus can be created by revolving two circles in three dimensions. For those interested an understanding of third dimension sacred geometric forms in relation to creation refer to the Metatron's Cube, the five platonic solids, the Fibonacci Spiral, Flower of Life, Golden Mean Spiral, and related geometric concepts.

Remember there is no creation that does not have a geometric form as its basic building block for manifestation. Holographic templates and their predecessor, morphogenetic fields are all based on specific sacred geometric forms.

1. Octahedron Holon (two square based pyramids connected at their bases) with one point facing up and the other facing down. Imagine the bases of the pyramids at waist level, so that the upper part of your body is inside the top pyramid and the lower pyramid surrounds the lower part of your body. Then imagine the feelings of safety and comfort. Continue holding the octahedron in your imagination as you continue to intensify these feelings of safety and comfort. Continue visualizing this image daily until by just imagining the octahedron you feel safety and comfort. Then you have reached a state of balance and comfort. With practice, you can amplify that safety and comfort and have no need of fear of any kind.

2. Banana Shaped Cylindrical Holon is used for strengthening the immune system. Imagine a cylinder positioned around your body where the top bends forward like a banana, facing to the front. At the bottom of the cylinder, the banana like shape points the opposite direction of the top. Visualize and hold the impression that the Holon as shiny silver in color. The visualization of silver (a "thought form"), increases the bodies immunity because of it's anti-bacteria and anti-viral properties. This banana shaped Holon also creates peace and calmness to strengthen the immune system.

3. Star Tetrahedron (Mer-Ka-Ba) is a very important three dimensional energy light body designed to surround a body. It contains three tetrahedrons, one is stationary, one spins clockwise and one spins counterclockwise. The Mer-Ka Ba is centered on the prana tube running down the center of the body. The two apexes of the prana tube connect the third DMC and the fourth DMC. You can inhale fourth DMC through the prana tube. In fact, you could survive within a vacuum by breathing through your prana tube.

The procedure for the activation of your Mer-Ka-Ba is outlined on pages 343-365 in "Ancient Search of The Flower of Life" Vol. 2, by Drunvalo Melchizedek. The importance of maintaining your Mer-Ka-Ba should be considered a very high priority. It is a sacred vehicle that has a value that could not be priced in dollars because of it's spiritual value.

If you have been on Earth and did not recently come from somewhere else, your Mer-Ka-Ba has been dormant for 13,000 years. Sixty-seven percent of the Research Associates (within the SERC) have been on Earth for over 13,000 years. Do you have a permanent Mer-Ka-Ba that is constantly spinning? Do you know what a Mer-Ka-Ba is? If not, it's time to find out if you plan to graduate and ascend to the New Earth. When you have any question about the functionality of your Mer-Ka-Ba use accurate pendulum dowsing to measure each tetrahedron's position, speed, and degree of centeredness. The electro-magnetic field around the Mer-Ka-Ba helps protect you.

The time to activate your third DMC electromagnetically designed Mer-Ka-Ba is "Now." You will need the Mer-Ka-Ba for your spiritual evolution and for a base for creating your other Light Body vehicles. Activation of the Mer-Ka-Ba can change you and your life for the better, forever. Keep in mind that the Mer-Ka-Ba is the foundation format for the creation of a Mer-Ka-Va, Mer-Ka-Na, Mer-Ka-Ra, and Mer-Ka-Vic. These upgraded Light Body energy forms will be required when you shift away from the third DMC states to the fifth DMC states on the "New Earth."

4. Dodecahedron - Icosahedral technology developed and patented by David Wheeler (www.davidwheeler.com) has been designed to structure the water you take into your body. Hydration of the body is a necessity for maintain health. The water taken in should have an appropriate spin (counter-clockwise North of the equator and clockwise for South of the equator) and appropriate clustered shape. The spin can be easily observed when you flush your toilet. You can request that a Spiritual team place this sacred geometric form around your neck. As you drink, the water passes through this dodecahedron, where it is re-structured. Then as the water enters your digestive tract as "Perfect Living Water," it can facilitate hydration and carry electricity when sufficient ions (electrolytes) are present.

The newly structured water greatly helps hydrate all body cells. We all know how important hydration of all body cells is. As David mentioned in his book the objective of developing this technology was to "empower people to become more integrated and whole based on the fundamentals of hydration and through a clear understanding how water related to health. Within the book, "Water Empowerment for Life," David

Wheeler states that, "freeing the dodecahedron from the icosahedral cage is the essence of water empowerment." The power of sacred geometric forms is beyond human imagination.

Future and Our Collective Consciousness

So what will the new fifth DMC Gaia (Earth) look like? We can all help answer that question. Several good books, channelings in magazines, and postings on the internet provide descriptions of the New Earth. In addition, during your meditation activities request to take a travel trip to the "New Earth" and look around. Certainly, you are quite capable of using your multidimensional nature to make that trip any time you feel ready and safe. Ask your High Self for assistance.

The power of "LOVE," followed by a transformation of consciousness, balancing, and healing of body, mind, and spirit can greatly influence the future of humanity. Closely observe the degree to which you Love God/Goddess, and yourself every moment of every day. Then transfer that Love to Your Family, Neighbors, The Trees, The Earth and all of Creation.

Remember who you are, a perfect creation made in the image of the Creators. Then develop an ability to keep an open mind and perfect your discernment to keep on your time line. Two very important books can help you understand these procedures. These are. "The Power of Now" and "A New Earth" by Eckhart Toole. Then after you read and understand these concepts, apply them to your Ascension preparation.

Perfecting Your Pendulum Dowsing

Dowsing is an art used by many throughout the centuries to locate water veins for digging wells and a multitude of other purposes. The tools of choice for dowsing water are a forked stick or a bobber. However, from a more practical perspective, where dowsing can be used to obtain meaningful data the pendulum is much more efficient. Pendulum dowsing has several advantages. There are millions of people in the world that use pendulum dowsing for a many different purposes.

A pendulum can be anything that can hang on a string or small chain. Generally, it is best to keep the chain about three to four inches long. The advantage of a small pendulum is that it can fit in a pocket or purse, thus always ready for use. Also, a small pendulum with a short chain responds more rapidly to your request. Remember your body acts as an antenna for the pendulum. A pendulum hanging on a stick is just that a pendulum hanging on a stick and has no practical purposes without a consciousness attachment.

Before you consider pendulum dowsing one very important consideration is your belief system. If you believe pendulum dowsing is dangerous it will be dangerous. If you believe pendulum dowsing is quackery -- it will be quackery. If you believe you will never be able to pendulum dowse, you will never be able to pendulum dowse. Your belief determines not only the dowsing procedure but also everything in your life. Thus, gain control of your beliefs and anything is possible. Thus if you believe pendulum dowsing can be helpful for you -- then sign up for classes or read some good books on the subject and get with it.

A word of caution is in order here. Anyone who broadcasts negative thought forms about the dowsing procedure can shut down your dowsing system. Therefore, avoid contact with closed- minded individuals who already know the answers for themselves and others. It will always be helpful to work with another pendulum dowser in a quiet place free from distractions. Alternatively dowse with a good dowser on the telephone. When dowsing make sure you are both on the same time line and tuned into the same target object or question. Otherwise, you can easily obtain separate answers, both of which are correct.

To use the pendulum, hold the chain between the thumb and first finger. Start the pendulum swinging and program it for a yes or no response by requesting that a certain movement indicate yes or no. For example, an up and down back and forth movement for No and a circular movement for Yes. Some prefer a back and forth movement to the right and left as a No response and a back and forth movement up and down as a Yes response. The response of the pendulum is influenced by the electrical (muscular) sensitivity of the person holding the pendulum. In addition, the swing of the pendulums is influenced by the super-conscious levels of mind, in response to a question.

To obtain specific numerical readings it is good to use a dowsing chart. Pendulum dowsing is a simple procedure used to access information about anything in the Universe. Learning how to pendulum does not require an understanding of what causes the pendulum to swing in a certain direction. However it is good to know what factors can adversely affect the pendulum swing.

One challenge may be in the formulating of the question. The question must be very specific to receive a specific answer. Generalized questions generally fail to receive a desirable response. For accuracy, the conscious mind must be totally controlled so as not to influence the pendulum's movement.

Anyone can consciously control the pendulum's swing to receive a "perceived" desirable answer. Such an answer has no value because of the limited understanding of the conscious mind. The conscious mind has derived its understandings from previously stored information based on past educational experiences, many of which were formulated from a very limited understanding of reality. Even the subconscious mind has limitations again because of its previous programming. Thus, the secret in perfecting one's pendulum dowsing is to tap into the super-conscious mind, a component part of God or Creator Source. A Source connected to all of reality, for your use.

If you are just now learning how to pendulum dowse it would be wise to work with someone who has perfected his or her dowsing skills. For accurate pendulum dowsing it will be very important to protect the dowsing system from outside interference or your tendency to control the answers. There are multitudes of factors that can interfere with the dowsing system. For example, disincarnate entities, solar flares, magnetic fields, electrical storms, and a weak connection to source energy when an individual's "Light Quotient" falls below a desirable energy level may cause your dowsing accuracy to decline. Keep asking that your "Light Quotient" be maintained at the appropriate level. Accurate pendulum dowsing involves keeping in contact with Universal consciousness for appropriate answers. Thus, it is always important to determine your connection to "Source" before dowsing. In addition, it is helpful to call upon various spiritual entities for protection and to assist in maintaining an accurate dowsing capability.

Many factors can reduce the efficiency of pendulum dowsing. For example, some very common interferences are initiated by "dark force entities." These spirit entities can purposely take control of your dowsing system with the objective of making you think you are receiving accurate answers. The consciousness of the dark forces can control the pendulum movements. When you believe that dark forces can influence the pendulum dowsing you will attract those dark forces. Therefore, secure adequate protection and know the dowsing system is free from the influence of adverse entities of any kind.

In addition, wind can interfere with dowsing. It is impossible to dowse while riding with a vehicle because of the sway. Electrical and magnetic interferences can affect the pendulum. These magnetic fields created by earthquakes and electrical storms can influence muscle activity (the basic communicator system for dowsing) and can cause an erratic swing of the pendulum. Solar flares can damage communications via satellites because of these massive electromagnetic impulses. Those same impulses can damage the electrical energy flow through the body and damage the dowsing. These solar flares can damage the human electrical systems rendering the body more susceptible to all types of adversities.

For those having difficulty in perfecting their dowsing accurately, you can take pendulum-dowsing classes. Pendulum dowsing is a tool for knowing about anything that may interest you. Pendulum dowsing is not a play toy. Pendulum dowsing is serious business. It is also the most efficient means I know of to verify intuitive knowledge. It is also a good tool for verifying the thought forms from the High Self. Similarly, you can verify along with discernment the validity of any entity you would like to have some form of communication. Following a request and permission from the High Self of another you can obtain an accurate understanding of their challenges about their situation. However never use pendulum dowsing without permission of the individual in question. That is, first receive permission from their High Self. Pendulum dowsing has changed my life for the better. Pendulum dowsing misused can be very destructive and damage your life. Thus, exercise caution when considering learning dowsing and work with your Spiritual team to be successful.

Read and study good books on dowsing. You can contact the American Dowsing Society for help. Log on to www.dowsers.org and check out their books and meetings throughout the country.